INTERPRETING POLITICAL
RESPONSIBILITY

Per Pino e Luciana

INTERPRETING POLITICAL RESPONSIBILITY

Essays 1981–1989

John Dunn

Polity Press

Copyright © John Dunn 1990

First published in 1990 by Polity Press
in association with Basil Blackwell

Editorial office:
Polity Press, 65 Bridge Street,
Cambridge CB2 1UR, UK

Marketing and Production:
Basil Blackwell Ltd
108 Cowley Road, Oxford OX4 1JF, UK

ISBN 0 7456 0827 2
ISBN 0 7456 0828 0 (pbk)

British Library Cataloguing in Publication Data
A CIP catalogue record for this book is available from
the British Library.

Typeset in 10½ on 12 pt Caslon
by Joshua Associates Ltd., Oxford
Printed in Great Britain by
T. J. Press, Padstow, Cornwall

Contents

Preface and Acknowledgements

Everyone who attempts to understand politics depends abjectly, whether they realize it or not, on the intelligence, labour and goodwill of an immense number of other people. It is not practical even to attempt to do justice to the range and intricacy of this dependence. But I would like at least to express my gratitude for the intellectual aid, encouragement and kindness of a set of closer friends and helpers over the years in which I have been trying to bring the character of political responsibility in the contemporary world into closer focus. I should like particularly to thank John Barber, Cynthia Farrar, Bianca Fontana, Paul Ginsborg, Heather Glen, Geoffrey Hawthorn, Istvan Hont, Susan James, Jonathan Lear, Graham McCann, Anthony Pagden, Pasquale Pasquino, Sandy Robertson, Quentin Skinner, Gareth Stedman Jones, Jim Tully and Richard Tuck.

David Held has been an exceptionally patient and helpful publisher.

At least half the pieces in this book were written at the Villa Anna in Vedasco. My thanks for its calm and beautiful setting and warm and generous hospitality are recorded elsewhere.

Chapter 2 was first presented as a lecture at Harvard University in 1986.

Chapter 3 was first published in Diego Gambetta (ed.), *Trust: The Making and Breaking of Cooperative Relations* (Basil Blackwell, Oxford, 1988) and is reprinted by permission of the editor and publishers.

Chapter 4 was first printed in Larry Gostin (ed.), *Civil Liberties in Conflict* (Routledge, London, 1988) and is reprinted with the permission of the editor and publishers.

Chapter 5 was first prepared for a conference of the United Nations University in Cambridge in 1984, organized by Dr Anouar Abdel-Malek.

Chapter 6 was first published by Terence Ball, James Farr and Russell Hanson (eds), *Political Innovation and Conceptual Change* (Cambridge University Press, Cambridge, 1989) and is reprinted by permission of the editors and publishers.

Chapter 7 was first prepared for the Centenary Conference of the Wharton School of the University of Pennsylvania in 1981 and first published in Richard J. Herring (ed.), *Managing International Risk* (Cambridge University Press, Cambridge, 1983). It is reprinted by permission of the editor and publishers.

Chapter 8 was prepared for a Political Theory panel of the International Political Science Association meeting in Paris in 1985.

Chapter 9 was first published in Patrick Chabal (ed.), *Political Domination in Africa* (Cambridge University Press, Cambridge, 1986) and is reprinted by permission of the editor and publishers.

Chapter 10 was first published in a symposium on the work of Roberto Unger and is reprinted by special permission of Northwestern University, School of Law, 81, *Northwestern University Law Review*, 732 (1987).

Chapter 11 was first prepared for the annual meeting of the Canadian Political Science Association in the summmer of 1986.

Chapter 12 was first prepared for an International Political Science Association conference on the Contemporary Crisis in Political Theory, in Ottawa in October 1986.

1

Introduction

Whatever else it may be, every modern state, at every point in its history, is both a strenuous ideological fiction and an eminently practical reality. Whatever else may be true about them, the vast majority of the human inhabitants of the modern world are each a subject of a particular modern state. (Woe to those who are not.) All modern states link rulers and ruled in a relation of assumed intimacy and massive social distance, the assumed intimacy for the most part representing the ideological fiction and the massive social distance the practical reality. But most modern states also describe their subjects as citizens and seek to implicate the latter, correspondingly, in their own sovereign acts. What modern state agency legitimately consists in is the collective agency of its own citizenry; and any contemporary state which cannot plausibly present its agency in these terms or which chooses not to do so faces persisting and acute difficulty in representing its agency as legitimate at all. In addition, every modern state also claims a wide and peremptory authority over very many aspects of its subjects' lives and an entitlement to determine in the last instance, by some legal process or other, just how widely that entitlement may reach. Defining the mutual rights and duties of states and their individual human subjects has been a central preoccupation of modern politics for several centuries and may perhaps be said to define the historical terrain of modern politics itself.[1]

What makes it so difficult to understand modern politics is not just the disparity between ideological fiction and practical reality, a disparity which is in fact coeval with state power itself. Rather, it is the tense and profoundly untransparent causal relations that obtain between the ideological fiction and the practical reality. No serious analyst of modern politics could fail to notice this disparity between ideological fiction and practical reality; and most are at least hazily aware of the consequential importance and the elusiveness of the causal relations between the two. But no analyst of modern politics thus far has hit upon a convincing strategy for bringing these relations under firm analytical control. Until they do so we shall certainly continue to fail – and fail fundamentally – to comprehend the nature and content of modern politics.

The essays in this book reflect a continuing attempt to develop a somewhat steadier understanding of what modern politics is really about. I hope that they offer some modest progress in this direction: a matter which readers must judge for themselves. But what they more definitely achieve is a clearer presentation of the costs of a number of contrasting approaches to the attempt to extend such understanding. In particular, they question throughout the felicity of one polar opposition in strategies of understanding which has had great imaginative impact over the last half-century: the opposition between a purely causal understanding of a world of fact and a defiantly non-causal understanding of human value, seen as constituted by the consciousness of individual human agents. The philosophical roots of this opposition go back at least to the European seventeenth century – to John Locke's contrast between nominal and real essences,[2] and in a sharpened form to David Hume's *Treatise of Human Nature* half a century later. Its contemporary fruits are still to be found in a scientistic (and epistemologically somewhat credulous) conception of political science and a style of moral philosophy (often epistemologically rather sceptical) which treats at least all sane human adults as appropriately morally sovereign over their own lives. Each of these conceptions has been carried furthest, notoriously, in the United States of America.

I doubt the ultimate intellectual coherence of either conception. But more importantly (and whether or not this doubt is in the end well founded) I am entirely confident of their incapacity to handle the tense and profoundly untransparent causal relations between ideological fiction and practical reality which lie at the very centre of modern politics. In itself this is a purely analytical conviction; and it would be possible to present the grounds for it in a variety of different ways. One might say, for example, that the claim to democratic political legitimacy, however muddled or fraudulent it may usually be, is of urgent causal importance in modern politics; or that politics today, as at every previous point in human political history, consists ultimately in human agency, and the latter, in turn, necessarily involves both an intentionality which is partially dependent on conscious human evaluation and a wide range of unenvisaged and potentially keenly undesired consequences. But it is not the purely analytical conviction (valid or otherwise) which principally concerns me. Rather, it is the profoundly aberrant quality of political

Why compare with physics with epistemology?

judgement generated by a scientistic political science and a moral philosophy constructed through an essentially apolitical process.[3]

It may well be the case that modern politics is just humanly unintelligible in principle: too complicated, too untransparent, and too unstable for the human mind to take in. But this will not stop particular human understandings of its character from continuing to have eminently material consequences: from defiling or beginning to rescue the human habitat, from defusing or indeed triggering the tightly coupled nuclear threat systems of the great world powers, from achieving a peaceful transition to capitalism and representative democracy in the communist world or reconsolidating the shackles forged by marxist–leninist revolutions for an indefinite future. The human attempt to understand politics may make little cognitive headway; but it is going to go on.

Political theory may be an epistemologically parlous enterprise when compared with physics or epistemology. But it cannot sanely turn its back, in proper humility at such epistemic insufficiency, on the very attempt to understand modern politics. Unlike history or moral philosophy, political theory cannot select a subject matter for its apparent epistemological tractability. It cannot confine itself to detached explanation or abstract prescription but has to set itself, as best it can, to judge how human beings now have good reason to act, both in the light of modern politics and within modern politics. All the essays in this volume are concerned in one way or another with this question. All treat politics, implicitly or explicitly, as a matter of agency within a more or less refractory practical context, a direct encounter between intentionality and consequences. All consider, more or less directly or ironically, the key virtue of human practical reason occasioned by the treacherous circumstances of this encounter, the virtue of prudence. Most concentrate, perhaps a trifle smugly, on the degree to which major aspects of modern political experience and ideology have failed to exemplify this virtue. The final essay, more incautiously, argues for one particular conclusion about the place of this virtue in modern politics. In effect it defends the view that the political consequences of modern conceptions of political legitimacy now demand the extension of prudence from the narrow social milieu of classical *raison d'état* to the adult citizen body as a whole.

There were distinguished precedents for this viewpoint in the political thinking of classical Greece;[4] and traces of it certainly survive in the understandings of Machiavelli[5] or even Rousseau. But most analysts of modern politics as a practical activity have essentially agreed with Thomas Hobbes (albeit usually with greater discretion) that the prudence of the modern citizen is (and should be) essentially exhausted in recognizing the imperative to obey their effective political sovereign.

Those who favour wider civic participation do so more for its putative moral edification of the individual citizens concerned than as a rational technique for improving the quality of state agency.[6] By contrast, those who explain (or celebrate) the workings of modern capitalist politics through the model of market rationality presume a high degree of prudence in the agents concerned. The entire utilitarian tradition of political interpretation turns, in effect, on the judgement that individual human agents standardly act in a well-considered fashion and on the basis of a clear understanding of their own interests. Inspection of the world in which we live does little to confirm these fond imaginings. If they are as delusive as I believe them to be, we need to change our approaches to the understanding of modern politics very drastically indeed; and our need to do so is every bit as much practical as it is analytical.

The essays collected here approach this somewhat strident conclusion crabwise and from a wide variety of angles.[7] All are concerned with the nature of modern political agency and the force, clarity and validity of the categories in terms of which such agency is conceived and justified. All adopt a pretty sceptical attitude towards modern political agency, questioning the extent to which states, individuals and intervening agencies today really know what they are doing. But the scepticism is not aimed at discrediting the project of effective political agency or at questioning the ideal or practical significance of political responsibility. The strategy of sceptical doubt is intended to assist clarity; and clarity about the potential scope of effective political agency and of political responsibility is seen as an evident prerequisite for enhancing the efficacy of political agency and for clarifying and strengthening the reality of political responsibility itself. For this reason the doubts are pressed just as vigorously against the categories which carry the professed good intentions and the assured self-righteousness of modern political agents as they are against the categories which claim to focus the systematic unintended consequences of their actions. Above all, they are pressed against the twin judgements that a systematic attempt to understand political causality entails a radical historical fatalism[8] or that moralizing under the rubric of individual ethical taste can offer a coherent approach to political value.[9]

The first essay, 'What is Living and What is Dead in the Political Theory of John Locke?', a public lecture given at Harvard University, begins from a repudiation of a foolish sentence in my preface to *The Political Thought of John Locke*,[10] which affirmed the latter's comprehensively moribund character in face of modern politics. It uses the perspectival advantages afforded by historical distance to question the intellectual security of the most popular and impressive recent recensions of Lockean political theory and to underline the superior strategic power and theoretical integrity of Locke's own understanding of the nature of politics, when set against those of his self-conscious modern heirs.[11]

The second, 'Trust and Political Agency', extends this contrast, setting Locke's emphasis on the practical centrality of the issue of trust for effective political agency against putatively more disabused modern conceptions which seek to comprehend politics through the concept of interest (or preference) alone. Seeing political agency in its entirety as dependent on eminently fallible judgement, it locates political legitimacy in modern politics not through the external application of a pseudo-authoritative criterion for the content of real interests but in the psychic and practical relation between individual subjects and their rulers, a relation which fuses the intimacies of affect, with widely varying discomfort, with the alien reality of economic, administrative and coercive structures. Seen in these terms, modern political legitimacy is an inescapable cooperative project for the denizens and operatives of a modern state. But it is also, even at best, a highly intermittent and sporadic achievement. The profound division of political labour which is ineliminable from modern politics requires, if the latter is to go well, the construction, reproduction and repair of structures of well-founded mutual trust within and between states. This is certainly a matter of well-considered risk-reducing institutional design. But it is also a ceaseless exercise in the communication of sharply discrepant understandings between rulers and ruled, and a permanent struggle to draw these understandings into greater harmony with one another. It is easy to make this conception of modern politics sound sentimental and naive. But its analytical validity is a matter of the harshest *realpolitik*, as the hapless rulers of Poland or Argentina (or perhaps even China, the Soviet Union and the United Kingdom) can testify at this moment. The struggle to mould identification is where modern politics most crucially takes place.[12] We may regret this. But we had better learn to recognize it.

'Rights and Political Conflict' attempts to illustrate the practical importance of this judgement in the context of one of the most bitter of Britain's recent domestic political confrontations, the miners' strike of 1984. It takes the preferred justificatory category of recent Anglo-American liberal political philosophy, the category of rights, and shows that the epistemological scepticism which characteristically lies behind this category today removes virtually all political force from it in the case of fundamental conflicts of interest. It is the most politically sceptical essay in the collection and I would be grateful to be shown why it is wrong.

'Liberty as a Substantive Political Value' reverts to the history of western political ideas to locate a decisive fissure between modern and pre-modern conceptions of politics, a fissure created by the need to identify and master the precarious relations between the dimensions of economics and politics in any serious modern political theory.[13] It is of the nature of modern liberty, as Benjamin Constant aptly conceived it, that there can now be no clear and compelling general theory of the political prerequisites for its practical realization (though there can certainly be compelling enough recipes for precluding it in principle). 'Revolution' considers the historical career of one of the more stalwart and widely applied recipes for precluding it in principle, underlining the point that it is not merely in the case of its modern liberal variant that the constitutive concepts which define and direct modern political agency offer a treacherous guide to the comprehension of its real character.[14]

The sixth essay, 'Country Risk: Social and Cultural Aspects', was prepared for the centenary conference of one of the great American Business Schools. Focusing on the intentionality of a type of modern political agency which prefers to see itself as essentially unpolitical, the large-scale capitalist corporation at home and abroad, it tries to bring out the importance of the gap beween intentionality and consequence in this instance too. Its relation to the class of agents in question is more explicitly ironical (and even more palpably ineffectual) than in the case of other chapters. But it does perhaps show that the overall strategy of understanding can be helpfully applied to rhythms of modern political existence which are rather different from (and at least as practically important as) its noisier ideological squabbles.

'Responsibility without Power' considers the incompatibility between an objectifying (and potentially fatalist) causal understanding of modern politics and the perspective of identification and agency in what for the present remains the most consequential and painful site of modern political choice, the sovereign nation state. It emphasizes both the lethal cognitive costs of abandoning either perspective and the impossibility of adopting both simultaneously and in a coherently related manner.[15] The role of ideological fiction in constituting the practical reality of any modern state forces it to accept a national responsibility for economic processes which are essentially international in character,[16] and in the case of states with thermonuclear armaments it also forces them to claim a degree of rational control in the domain of military strategy which is sadly at odds with the facts. The most important implication of this chapter is the analytical and practical importance of disentangling the real causal capacities of modern political agencies from the massive inherited ideological encumbrance which prevents us from thinking realistically about what we really now have good reason to do in modern politics.

'Responsibility without Power' considers these issues principally in relation to the wealthier and more heavily armed of modern states. But the same issues are examined on more austere terrain in 'The Politics of Representation and Good Government in Post-colonial Africa'. This essay explores the acute potential conflicts between political accountability and economic prosperity in the states of sub-Saharan Africa and the comparative vulnerability within them under these conditions of the former value.[17] While fully accepting the recent emphasis of the French political scientist Jean-François Bayart on the vitality and complexity of the political process in contemporary African states,[18] it also emphasizes the weak capacities of the subject populations of particular African states to constitute themselves as effective collective agents, and the severely limited success of Africa's contemporary societies in securing effectively institutionalized political representation for most extended social interests.

Chapters 10 and 11 turn to two of the most vivid recent defences of the perspective of agency against that of social and political fate, those of the Brazilian legal theorist Roberto Mangabeira Unger, paladin of the Critical Legal Studies Movement, and of the Canadian philosopher Charles Taylor. Of these two writers, Unger is the closer in analytical orientation (if not always in political judgement) to the perspective of the present essays. His insistence throughout his writings on the untransparency and provisionality of existing social, political and economic routines, and on the role of imaginative habituation in perpetuating them, makes him a belligerently modernist theorist of politics, and is convincing enough in itself. But it prompts a flippancy about the practical difficulties of political judgement and an impatience with any systematic attempt to understand political causality which (if they are accepted) preclude contemporary political agency from aiming honestly at the genesis of structures of well-founded mutual trust. By contrast, Charles Taylor's insistence on the permanent presence and the evaluative depth of human intentionality makes him a more scrupulous and less hasty critic of the fatalist perspective. But his comparative inattention to political and economic causality as such gives his thought a weaker and less decisive purchase on politics itself.

'Reconceiving the Content and Character of Modern Political Community' seeks to draw some of the morals of these arguments. In particular, it insists on the need for all three of the types of understanding of their nature which combine to make modern societies what they are[19] to learn a more delicate and prudent awareness of each other's presence.

The basis of this need is not elusive. At present there is every reason to believe the bearers of official, amateur and professional social theory to be equally feckless in their grasp of the prospective consequences of enacting their own presumptions, and equally regrettable contributors, accordingly, by their agency to the impairment and imperilling of collective human life. The essence of my complaint about contemporary academic consciousness is its systematic unsuitability for defining this predicament, let alone for contributing to its alleviation. By dramatizing the predicament itself I hope to help to steady the intellectual nerves of those who would like to contribute more directly themselves to this alleviation.

To offer prudence as the intellectual fulcrum of a modern political theory is to reject the sufficiency of a heavily moralized conception of personal agency, a fetishization of routine, or an essentially autonomous governmental practice of domestic or geopolitical manipulation as approaches to the understanding of modern politics. But it is to identify an awesome collective task, not to invoke an existing level or style of cognitive prowess. The most important and dismaying fact about modern politics as a whole still remains that as yet we have no coherent conception of how to judge, exemplify, realize, sustain or create structures of effective political responsibility at any level from individual human agents to the governments of the great world powers or the United Nations itself. In politics today, we do not really understand what we are doing and we do not grasp what is being done to, or for, or against us.

Cambridge
November 1989

2

What is Living and What is Dead in the Political Theory of John Locke?

I would like to begin by making clear that my argument as a whole is in effect a repudiation of a single (and peculiarly ill-considered) sentence in the preface to the book about Locke which I published twenty-one years ago.[1] I begin in this way because what led me to make this all too exposing avowal in the first place was a misunderstanding which has some more general importance.

The offending sentence itself is dismayingly unequivocal. It reads blankly 'I simply cannot conceive of constructing an analysis of any issue in contemporary political theory around the affirmation or negation of anything which Locke says about political matters.'[2] Or, more freely translated, everything in the political theory of Locke is well and truly *dead*. The sentence was intended, plainly enough, as a challenge – perhaps even almost as a boast. It was certainly not intended, as it now dispiritingly reads, as a ludicrous confession of intellectual myopia. But its importance lies not in its only too sincere expression of stupidity but in the error which led me to make it at all. To see that error clearly it is necessary to concentrate one's attention less on the sentence itself than on the point which I had in mind in penning it: the effect which it was intended to have upon the affronted reader. The judgement which I particularly wished to press upon that reader – and which the book as a whole was intended to thrust home – was a judgement about how to understand the thinking of another human being in a very distant and in some respects culturally exceedingly alien environment. And the point which I especially intended to emphasize was the need to consider that thinking as an internally related, though no doubt less than perfectly integrated, whole – a theory or structure of theories – and *not* as an assemblage of discrete individual propositions or assertions, each and every one of which would be readily detachable from all the others and any of which could be both understood and epistemically assessed firmly on their own. I was too ignorant at the time to know it; but I am pretty confident in retrospect that this point of view, expressed more clearly than I could have expressed it then or could indeed express it now, is one which can realistically hope to find an intellectually authoritative welcome within one of the most powerful currents of modern philosophical thinking – the holistic or, in some versions, the anti-realist strand which has its roots in the American pragmatist tradition and especially in the thought of Quine.[3]

This sort of holistic perspective can obviously be adopted with very different degrees of intellectual rigour and precision. (I certainly adopted it myself in 1969 very vaguely indeed.) In its strongest form, as an approach to the explanation of linguistic meaning or of mutual human understanding, it can make it very hard to grasp how there can be *any* such thing as linguistic meaning or how mutual human understanding is ever possible at all. In its weakest forms its force, within the practice of understanding, is perhaps merely admonitory and negative: a simple reminder of the hazards of jumping too quickly to the conclusion that one understands someone very different just because *some* of what they prove to have said is something which one could easily imagine saying for oneself. There is nothing wrong with these latter and weaker forms as far as they go, apart from their severely limited intellectual interest. (It takes a real historian to extract intellectual *excitement* from the thought that one can fail to understand someone else.) The strongest and most bewildering form may in fact be simply correct. But at the more mundane level of particular attempts to understand other people or other cultures, dead or alive, the zone which seems most attractive – of most practical help in securing such understanding – lies rather feebly somewhere in the middle of the continuum. In this unexhilarating (and perhaps philosophically unenticing) middle ground one can sense the practical strain, the sheer degree of resistance encountered, in any attempt to penetrate a truly alien web of beliefs, without instantly capitulating to the overwhelming futility of hoping to understand anyone else at all ever. (And if not anyone else, how on earth even oneself?)

The point which I especially wished to press upon my readers – and which the book certainly labours *ad nauseam* – is that Locke was a Christian thinker. This, of course, was not a biographical fact about him as a historical individual which had altogether escaped previous commentators. But it is, I think, fair to say that it was one whose significance most of them had not altogether contrived to fathom. I did not mean by it, of course, merely that Locke was a thinker who just happened to be a Christian (although he might equally well have been a Buddhist or a Hindu or a belligerently materialist atheist). I meant that his thinking in its entirety was shaped and dominated by a picture of the earthly setting of human life as a created order, an order designed and controlled by an omnipotent, omniscient and also, mercifully, benevolent deity: the God of the Christians. I didn't of course wish to imply that each and every item of his beliefs and of the views which these led him to put forward conceptually depended directly and necessarily upon that overall picture of the setting and significance of human life. It would not be easy to trace its impact, for example, in the directions which appear in his *Collected Works* for the cultivation of fruit trees;[4] nor did I wish to imply that there are not structures of argument or analysis in every one of his more important works which can (and in some sense *must*) be understood quite independently of the overall strategic setting within which he chose to formulate them. But what I did wish to stress – and retain my confidence that I was entirely right to have stressed – was not just that it would never be safe in reading Locke to presume in advance that this overall framework was simply irrelevant to the exact comprehension of an individual passage or work but also, and more importantly, that this framework would often in fact prove to be of fundamental importance for assessing the force or weakness of many of the arguments which he chose to put forward. It would be of fundamental importance precisely because from Locke's own point of view, his perspective on his own intellectual agency,[5] it was a premise and often an indispensable premise of the arguments which he offered and the conclusions which he hoped to establish.

The view that the historical Locke was in fact a Christian is less often called into question now than two decades ago; and there is even, at least among historians and a segment of political theorists, more readiness than there used to be to acknowledge that his Christianity may have been of some importance in determining the content of his moral and political beliefs. Philosophers, by contrast, have not for the most part found the claim that Locke was in fact a Christian of arresting interest. And in so far as they confine their concerns to assessing the merits and weaknesses of his epistemological or ontological conclusions, it is perfectly possible (though in my view some way from being certain)[6] that they are right to find it simply irrelevant. But what they are certainly *not* right to presume is that Locke's Christianity can be defensibly regarded as irrelevant either to his ethics or to his political theory. To suppose anything of the kind is not just historically careless. Indeed it may well not be *historically* careless at all, but rest instead on a frank, relaxed and massive indifference to history as such. So that Locke is not here well understood as the name of a real dead person, but rather as that of a poor stuffed doll tossed casually into the arena to show off the fearsome destructive powers of the splendid intellectual carnivores which prowl the ground to their admiring audience. Whether or not one enjoys this form of bloodsport is very much a matter of personal taste. But it is at least permissible to doubt whether the practice of 'telling men of straw that they have no brains'[7] (to steal a phrase of John Passmore's) really is very compelling testimony to anyone's intellectual acumen. In any case, whether such historical negligence is inadvertent or deliberate, my point is that at least in relation to Locke's ethical or political views it is also most emphatically philosophically inept.

The main interest of the present essay is that this particular instance of philosophical ineptitude has important implications not just for the interpretation of Locke as a historical thinker (a topic of interest principally to historians) but also for contemporary political philosophy (a topic plainly of interest to very different audiences and which I certainly believe to be relevant, for better or worse, to the vast majority of human beings).

What implications, then, does the deeply Christian imaginative frame of Locke's ethical and political thinking actually have for contemporary political philosophy? And what in particular does it imply for determining which elements in his ethical and political thinking truly are gone beyond recall and which elements stubbornly remain alive? There are perhaps four elements in his political thinking which are widely regarded – particularly in North America – as obviously and vividly alive: a theory of human rights as prior to and independent of the claims of political authority; a theory, more particularly, of the basis of legitimate appropriation and the consequent standing of rights to property; a contractarian approach to the understanding of legitimate authority which relates such legitimacy more or less deviously to the consent of those over whom it is exercised; and a relatively distinct theory of human rights to freedom of belief or expression, grounded fundamentally on the involuntariness of the condition of believing something to be or not to be the case. Of these four elements only the third – the contractarian approach to the understanding of legitimate authority – does remain coherently and unfactitiously alive – and even that only in a distressingly plastic form. What has killed off the others as Locke conceived them, or on the whole as they have been rethought by subsequent and more secular thinkers, is principally the extinction of Locke's Christian conception of the nature of the human habitat and the role of the human species, at least as an animating frame of current theoretical understanding.

Since there are of course still a great many Christians, particularly in the United States, Poland and some of the more beleaguered parts of Latin America, the dependence of so much of Locke's political theory upon his Christian assumptions *might* simply mean that his theory, while dead for those who are not Christians, is at least fully alive for all those who remain such – or at any rate for all among those who remain such that happen to share Locke's distinctively Protestant religious sensibility. That possibility would at least give us a clear answer to the question which I set myself to resolve. But I believe that this resolution at least is definitely quite wrong, and that, among other demerits, it greatly exaggerates the extent to which the intellectual currency of Locke's thinking on these questions could be sustained merely by an overlap in strictly theological convictions. It is an interesting and rather puzzling question just why this should be so; but my grounds for believing that it in fact is so do not require an answer to that question. They merely involve a reasonably close attention to the conceptual structures and patterns of argument employed in political understanding by all but the most intellectually uncouth of present day Christian believers. (The most plausible exception to that claim today is probably the somewhat intellectually volatile field of liberation theology: but I suspect that even there the judgement can readily be defended with just a little intellectual agility.)

Thus far nothing that I have acknowledged actually requires the repudiation of any claims advanced in my *Political Thought of John Locke*, though the qualifications offered on the question of the contractarian approach to the understanding of legitimate political authority do suggest that my report of the demise of Locke's political theory may in that respect have been, as Mark Twain said of reports of his own death, a trifle exaggerated. (The book was published in 1969, before the recent revival of contractarian political thinking had yet established its now commanding presence, let alone its increasingly formidable amplitude.) But what I do now have to repudiate here is the singularly explicit assertion that there were (and are) no other and at least equally momentous elements in Locke's political theory which remain intractably and vividly alive. In particular what I failed completely to see (though I might perhaps with a bit more guts and perseverance have come just within sight of it by the time I reached the book's somewhat exhausted finale) was just how vital and how deeply intelligent was Locke's understanding of the nature of politics as a purely human activity (an activity for humans for whom God has since gone off the air). What I did see was Locke's own sense of the *bleakness* of such a condition: its frailty, urgency and radical lack of existential solace for human beings as social creatures.

But what I missed, and missed completely, was the bracing imaginative force of this steady and unsuperstitious vision, its grim but potentially profoundly energizing realism. What I missed was the force of certain kinds of negation, of holding back assent, in the face of a domain of human experience where the will to credulity has raged with such terrifying vigour throughout the modern history of our species. Modern political theory, in so far as it is normative in its bearing (and the vast bulk of it that is not self-evidently trivial certainly *is* normative in its bearing whether consciously or unawares) is drenched, saturated with credulity. There are many aspects of Locke's own beliefs which many of us today have no option but to regard as credulous. But in his conception of what politics is like and what, in the world and between human beings, it really means, I find astonishingly little credulity, astonishingly little capitulation to the tug toward self-deception, to the will to fantasize a lasting and readily accessible social ease, or a peace that cohabits comfortably with understanding and might well go on for ever. To reach this steadiness of vision would in anyone be a tremendous triumph over the will, that lonely and indefatigible enemy of every once Puritan child. And in the case of Locke, whose disposition certainly contained many elements as nasty as those of the rest of us, that triumph, I now think, made him not merely a great thinker but also a very great human being, an attainment for which *some* aspects of his disposition did little, if anything, to equip him.

What I should like to try to do in this essay is first to explain just why the elements which I take to be dead in Locke's political theory – in the teeth of extremely distinguished disagreement – are in fact so; and secondly, and more adventurously to try to convey just what it is that I take to be so obstinately and crucially alive.

The feature of Locke's political theory which is least likely to be regarded as well and truly dead, particularly in North America, is his view that human beings have rights which are prior to and independent of the claims of political authority.[8] I am not myself at all convinced that this is in fact so, though it is an engaging view and one whose natural political drift I largely applaud. But what is quite certain is that if it is indeed the case that human beings have rights and if there really are clear and cogent answers to the question of what gives them these, and only these, rights, then the reasons why Locke supposed men and women to possess them cannot for most people now alive be good reasons for believing them to do so. For Locke rights were not just a *façon de parler* or a contingency of sentiment or cultural attitude[9] but what it is helpful to see as a legal fact, a fact of value. The idea that there can actually be facts of value (or legal facts independent of any system of humanly enforced law) has been regarded with considerable contempt by many modern philosophers. They may be quite correct so to regard it, though I do not myself in the former case as yet altogether see why.[10] But for Locke it was the single most important premise of his intellectual system that there are such facts, not of course facts that are epistemically or ontologically at all similar to facts of nature, but facts about an order of authoritative law and about the crisp and decisive implications of this order of law for how all human beings have good reason to act.[11] Locke's theory of rights rests foursquare upon this picture of a divinely created universe, of the purposes of its concerned creator, and of the role for which that creator destined human beings. Without that theoretical frame Locke himself actually did *not* believe that human beings *do* possess rights at all; and there is sharp and chilling evidence that he did not believe so in the short and brutal shrift which, in the *Letter on Toleration*, he gives to atheists.[12] Those who close their eyes (somewhat inconsistently, he seems to see atheists as *choosers* of their own beliefs) to the structure of divine purposes legible in the universe which they inhabit evict themselves from the legal protections that all other human beings enjoy and turn themselves, gratuitously but deservedly, into foes of every other member of the species to which they belong. They do so not by actually harming anyone else at all; but by rejecting, even desecrating, the whole framework of assumptions on which for Locke all human decencies and hopes in the last instance rest. That is not merely *not* a very tolerant point of view: it cannot soberly be said to show the least regard for the rights of human beings as such, free-standing and left to their own devices.

Of course there are parts of the world in which over lengthy tracts of time some human beings certainly do have rights. Citizens of the United States of America in particular have quite a rich array of rights – some no doubt more effectively observed than others. But they possess those rights by historical and political inheritance, as a product of – at a minimum – almost two hundred years of constitutional history. And that history offers no licence at all for viewing their possession of these rights as in any sense *prior* to the claims of political authority. Nor, for that matter, do the tense political antecedents of that continuous constitutional history in the victorious struggle for national independence from colonial overrule provide any such grounds either. It is certainly a cultural truth that Americans are apt to regard their possession of rights as self-evident. But self-evidence in this regard is firmly in the eyes of the beholder; and it is the political history of a culture, not the nature of the universe or the properties of the human species as such that have put it there. Rights theories certainly offer an evocative idiom for expressing some sorts of moral intuition; and in a country which had considerable difficulty in disembarrassing itself of slavery as a legal institution and which may never wholly escape from the social consequences that are the legacy of that institution it would be silly to disparage the political point of expressing certain moral intuitions in this particular way. But once moral theorizing is seen firmly as merely a human activity and once the intuitions which it seeks to cast more clearly and compellingly are recognized as historically intelligible facts of culture, it is very hard to see how rights can hope to retain the peremptoriness, the rigidity and the conclusiveness which they expressly assert and which is, in most instances, the political point of proclaiming them at all.[13]

For Locke all the rights human beings have (and which they certainly do possess prior to and independently of all human political authority) derive from, depend upon, and are rigidly constrained by a framework of objective duty: God's requirements for human agents. Within this setting, but as he supposed only within this setting, the claims of right are indeed decisive and all human beings have a duty to observe them and to enforce them. In his thinking about rights there is none of that suspicious combination of theoretical plasticity and arbitrary pretension to conclusiveness which is the distinguishing characteristic of modern rights theorizing: a combination which I at least suspect to be ineliminable on the basis of any remotely convincing modern formulation of meta-ethical views.

Much the same holds good – and for rather similar reasons – of Locke's theory of the basis for legitimate appropriation and the consequent standing of rights of property. Because of the importance of quarrels over property rights in modern domestic and international politics, and at a more academic level because of the prominence of arguments about distributive justice in modern political philosophy, this is probably today the most resonant feature of Locke's ideological legacy. (A prominent American disagreement about the nature and standing of social justice, for example, can be well understood in effect as principally a dispute about which of two elements in Locke's theory – his conception of legitimate appropriation or his contractarian approach to the understanding of legitimate political authority – ought in the end to be master.)[14] In that dispute I would certainly side with the contractarian approach, but less because I see great determinacy and force within that approach than because I cannot begin to see how Locke's understanding of the basis of legitimate appropriation can retain any force at all when extracted from the framework of his overall theory.[15]

I put this last point rather stridently and I do not mean by it that there are no elements in Locke's understanding of property which still make any sense today. Of course a number of features of his understanding continue to make *some* sense today: the special relation of human agents to their own bodies (and also minds),[16] the emphasis on the historical role of labour in reshaping the human habitat and on the direct and relatively transparent claims to enjoy its fruits that flow from physical and mental exertion. But within the deeply opaque causal structures of a modern domestic and international economy, these considerations too have taken on (and could hardly have been prevented from taking on) a plasticity and a rationally unwarranted shrillness very similar to that which has overtaken the idiom of rights theories.

The contrast which I wish to underline is once again a contrast with the comparative solidity and externality of Locke's theory. It is not that that theory itself is especially satisfactory even in its own terms. It gives a pretty unclear account even of the dimensions of property rights which it was its principal purpose to expound: the relations between the standing and content of property rights *within* a particular positive legal system and the standing and content of property rights over against the abusive dictates of such systems of positive law.[17] (This vagueness, in its turn, is largely a consequence of the unclarity of Locke's conception of the relations between the role of the positive law of a legitimate political society as an explication in practice of the content of natural law and the historical possibility that each and every one of the positive laws of even the most legitimate of political societies may just contingently happen to *be* violations of natural law.[18]

Nor does Locke succeed in offering a particularly clear and convincing account of the degree to which human labour operates causally as the source of use value. Professor G. A. Cohen has recently shown in a very clear and thoughtful lecture to the British Academy[19] that chapter 5 of the *Second Treatise* provides quite inadequate grounds, even on its own terms, for Locke's attribution of the vast preponderance of human use value to labour as opposed to natural goods: an attribution which is of course of the greatest importance in explaining his overall conception of the scope of legitimate appropriation. Cohen does, however, also acknowledge, perhaps a little casually, the presence of a further argument, added by Locke in his final revision to paragraph 37 of the *Second Treatise*, that the appropriation of land constitutes an addition to, rather than a subtraction from, the stock of natural goods because of the massive increase in productivity which it renders possible; and that the man who appropriates ten acres accordingly, and renders them capable in consequence of producing more than a hundred acres of uncultivated land, may, as Locke put it, 'truly be said to *give* ninety acres to mankind'.[20] Since this argument, descending lineally from Adam Smith to Schumpeter and Hayek, is still the single most powerful and resonant moral and practical defence of capitalist production its intellectual inauguration perhaps deserves rather crisper attention.

But despite its power in comparison with other defences of capitalist production this argument also has rather evident weaknesses and weaknesses that are difficult to allay once it is removed from the theoretical framework for which Locke designed it. For Locke human property rights were to be understood on the basis of a world given by God to human beings for God's own purposes. When Locke says in paragraph 35 of the *Second Treatise* that 'The Law Man was under was rather for *appropriating*',[21] he means exactly what he says. The earth was given by God to mankind in common but it was given to them under the terms of a law which prescribed what they were to do with it.[22] All human property rights which genuinely amount to *rights* against other human beings (which aren't simply arbitrary and unjustified instances of force or fraud) are simply instrumental contributions to mens' or womens' fulfilment of the historical project for which God has destined the human species. Because the whole earth was made by an omnipotent creator and made for His own good reasons it was a compelling theoretical presumption within Locke's theory that there was one and only one way at any time that natural goods ought to be appropriated to human use and at best a pretty restricted range of ways in which the goods themselves ought to be enjoyed. But in no modern theory could it possibly be a sane presumption that either of these conditions obtains. The accumulated history of the politics of capitalist societies shows plainly – to anyone prepared to lend it even the most cursory attention – that there simply is no single clear and authoritative principle or standard or ground of legitimate appropriation. There may sometimes be good prudential reasons for taking existing patterns of appropriation largely as given and merely adjusting their more blatantly obnoxious features to the outraged sensibilities of bystanders or victims. But these reasons are an accommodation to facts of power, not to intimations of justice. The causal law human beings are under now is certainly one for appropriating: we cannot drift woozily back into Elysium. But there is no reason whatever to believe any longer that there *is* any definite and authoritative answer to the question of who should now own what – and not much reason to believe that the question itself even possesses a clear sense. Locke's analysis of property may have been a trifle disorganized and unstable in its outlines; but in contrast with the sheer ideological flimsiness of all modern evaluations of appropriative outcomes its solidity looks as enviable as it is irrecoverably beyond our reach.

The third element in Locke's theory which most modern liberals would assume to be comfortably (and comfortingly) alive in his celebrated defence of toleration: of freedom of religious belief and expression. But here too, I think, a more careful assessment requires us to judge differently. In particular it requires us to distinguish sharply between the grounds which Locke offers for his conclusions and the content of those conclusions themselves. And once we have drawn this rather obvious distinction it then underlines the yawning chasm between the implications of Locke's arguments for tolerating varieties of Christian belief and practice within a Christian state and society and the implications which they would bear for freedom of thought and expression more broadly within a secular state or a more intractably plural religious culture. Locke's arguments themselves depend upon two key premises (though they naturally marshal a variety of further considerations as they proceed on their way). The first premise is a premise about the nature of human belief: that belief is essentially – or at least to an overwhelmingly preponderant degree – *not* a voluntary matter: that humans do not and very largely cannot choose their beliefs. (One of the trickiest aspects of Locke's philosophy from his own point of view came from the strain of attempting to combine this thesis with his guilt-ridden post-Puritan conviction that human beings *are* nevertheless unequivocally responsible for almost all their less edifying beliefs.)[23] The second premise of his argument for toleration is explicitly Christian. The primary personal duty and rational prudential preoccupation of any human being fortunate enough to enjoy access to the Christian gospel was the committed quest for the salvation of their own soul. Christian worship was an indispensable element in this quest; and Christian worship logically required (could not *be* worship if it lacked) the sincere expression of individual devotion in forms of action, which that individual saw as and felt to be appropriate expressions of his or her devotion.[24]

Atheists of course have – in their own eyes – no need for religious expression (as well as no inclination whatever to indulge in it). But for Locke, as we have already seen, they also have no right even to the content of their own beliefs. For Locke indeed – and unlike his Huguenot contemporary Pierre Bayle[25] – atheists are such a *practical* menace that they threaten the very existence of a society. And because of the degree of threat which they pose – a sort of spiritual equivalent of AIDS in the most hysterical and contemporary understandings – they actually in Locke's eyes lose the great majority of human rights altogether.

There is no reason to believe that Locke thought very carefully about this question – though he certainly felt extremely strongly about it. But what needs to be emphasized is that what he did think about it entails that he did not suppose that all human beings are in fact entitled to freedom of belief: let alone to anything that could possibly be mistaken for freedom of expression. Furthermore the component of his theory of toleration that passes most comfortably into a modern secular point of view – his comparatively steady insistence on the predominant involuntariness of belief – cannot on its own furnish a very robust basis for a firm and convincing entitlement to freedom of expression. In particular it can hardly serve to establish that priority of the dignity of belief (whether compulsive or not) over the offended sentiments of the listener which any worthwhile doctrine of freedom of expression imperatively requires. (There is, after all, only a need for freedom of expression where what is to be expressed is likely or certain to wound or outrage the feelings of fellow human beings. And the view that human beings by and large cannot, at time t, choose their beliefs is hardly better grounded than its natural concomitant: the view that they by and large cannot, at time t, choose their feelings either.)

$\rightarrow$ In my view, accordingly, it is only the second of these four elements of Locke's theory – the contractarian approach to the understanding of legitimate political authority – which is in any reasonably integral sense still firmly alive. And even in the case of this element the form in which it does survive represents a quite sharp mutation from the form it took within Locke's own theory.[26] One can see this plainly enough simply by noting that within Locke's theory the contractarian account of political legitimacy followed from and depended on his overall account of the rights which human beings enjoy under the law of nature: rights which, as already noted, themselves in turn depend upon the duties to which human beings are subject under that law. What this feature of his theory implies – crucially – is that for Locke in the *Two Treatises of Government* (and unlike in his earlier writings)[27] the burden of proof of the legitimacy of political authority falls upon *it* and not upon individuals or communities as bearers of rights. It is hard to see how this feature of his theory could be validly retained as a *premise* (though it might of course be delivered as a conclusion) of a modern recension of Locke's contractarianism. Today it simply is not theoretically clear *a priori* in any collision between institutionalized forms of collective secular life and dissident individuals or groups challenging their authority, which way the burden of proof does lie. Forms of collective social, political and economic life are every bit as much there as single individuals and it is just sheer ideological effrontery to pretend that perhaps they may really not be there or there may be no pressing occasion for recognizing them to be so.

What force then can a contractarian approach hope to retain, once sundered from any foundation in an authoritative general theory of human or natural rights? In what sense, if any, does it make sense to see modern political legitimacy (whatever that may be) as resting upon the consent of those over whom its authority is exercised? In Locke's own account the precise status and character of consent was pretty muddily treated, but it seems fair to summarize it in two distinct components: a theory of the preconditions for the existence of *any* legitimate political authority, which definitely requires historically actual or express consent (conscious choice) at some point in time, and a theory of how particular human beings become subject to political obligations, which is very considerably shiftier and vaguer in its demands. It is not entirely textually justifiable (but may nevertheless be analytically helpful) to see the former reading of consent as requiring historical agency and the latter as resting on a more nebulous conception of hypothetical consent.[28]

As numerous recent writers have pointed out it is a pretty forlorn business to hope to construe the causal character of the politics of any territorial society, today as in the past, in terms of actual or express consent.[29] Transitory instances that might excusably be mistaken for it do show up at intervals in at least some modern polities – contested elections and so on.[30] But it is apparent enough that these ceremonies play an exceedingly tangential role in determining the direction in which political power is exercised – and no modern thinker has really contrived to indicate how human beings today could hope to have good reason to appreciate through time the consequences of their playing a more salient and decisive role.[31] (The politics of existing within a world economy are alienated beyond redemption.)

A theory of hypothetical consent as the criterion for modern political legitimacy is obviously less vulnerable to confrontation with experience. But it is also in my view certain to disclose itself under reasonably close examination as resting necessarily on some prior theory of the right or the intrinsically good – and thus as not in the last instance being a theory of *consent* at all.[32] Since I certainly have nothing worth saying to offer on what a general theory of the right or the intrinsically good ought to be *like* or how it could hope today to enjoy rational authority for all human beings, I shall pass those issues by firmly on the other side.

What then exactly is the *merit* of the contractarian approach to the understanding of political legitimacy, if resting its authority on consent must be either a brazen ideological deceit or a theoretically confusing formula for resting it in fact upon something quite different? The merit itself is exceedingly simple. It lies, I think, in what the contractarian approach takes to be the *starting point* for the understanding of politics and political value. Here we all are, loose in history and dubiously at ease within ourselves and with each other. What are we going to do about it? This is certainly *the* political question: and an eminently practical and exceedingly insistent one too. But it is hard to see how it can in itself also be the *answer* to that question.

What it underlines is that in the understanding of politics all human beings alive at the time *must* be taken in the first instance just the way they are – not just as sites of their own evaluative beliefs and choosers of their own choices, but also with all their factual and causal beliefs and all their dispositions and attitudes intact. To see politics in this way is in fact a stiff imaginative discipline for almost anyone: maybe an impossibly stiff imaginative discipline.[33] And it is of course more a reminder of what the political problem is than a distinct contribution to meeting it. But by the same token it is also neither intellectually nor practically at all bad going to have *succeeded* in identifying what that problem really is. For to be reminded of the political problem in this way – to have it drawn firmly to one's attention – is to be shown that the political problem *has* no general solution: that it can be met only by a series of more or less deft and honourable improvisations. And that it cannot be met any other way not because of some deep and befuddled providentialism – some view that anything at all (God, the forces of production, the history of liberty or progress) is *in charge of* human history, but simply because *nothing* is in charge of human history: because we make that history together as best we can as we go along, through our own more or less ill-considered actions. This, of course, is an old conservative truth and one which it is essential to distinguish sharply from the rich medley of conservative falsehoods that customarily accompany it.

Locke himself definitely hoped (and as far as we know he also always fairly confidently supposed) that this was not in fact altogether true: that the Christian God, by contrast, was in the last instance fully in charge of human history.[34] But what is important today is that the main set of categories which he elaborated to interpret the *role* of men and women within God's history can in large measure stand free of that setting and serve still to interpret their political fate when left severely on their own. The principal categories which he developed for this purpose are again extremely simple and they neither depend upon, nor themselves imply, the conception of the laws of nature and of men and women's rights under that law on which the principal modern recensions of Lockean politics are apt – overtly or covertly – to rely. I take these categories to be in essence three. A conception of what makes a human being at least in the vast majority of instances, a single particular person; a conception of what makes a human society the society it actually is; and a conception of what the better features of any human society must in the end depend upon. That is, a theory of agency and personal identity, a vision of the nature of human society as the unintended product of an immense variety of human contrivances, and a view of the natural and historical basis of any acceptable and lasting form of human social cooperation as the genesis and reproduction of mutual trust.

The first two of these elements had deep roots in Locke's own personal religious preoccupations. The point of the first, expressed most graphically in his famous account of what it is to be a person at all, was to fix the terms of agent responsibility for human beings: to define a human person, as he put it, *forensically* – by picking out what makes that person responsible for all, but only for all, of their own actions.[35] Locke's own principal concern in this analysis was to explicate what it is about human beings that makes them 'capable of a law' and hence justly subject to punishment for breaches of it and subject in some cases to his own rather relaxed interpretation of eternal damnation (which is not overwhelmingly easy to distinguish from what most people today mean by just being dead).[36] There is nothing especially distinctive or impressive about this conception of agent responsibility. What is salutary about it is principally its *prominence* within his overall strategy of understanding.

The second element, the insistence that what a human society *is* is the unintended consequence of a vast array of past human contrivances, is a little more bracing: not because many today are apt to have much motive for openly denying it, but because its implications register very poorly in the social and political imaginations of most denizens of the modern world. For Locke its principal importance was to deny the providentialist presumptions of Filmer: to denaturalize and disenchant existing shapes of human social life, both as structures of power and as inventories of more or less widely shared meanings.[37] Here I think Locke's understanding was in fact analytically as modern and as disabused as understandings come: giving full weight to the reflexive historical role of human intelligence without sentimentalizing the degree of purchase which that intelligence can ever hope to achieve upon the full concreteness of any particular historical social order.

But it was principally the third of these elements – the degree to which the political texture of any decent human society depends and must depend always upon trust – which does distinguish Locke's understanding both from those political thinkers in the natural law tradition who precede him and more importantly from the many distinguished thinkers who followed after him. The view that trust-worthiness, a modicum of rational dependability, is the first virtue of human social institutions – in a sense prior to, and altogether less dispensable than, justice – is a despondent view.[38] It locates the possibility and uncertainty of trust in the deep ambiguities of human nature: not just in the largely cognitive capacity for giving and receiving undertakings (for promising and being promised) which features more or less prominently in every pre-modern contractarian thinker, but also in the sometimes warm but always erratically reliable capacity for animal companionship on which any durable and reasonably pleasant form of human cooperation depends for its practical viability.

For Locke the political task is always principally an exercise in practical skill. But what that skill essentially consists in is the construction of moral order in the face of the permanent possibility of chaos. To construct such an order is in the first place to design institutions which economize on trust, which do not strain its elasticity beyond the breaking point. The purpose of political society – known standing laws, impartial adjudicators and the accumulated executive power of the law of nature of the community's members to furnish these goods with effective physical protection – is precisely to economize on trust: to bring men's over-whelming need for trust within their all too finite reach. What the state of nature most pressingly is is a condition in which the need or demand for rational trust hopelessly exceeds the available supply. But to economize on trust is not to eliminate the need for it. The best designed of human institutions are only partial strategies for mitigating this need. There can be no total strategy for meeting it for ever, for writing it out of human political history. (Notice how hard it is for all modern ideologies of domestic political community to face up to that harsh fact.)

But what then is the advantage of seeing the political task as the design of allocative and coercive institutions that economize on trust and the adaptation and sustaining of such institutions so that they continue to merit it? Principally within modern political theory, I think, that it recognizes the overwhelming importance of the political division of labour in any real society. The weight of the political division of labour is something which modern moralizing theories of politics find it almost unendurable to acknowledge.[39] (It is also something that often leads those modern understandings of politics that do acknowledge it to demoralize political relations across a society in favour of a sinister narcissistic obsession with the pathos of the exercise of power.)

What lends Locke's understanding of politics its imaginative power is not the special insight of any one of these three elements, each of which can readily be matched in the thinking of many other sometimes more exciting and frequently more up-to-date thinkers. Rather it is the conjunction of all three. Even this conjunction, of course, has nothing magical about it. It ends no arguments and grounds no conclusive claims to authority. But that is its virtue, not its weakness: the index of its sober realism. A theory of social justice is a fine thing, a good thought in a naughty world. But it is the naughty world which has to be dealt with. As we look around that world: at the governments of the United Kingdom and the USSR, of the United States and El Salvador, of Ethiopia and India, theories of social justice sit very lightly on it and shape in practice very little of it indeed. Rational trust, likewise, plays a pretty modest role in the politics of any modern state. Locke's view of the political project still has a huge distance to go. But it is a view which captures – and captures most evocatively – what politics is still like: captures it without superstition but also without despair.

Locke saw politics this way; and I do not know of any other modern thinker who quite contrived to do so. And because he saw it this way and because this is the way it still is and is likely always to remain, we *do*, I think, have good reason to nerve ourselves for the full unfamiliarity of his vision – its unblinking historical distance – and to use it in all its integrity and imaginative force to help us to think again.

And what could be more alive than that?

3

Trust and Political Agency

Trust is both a human passion and a modality of human action – a more or less consciously chosen policy for handling the freedom of other human agents or agencies. As a passion, a sentiment, it can be evanescent or durable. But as a modality of action it is essentially concerned with coping with uncertainty over time.[1] A human passion, let us agree with David Hume, is an original existence.[2] Human beings can certainly affect their own feelings through time, by more or less ingenious strategic dispositions.[3] But they cannot at a particular time simply choose these feelings. In contrast – and on any defensible theory of the causation of human actions – they can and do often and decisively choose their own policies and modalities of action. On a holist view, to be sure, these choices may in the last instance be made for them by structural features of the economic, political or social setting of their lives.[4] But the most intrepid holist view denies merely the analytic or explanatory significance of individual choice. It does not (and, to be coherent, it *must* not) deny either the phenomenological reality or the causal efficacy of individual decisions as such. (To lengthen a causal chain is not to remove from this its later links.)

The claim that trust is central to the understanding of political action plainly needs to be stated with some care. Defenders of absolutism throughout the ages, from Bodin, Richelieu and Louis XIV to Stalin and

I am extremely grateful for the challenges levelled at the first version of this paper at the Kings seminar on trust, especially by Frank Hahn and Bernard Williams, for the editorial suggestions of Diego Gambetta, for the stimulus of two papers by Alan Silver and, once again, for the extensive assistance of Quentin Skinner.

Mao Tse-Tung, have sought to present their own putatively legitimate political authority as founded in fact upon the profound and pervasive trust of its faithful and law-abiding subjects, contested only by the wilfully and inexcusably contumacious. But one may doubt in fact whether the passion of trust can ever have been a very prominent characteristic of intricate and massively inegalitarian political relations – perhaps indeed of any political relations of substantial demographic or geographic scope.[5] Certainly it is scarcely a prominent feature or a natural consequence of either of the leading forms of contemporary state: the huckstering interest-brokerage of advanced capitalist democracies or the petulant accents of monopolistic party authority in existing socialist states. Nor, it may be as well to add, would there be any great cognitive appropriateness in the passion itself being at present markedly more widespread in political relations. The absolutist case for the benefits of subject docility continues to have plenty of utilitarian force: lowered expenditures on surveillance and repression, the smoother concertation of productive energies for projects many of the benefits of which are likely to extend far beyond ruling circles. But for a belief to be consequentially advantageous is very far from its being true.

Trust as a human passion may rest on close familiarity or massive social distance. Many have trusted their Queen (or Stalin) as implicitly as ever they have trusted their spouse or favourite sibling. The essence of trust as a passion is the confident expectation of benign intentions in another free agent. Compare Hobbes's sharp behaviourist account:

> *Trust* is a Passion proceeding from the *Belief of him* from whom we *expect* or *hope* for Good, so *free* from *Doubt* that upon the same we pursue no other Way to attain the same Good: as *Distrust* or Diffidence is *Doubt* that maketh him endeavour to provide himself by other Means. And that this is the Meaning of the Words Trust and Distrust, is manifest from this, that a Man never provideth himself by a second Way, but when he mistrusteth that the first will not hold.[6]

Since at the moment of experience it is necessarily unchosen, trust as a passion cannot be in any way strategic, though of course like any other psychic state it can in practice prove to have either good or bad consequences. As a modality of action, however, trust is ineluctably strategic, however blearily its adopter may conceive the circumstances in which he or she comes to adopt it, and however inadvertently they may carry through the adoption itself. When it proves to have been strategically well conceived, trust as a modality of action may well generate its passive concomitant. But when less happily placed, naturally, it is more apt to generate acute anxiety, or even paranoia. To see trust as a modality of action as central to the understanding of politics is certainly not to commend a strategically inept credulity or a sentimental misconstruction of the intelligence, ability or benignity of the great.

How, then, should we see the claim that an assessment of the presence or absence of trust and of the cognitive justification or folly of trust must be among the central elements of any adequate understanding of politics?

It may help initially to contrast this claim with a range of other understandings of the character of politics with which it is clearly incompatible. One such understanding is given by a common version of anarchism. We may take this to assert: first, that centralized coercive power can never be justified; second, that it is never a precondition for organized social life; third, that it never (or at least seldom) on balance has consequences more desirable than those which would follow from its absence; fourth, that human beings who belong to a single community potentially have both the will and the capacity to cooperate with each other to whatever degree such cooperation will be necessary to serve their several (real) interests; and fifth that individual communities in their turn have both the potential will and the potential capacity to cooperate with each other to the same degree. The serious case in favour of anarchism is, as Michael Taylor has well argued, a case in favour of the efficacy of community.[7]

On this view centralized coercive power, whenever and wherever it is present, can only be a ground for acute rational distrust and resentment; and whatever grounds for interpersonal and intercommunal distrust may emerge and persist at different times and in different places can be sufficiently and best dealt with by interpersonal and intercommunal cooperative responses which do not rely on the concentration and alienation of coercive power. (Anarchism is a singularly optimistic doctrine – but only in its more utterly inane forms does it actually presume that human life can go on over any length of time and extent of territory without there arising occasions for the exercise of coercion. The core conviction of anarchism is the conviction that such coercive capacity must never be permitted to congeal, settle down into a distinct institutional complex under the control of a distinct set of persons.)

If one asks why anarchists are so confident of the validity of this conviction, the answer must be that they believe both that organized coercive power is inherently untrustworthy and that unorganized coercive power can readily and routinely be at least inherently more trustworthy. In this sense anarchism depends upon (or can be expressed as) two key presumptions: first, concentrated coercive power cannot be made trustworthy (or, less utopianly, it cannot be made *sufficiently* trustworthy for its existence to be endorsed); second, dispersed coercive power (what Locke called 'the executive power of the law of nature'[8]) just is trustworthy, or at any rate it can readily be made and kept trustworthy (or less utopianly, it can readily be made and kept *sufficiently* trustworthy).

The anarchist thesis is that there is nothing wrong with the state of nature; or, that there is nothing wrong with it which is not even more dramatically wrong with organized and concentrated coercive power. Of these two beliefs the second, especially since the invention of nuclear weapons, is very substantially more plausible than the first (indeed, in a wide variety of settings at different times – from Buenos Aires to Phnom Penh – it has been proved very evidently valid.) It is helpful to present the deficiencies of anarchism as a theory not by stressing its exceedingly skimpy and implausible conception of the causal determinants of collective social life and its vicissitudes (a charge which can scarcely be denied), but rather by underlining its blatantly capricious views about the incidence of trust in human social relations.

The anarchist judgement that organized coercive power cannot be made entirely trustworthy, while despondent, has much persuasive force and is in fact shared with a number of thinkers who are certainly not anarchists.[9] What really marks anarchism out as a political theory is the judgement that dispersed coercive power either is in itself, or would be if instantiated, or could readily be caused to become, quite sufficiently trustworthy for the living of acceptable human lives. At its most optimistic anarchism simply consists in the universalization of trust towards all humans who are not themselves bearers of concentrated coercive power. Its sociological realism therefore varies very greatly with historical setting, from the Nuer ('deeply democratic, and easily roused to violence'[10]) to the *classes dangereuses* of a great third world metropolis like Cairo (or Beirut) or a centre of advanced capitalist civilization like Manhattan. As Locke pointed out,[11] and as most subsequent social and political thinking has amply confirmed, this sociological realism diminishes markedly with a deepening division of labour, enhancement of productive power and widening of economic inequalities. To restore to anarchism a measure of sociological plausibility, it would be necessary to extricate an anarchic community from the modern world economy and to reconcile its members to decidedly more modest standards of living than those which prevail in, for example, Sweden or Spain or the Soviet Union. It would also be necessary to reconcile the existing holders of territorial sovereignty (and perhaps their neighbours) to this withdrawal. The problems of anarchism so conceived are certainly problems of its potential stability within a world of comparative economic dynamism. But they are also, and at least as acutely, problems of its mere accessibility within that world.[12] As a policy, accordingly, anarchism prescribes the universalization of trust in conditions which it gives no good reason for supposing will prove available. As a strategy for conditions which are at all likely to obtain, it has, therefore, very little to recommend it. In anarchism trust as passion swamps trust as potentially well-considered policy.

A second understanding of politics which regards trust as potentially unproblematic, because dependably available under some particular circumstances, is marxism. In contrast with anarchism, marxism certainly has an explanation of why rational trust is unavailable in principle in many (perhaps thus far, most) historical circumstances, and of why in contrast it is (or will be) available in others. It does, in that sense, have some explanation of the asymmetry for which anarchism provides no explanation whatever. And it certainly offers a sociologically fuller and more realistic representation of the practical settings within which rational trust cannot hope to be reproduced. (It is decidedly weaker on the settings in which it *can* reasonably hope to be reproduced.)

Like anarchism, unfortunately (and partly because one key element in its political theory simply *is* a form of anarchism), marxism's grounds for rejecting the dependable availability of rational trust where it sees this as absent are decisively more cogent than its grounds for affirming this availability where it presumes it to be potentially, readily, or even necessarily present. The core marxist view is that rational trust is precluded in principle by exploitation. It is unavailable, plainly, in a slave or feudal mode of production, and equally unavailable under capitalism. The theory of surplus value may be of little or no use for economic analysis; but it does offer a vivid idiom for disputing the justice of capitalist property relations. Justice may or may not be precluded in principle by capitalist relations of production;[13] but it is scarcely routinely encountered in practice under such relations. There is plainly a strong case for claiming, as both marxists and modern liberals like Rawls and Dworkin do, that rational trust is precluded by a structurally unjust social order. Contrast, however, the flimsiness and aberration of the judgement that rational trust will readily be generated (let alone guaranteed) by the presence of a structurally just social order: a society in which all productive property has been subjected to collective ownership or its modern liberal surrogates.

There are many difficulties to this ingenuous expectation:

1 Can a structurally just social order be coherently conceived even in principle? Is it possible to furnish a non-contradictory and reasonably full description of such an order? (Modern liberals here can at least not be accused of failing to try.)
2 Could a structurally just social order be causally viable in principle? Is rational economic planning a real causal possibility? Does not the

democratic organization of an economy necessarily demand: one person, one economic plan? Could there be cooperative ownership and control of productive property and reasonable economic efficiency without in due course engendering just those arbitrary and unjust disparities of property rights which are characteristic of capitalist economies? How can such a social order be reconciled with the ineluctable existence of a political division of labour? How, within such a social order, are we to understand the cultural self-formation of society?

3. Is a structurally just social order (could it ever realistically be) causally accessible in practice?[14]

There certainly are very drastic doubts as to marxism's capacity to resolve both the second and the third of these sets of difficulties, a central problem about both being the recalcitrant presence of a highly obtrusive division of political labour: a set of institutional structures for political action, reproduced through time. Marxists at present scarcely have much claim to rational trust over the purely economic effectiveness of a productive system founded upon communal or cooperative property.[15] But even if they did possess such a claim they would remain drastically inadequate in their conception of politics. The political creation and reproduction of a structurally just social order is presented within marxism as an occasion for rational and unproblematic trust on the part of all those who are not structurally opposed to its inauguration in the first place. But even if it were in fact historically possible to create and reproduce such an order, the choice of strategies for attaining it, and the assessment of commitment to doing so, would always remain savagely demanding exercises in appraising the rationality of trust.

A third understanding of politics which regards trust as politically unproblematic does so from a dramatically contrasting point of view. It insists that we have no option but to take the concentration of power in human societies as given, and that we must take the less edifying motives and the less impressive levels of cognitive insight of most human beings as equally given. (That is what human society and human beings are like: that *is* the existential reality of human society.) Classical natural law or natural right theories it sees as confused, sentimental and in bad faith. The world and human beings are to be taken the way they are and are going to remain. Coercive power may sometimes be humanly ugly; but it is here to stay and is, moreover, certainly no uglier than the more socially extended impotence that it confronts, reproduces and, to a large degree, protects from a still worse fate.

This putatively realist perspective can be expressed in notably

unapologetic terms – as it is, for example, by Thrasymachus in Plato's
Republic and, to some degree, by Machiavelli in *The Prince*, and
subsequently by Nietzsche. Thus presented it is a perspective on power
from the viewpoint of the powerholder (or of claques of intellectuals who
more or less grovellingly identify themselves with the powerholder). But it
is commoner for it to appear in a decidedly more apologetic vein,
explicating not the pleasures of exerting coercive power but the practical
services which this can and does furnish to those over whom it is exercised.

An instructive thinker to consider in this respect is Joseph de Maistre,
who combined a strong feeling for the absurdity of rationalist politics and
for the massive role of the heteronomy of ends within political experience
with a powerful utilitarian critique of the actual consequences of rationalist politics in revolutionary France and a gleeful providentialist celebra-
tion of the extent to which the victims of revolutionary violence on all
sides had it coming to them.[16] De Maistre, to be sure, is scarcely a
promising starting point for constructing a modern political theory. But
the way in which he conceived politics is sufficiently unlike our own to
bring out some aspects of the latter with some sharpness. In particular he
makes it clear that it is possible to reject the view that the problematic
availability of trust is of any great significance for the understanding of
politics on grounds other (and intellectually more bracing) than
misplaced credulity over the merits of particular political agencies. A
necessitarian theodicy which sees political society as something for
which human beings are not genuinely causally responsible – and for
which they are in principle incapable of making themselves fully causally
responsible – is less than enticing for most inhabitants of the modern
West. But it is important to note how little it differs in its practical
implications from the alienated and egoist individualism characteristic of
the most sophisticated contemporary thought.[17] There is, therefore,
considerable admonitory force to de Maistre's point of view; and there
are certainly today still a fair number of human settings to which it
directly applies. (Who has the least idea how South Africa, or
Kampuchea, or the Lebanon, or even Afghanistan could be turned into a
humanly acceptable habitat once again?)

Over considerable areas of the world, however, it is now reasonable to
believe that establishing or sustaining a social frame that facilitates
human flourishing does depend on establishing and sustaining structures
of government and responsibility which in some measure merit and earn
trust.[18] Where such institutions already exist and happen to be operating
successfully it is reasonable for individuals to feel a stolid indifference
towards the exertions which have brought them into being and to see
them merely as occasions for current confidence. But where they have yet

to be established, the need for more direct and exigent forms of trust is altogether more importunate. Whether or not such structures will be established depends upon two sorts of factors. It depends obviously, and passively, on the way things already are, on the historical inheritance of the society in question: the weight of all the dead generations and several generations still in part alive, pressing like a nightmare on the brains of the living. But it also depends, *pace* de Maistre, on human agency; and this in its turn depends upon human intelligence and practical skill.

This last is a delicate claim, but it is of fundamental importance. Much of human life, plainly, is shaped by forces which no human beings at all at the time of happening genuinely understand; and some of these forces are of a character that even a few select human beings who did happen to comprehend them could scarcely significantly affect. There are important cognitive perspectives on human life (for humans themselves often perspectives of a retrospective kind) which are views from well above or beyond politics. At a given time these perspectives are views through the eyes of God or perhaps through those of an idealized Martian observer. A political perspective upon human life, if it is to be coherent, must necessarily be more modest. It is a view focused on, and restricted by, human capacities: by the possible consequences of possible intended actions. It is within this – world-historically somewhat mole's eye – view of human circumstance that the incidence of well-founded or ill-founded trust occupies such a key position. It does so because within this perspective what happens to a human society *does* depend both on the intelligence and practical skill of at least some of its members and on the use which they elect to make of their freedom of action. What trust fundamentally is is a device for coping with the freedom of other persons.[19] It is because of the phenomenological plausibility of this conception of trust that it plays such a prominent role in shaping collective life.

Most of what is true and worth saying about the role of trust in making possible human flourishing is severely particular. (To get a sense of the extravagant and unnerving variety of these particularities it would be an instructive exercise to set oneself the task of reducing the disarray of British politics today to a set of relatively clear and confident prescriptions for action by any conceivable agency. Perhaps, indeed, to do the same with the politics of any modern society at any time.)

But to develop a clearer sense of the bearing of trust on political agency in general it may be more helpful to consider a pair of seventeenth-century generalities. We may take these, conveniently, from the political theory of Locke,[20] though the viewpoint which they represent was characteristic of a wide range of European political thinkers of the period of the wars of religion of the sixteenth and seventeenth centuries.[21] The first of them is the claim which Locke shared with many natural law thinkers before and after him that the fundamental bond of human society – what makes it possible for human beings to associate with each other as human beings at all – is *fides*, the duty to observe mutual undertakings and the virtue of consistently discharging this duty. Truth and the keeping of faith, as he put it elsewhere, 'belongs to Men, as Men, and not as Members of Society'.[22] As human beings actually exhibit it (or fail to do so), it is a socially acquired attribute. But for Locke it both helps to explain what makes benign social existence possible at all and sets a standard for judging how far social existence is indeed benign. Locke himself believed that such mutual dependability could only be rationally and stably coherent when backed by the sanctions of an avenging deity: 'the Hand of the Almighty visibly held up, and prepared to take Vengeance.'[23] But he was far from insensitive to the psychic impact of human socialization.[24] His eighteenth-century critics were far more sanguine about the efficiency of socialization,[25] anticipating the verdicts of Talcott Parsons and, with a rather different emphasis, Michel Foucault. No modern political thinker has mustered a very impressive treatment of this issue.

Most seventeenth-century natural law thinkers laid particular emphasis on the promise as a type of social performance on which human cooperation depends and on the role of language in defining the scope and limits of human commitments to one another; and Locke was emphatically among them. But his root conception of what makes social existence possible does not really depend on the role of words in expressing such commitments. Rather, it depends (and in ways which perhaps extend relatively unforcedly to some other species) on the presence or absence of relatively well-founded expectations about the conduct of others, expectations which can serve, until too harshly violated, as premises for partially cooperative conduct of one's own. What the root conception consists in is a picture of the conditional meshing of mutual interaction.

One great political merit of this root conception is that it discourages excessively credulous and optimistic expectations, recognizing that such forms of interaction arise and persist because all human beings need and rely upon a large measure of cooperation from others, but also recognizing that all may at any time discover that such cooperation is in fact unavailable. In some measure it certainly is true, as Locke put it, that men 'live upon trust'.[26] But the twin of trust is betrayal. There is no occasion for trust without the possibility of betrayal. However indispensable trust may be as a device for coping with the freedom of others, it is a device with a permanent and built-in possibility of failure.[27] The central, if equivocal, role of mutual commitments and understandings in rendering social cooperation possible is one important seventeenth-century generality which needs to bulk a great deal larger in late twentieth-century political theory. In so far as political life is conceived exclusively in terms of manipulation and ideological befuddlement, the issue of trust need not feature prominently within it. But even in this vision those whose role it is to manipulate and befuddle will in practice face the constant problem of how to concert in carrying out their venture. In so far as politics is conceived at all in terms of agency, the cooperative and strategic interaction of individuals and groups, the issue of the rationality of trust is ineliminable from it.

A second seventeenth-century generality with an equally strong claim to a place of honour in modern understandings of politics is the vision of the nature of legitimate political authority as a structure of well-founded trust set out in the political theory of Locke, and particularly in his *Two Treatises of Government*. This theory is expounded as a theory of duties and rights; but it survives in modern ideological practice, particularly in the United States of America, as a theory of rights which have sloughed off their concomitant (and markedly demanding) duties – and lost along with them the theoretical basis which gave the right claims whatever intellectual force they initially possessed.[28] But in Locke's own thinking the right claims are principally important for estabishing one categorical distinction: a distinction between political units within which governmental power is essentially legitimate and those in which it is essentially illegitimate. Locke's account of this distinction is a bit rough and ready,[29] though it is a marvel of intellectual intricacy and elegance in comparison with any realistic twentieth-century reflections on the same issue.

Anarchists, of course, deny that there can ever be legitimate governmental power, while providentialist thinkers like de Maistre, in well-merited revenge, deny that there can ever be illegitimate governmental power. But on less flighty views it is perhaps evident enough that there can be, though all too often there is not, at least imperfectly or partially legitimate governmental power. (The possibility of *wholly* legitimate governmental power seems a great deal to ask for, at least within this world.) The view that a number of existing governments are blatantly illegitimate arises naturally out of listening to the morning news or reading the front pages of a reasonably honest newspaper – in any country that permits reasonably honest newspapers. The view that a number of existing governments are at least partially legitimate is perhaps harder to defend, at least to an audience of trained social scientists. But there can be little doubt that if most of the past population of the world were to be transported into many countries in the present, they would (once they had recovered from the shock of arrival) be extremely clear that the governments of these countries had gained markedly in legitimacy over their historical predecessors. Modern political theory is obsessively interested in the question of what could make a modern government truly legitimate; but it has not succeeded in developing at all a convincing way of handling this question.[30] Locke, on the other hand, distinguished sharply between true civil societies in which governmental power derives in more or less determinate ways from the consent of their citizens and political units which possess at least equivalent concentrations of coercive power but in which there is neither the recognition nor the reality of any dependence of governmental authority on popular consent. For him, legitimate political authority was itself a product of human will and action, a verdict in one version or another essentially common to all major seventeenth or eighteenth-century contractarian thinkers.[31] Within illegitimate governments, in Locke's view, the psychological relation of trust between ruled and ruler was likely for the most part to be absent, though it was also apt to be affirmed by those in authority with particular unctuousness. The more complex and the more economically differentiated the society in question, the more likely it was to be absent.[32] It was within the former, true civil societies with governments of at least partial legitimacy, that the category of trust played a second important role in Locke's understanding of the nature of politics.

What legitimate governmental authority is, Locke insists, is a range of freedom to act on behalf of what the governors take to be the rights and interests of the members of a society. To possess this freedom of action the governors must be in some ways released from the control of those over whom they govern. But in a legitimate political society they are accorded the discretion and the coercive power that they need, solely in order to serve their subjects; they claim it solely for this purpose; and they use it, to to the best of their abilities, solely for this purpose.[33] In legitimate political societies, accordingly, governmental power is in fact conceived both by rulers and ruled as a trust and (with whatever modifications are due for the moral and cognitive limitations of both rulers and subjects) the psychic relation between rulers and ruled can also consequently aspire to be one of trust: confidence, the giving and receiving of clear, veridical and carefully observed mutual understandings, a relation of trust deservedly received and trust rationally and freely accorded. Seen in this way, politics at its best is an intricate field of cooperative agency, linking a multiplicity of free agents, none of whom can know each other's future actions but all of whom must in some measure rely upon each other's future actions.

The most striking feature of Locke's conception, to a modern eye, is its readiness to conflate two issues which most (though not all[34]) modern traditions of political understanding regard as so drastically discrepant as to be essentially irrelevant to one another: the psychic and practical relations between individual citizens across the space of private life, and the structural relations between bureaucratic governments and the subjects over whom they rule. It is fair to say that Locke (who had some experience with the seventeenth-century version of bureaucratic government) sees these relations as connected in meaning rather than identical in practical character. But it is also fair to underline that his political theory as a whole represents a determined resistance to the depersonalization and demoralization of political authority which already in his day constituted the main thrust of modern political thinking.[35] This resistance was strongly linked to his uniquely individualist analysis of the basis of political legitimacy and to the sometimes exceedingly radical political implications which he drew from this analysis.[36]

The point of his emphasis on the personal and moral character of political relations was not to embrace the political routines of a decaying feudal order,[37] founded very explicitly upon *fides* as a concrete social relation of an eminently instrumental character.[38] He had, in fact, little more enthusiasm for factious grandees or a Frondeur nobility than Cardinal Richelieu himself.[39] Nor was it to herald or applaud the emergence of a social and economic order in which all human relations aspire to the condition of overt and definite contracts.[40] Nor, indeed, was it in any way to slight the merits of, or discourage the search for, risk-reducing and trust-economizing institutions over time. The very purpose of political society itself is precisely to stand in, by clear and predictable legal and judicial arrangements, backed by effective powers of enforcement, for the erratic and dangerous conditions generated by the collision of institutionally unrestrained human partiality. The best condition open to human beings, in his eyes, was the enjoyment of an environment in which men were fortunate enough to be able to have well-founded confidence.[41] But the thread which ran through all his political judgements and which set him so tenaciously against the modern penchant for purely institutional solutions was the vision of the most benign of human environments as in the end a habitat created and sustained by free human agency.[42] Since any state as its subjects actually encounter it at any point in time behaves as it does merely because a particular set of human beings chooses one course of action rather than another, the most important single point about a state's claims to authority always remains that they are claims of particular human beings to be obeyed.[43] (It was not a trivial matter to elect Ronald Reagan

President of the United States.) In political agency what there is in the end for human beings to reckon with is only their judgement of how other human beings can be expected to act. No one can *know* how another human being will act in the future. Trust is a policy apt for conditions where knowledge is unavailable, as, in the case of the free acts of another person, it (in Locke's view) will always remain. Trust does not have to be any more credulous or sentimental than the judgement of those who decide how to allocate it, though it will in practice, naturally, not be any less so either.

There is, to be sure, an alternative to trust: a consistent and strategically energetic distrust. But even in a small *latrocinium*[44] this is apt rapidly to paralyse all capacity for cooperative agency. Across the space of national, let alone global, politics this perspective, if held with any pertinacity and clarity of mind, will crush political energy and creativity in a sense of overwhelming futility. For most human beings to envisage politics as a relentless quest for the maximization of their personal advantage is to consign its practice to a sorry blend of immediate impotence and protracted disappointment. Indeed for most human beings most of the time, from the narrow viewpoint of instrumental advantage, there is almost everything to be said for pushpin over politics as a field for the expenditure of their energies. Those who live off politics, of course, can narrow their evaluative sights without condemning themselves to miscalculation or absurdity. But only an ampler array of values and a less parsimonious conception of what is worth doing can rescue politics for most as a relatively sane and coherent preoccupation. Locke in effect foresaw this quite early in his life when he acknowledged the radical contradictions between human terrestrial interest.[45] The busily opportunistic optic of game theory has done much to confirm his assessment. (It has also, of course, identified a bewildering array of impediments to rational cooperation that are quite independent of assumptions about individual motivation or interest.) A purposeful determination to avoid being a sucker, we now know, if generalized to the human race, would subvert human sociality more or less in its entirety.[46]

In the extraordinarily complicated division of labour on which modern social life necessarily depends no one could rationally dispute[47] that human beings need, as far as they can, to economize on trust in persons and confide instead in well-designed political, social and economic institutions. (The yearning for transparency in modern social organization is at bottom a muddled longing to combine the reassurance of institutions that rely minimally on trust with the directness of unmediated personal relations, to synthesize the charms of free agency which dictate ignorance of the future with the advantages of knowledge which preclude this.)[48] One of the main battle lines in modern political theory has been the dispute as to how far such economy of trust can go. On the one side are ranged thinkers from James Mill[48] and Bentham[50] to Anthony Downs[51] and the younger Robert Dahl[52] who insist on the possibility (or in some cases on the actuality) of institutions which produce a predictable 'common good' from the consequences of the rational pursuit of interest by individual role-players. On the other are arranged thinkers, from Locke and Macaulay[53] to Mancur Olson[54] and the older Robert Dahl[55] who insist on the antinomies of individual egoism or stress the key role of improvisatory leadership in facilitating the production of collective goods. (For important recent examples, note Olson's sombre assessment of the incremental encroachment of political agency on market rationality[56] within the political systems commended by Mill, Bentham and Downs, or Schumpeter's bleak insistence, in anticipation of the travail of post-war European social democracy, that no one could rationally welcome direct political sovereignty over an entire economic process.[57])

In this setting Locke's insistence on the centrality of trust was already in some respects archaic by his own day. Even in the feudal monarchies of medieval Europe the impress of Roman public law had prompted a strong theory of the priority of claims of public utility over those of private right, in determining the content of the *rationes status*, and thus in guiding the ruler in the discharge of his or her responsibilities.[58] It was a priority which might on occasion fully license a breach of *fides* between ruler and individual subject or an emergency encroachment for public purposes upon private property throughout the realm. (The latter claim, notoriously, was one which Locke in contrast with Richelieu[59] was especially anxious to repudiate.) In the trenchant pages of Machiavelli's *Prince*[60] the idea that a ruler would be well advised to (or even that he could possibly afford to) confine himself to telling the truth and keeping faith with his subjects was held up to vivid scorn. More recently, and more pertinently, Cardinal Richelieu and his busy apologists had pondered long and hard on the questions of how far public utility, the *raison d'état*, could justify the breach of a ruler's solemn undertakings to individual subjects or to foreign or domestic heretics.[61]

There is an important parallel in these construals[62] between the clash of feudal defenders of private right and personal faith with modernizing monarchs and intellectuals pressing the claims of state interest and more recent encounters between utilitarians and exponents of the primacy of justice. True, the crucial thought experiments considered have changed a trifle over the centuries. Utilitarians today clash with rights theorists over the issue of whether it is ever legitimate to torture an individual to save the city,[63] a question over which it might be hard to muster a single medieval critic of the utilitarian viewpoint.[64] Medieval conceptions of a truly hard case centre more on the regulation of sexuality than on the infliction of pain. Could it be legitimate, for example – a lesser evil – to commit adultery with the wife of an intending tyrant in order to save the city from destruction?[65] Would the Pope's *plenitudo potestatis* entitle him to dispense from her vows of chastity a fetching young nun, if marrying her to a tyrannical Saracen emperor would deter the latter from destroying the Christian faith and all the faithful along with it?[66] (Philosophical examples have gained little in unreality over the last seven centuries.) Even in the early Middle Ages, however, it is plain that contemporaries had a clear sense of the claims of utility in the discharge of public office. When Pope Zachariah deposed the last of the Merovingians from the crown of France and absolved his subjects from their oaths of loyalty, he did so quite explicitly because the latter was *inutilis* for the exercise of his *potestas*.[67]

In the context of this clash, however, Locke's espousal of trust assumes a rather less archaic character. For him the political primacy of *fides* is certainly not a matter of the priority of private rights over public utility. What divided him on this score from Richelieu and other exponents of the claims of state authority[68] was not any lack of sensitivity to the *rationes status*.[69] Rather, it was a more disabused and less alienated conception of the state itself. For him the state was only an organizational system through which some human beings are enabled to act on behalf of (or against) others. Above all, it was an eminently fallible human contrivance: not a divine provision. Men and women need in their rulers a power of agency which they can themselves only very marginally control. The subjects of every state are committed permanently by their political subjection to acts the character of which they cannot know and the consequences of which may embellish or devastate their lives. In so far as these actions are genuinely undertaken on behalf of the public good and in so far as their consequences in fact subserve this, human beings can ask no more of politics, even if the means deployed are sometimes ones which under other circumstances would have been open to moral censure. (Locke is certainly in some sense a theorist of individual human rights; but he is most emphatically not a theorist of the priority of private right over public utility.)

In political life after a certain stage of economic development the only policies which are open to human beings carry massive risks. In particular they expose men and women to appalling harm through the treachery or fecklessness of those in a position to exert concentrated coercive power. Trust in the relation between ruler and ruled is not a supine psychic compulsion on the part of the latter. Rather, it is an eminently realistic assessment of the irreversibility of a political division of labour and a sharp reminder, from the latter to the former, of the sole conditions that can make that division humanly benign.

There is no doubt that Locke's conception of political legitimacy is a remarkably optimistic picture. But its optimism is conditional and in no sense absurd. For, unlike the anarchist view or the marxist vision of the socialist or communist community, it is a picture of a continuing and inordinately demanding collective human project. It is *not* a picture of a state of affairs that is effortlessly and routinely available at any stage of history, still less of one which depends on something other than myriads of intended and free actions. It is a goal at which to aim, not a destination at which it is reasonable to expect ever fully to arrive, let alone to remain for ever. Locke did not expect well-founded trust to be actualized at all ⟶ *textual proof.* frequently even in an essentially legitimate political society. But he thought that in political communities which were fortunate enough to be essentially legitimate the problems of political agency for all socially and politically active groups were always problems of how best to construct, reproduce or repair structures of well-founded mutual trust. Even in political units which were far from being legitimate, he supposed that all socially and politically active groups whose aims were not intrinsically malign had reason to do their best to establish structures of well-founded trust – at least at reasonable risk to themselves and in so far as they stood any reasonable chance of success.

How do these two Lockean conceptions bear upon the understanding of modern democratic politics? There are two distinct and not readily compatible conceptions of a democratic political order current in the modern world. One of these, harking back to the institutional forms, if not to the social or economic realities, of the ancient *polis*, denies the need for and the legitimacy of any clear division of political labour. This view is fully current as ideology in contemporary political conflict (to say nothing of contemporary western higher education). But in a world of economies of immense intricacy, all of which are founded upon an elaborate social and economic division of labour and none of which, plainly, could maintain their productive efficiency on the basis of any less elaborate organization, it is a view in very evident bad faith – where it is not simply hopelessly confused. (It is not infrequently both.) As a view it neither has had nor could ever have any very firm and lasting purchase on the real political history of societies, being based on the systematic rejection of the attempt to consider, let alone control, political causality. But none of this implies that it is a view devoid of political consequences: on the contrary.

It certainly is not true, as Moses Finley made exceedingly clear,[70] that the participatory democracy of the ancient *polis* dispensed with an elaborate division of political labour. All modern states likewise display and depend on an elaborate division of political labour. Indeed what a modern state in large measure actually *is* is a strongly institutionalized division of political labour, though not one which in any sense occludes the exercise of coercive force. The interesting question in modern political theory is not whether there is going to be a political division of labour. (There is.) It is the question of what forms that division is going to take and what are going to be the consequences of its taking those and not other forms. More acutely still it is the question of what, if anything, could make such a political division of labour at least partially legitimate.

There is no extant model of the most minimal plausibility which suggests that such legitimacy could be sustained other than momentarily and in extreme crisis without at least freedom of political speech and association and the right to organize and choose political representatives on the basis of the opinions that citizens actually hold. There are not many places in the world today where these conditions are plainly satisfied. We know, too, rather close to home how painful it may be to satisfy them in, for example, Armagh or Belfast or Haringey or Brixton. But even within a political order which *was* legitimate by these criteria the issue of how to conceive an acceptable division of political labour or an acceptable structure of representation remains an extremely demanding one.[71] The favoured political agency for modern representation has been the political party, a vaguely conceived and in practice a notably unreassuring mode of human agency. Faced with the choice between a state with a variety of competing political parties and a state evasively related to a single monopolist political party which determines its own membership, it is not hard to see the merits of the former model. But in the less auspicious periods of modern capitalist democratic experience (themselves related to the less promising periods of modern capitalism's economic experience) it is discouraging how far their sole convincing ideological merit has become their not instantiating the latter model. A state founded upon political parties may well be a necessary condition for modern political legitimacy of any real durability. But it is distressingly far from being a sufficient condition.

What might serve to flesh it out a little, and render it more of an aid in practical political thinking, would be a more strenuous attempt to think through the character of a modern political party in terms of the project of constructing, reproducing, or repairing structures of well-founded mutual trust. Any such attempt would have fully to acknowledge the reality of the distinction between leaders and led; and it would have to give a much clearer account of the attributes that leaders need to display if trust in them is to stand any chance of proving well founded. It would need to construe the party as agency of representation more as a medium of social identification and less as a structure for the manipulative pursuit of interests.[72] But by the same token it would also need to distinguish more sharply than is customary in modern political ideologies between trust in the good intentions of more or less professional politicians and trust in their practical capacities. Trust in either might often be an agreeable start. But if it is necessary to choose between the two it is on the whole wiser in most circumstances (the more so, the more democratic or legitimate the polity in question) to opt for trust in the practical capacities. Politics is not on the whole good for the character; and it is unlikely that there really are sound reasons for viewing the intentions of most of those who have devoted decades to it with unreserved trust. But this provides no reason for welcoming the chance of being ruled by the well intentioned but hopelessly ineffectual. Modern political theory, both liberal and socialist – because it is so vacuously and evasively moralistic – gives quite inadequate weight to the human importance of practical skill in politics. Here, especially, we can see how misguided it would be to hope to replace trust as policy (the properly sceptical choice of human political expedients) with trust as passion (in its characteristic modern form, an unreflective confidence in the efficacy and decency of existing institutions: state, party, government, union or firm).

With this caveat in mind we may take as a final plain illustration of the soundness of Locke's insight into what politics is really about and really like a quite novel problem of practical trust – the problem of human coexistence after the point at which human beings have learnt how to exterminate themselves.

Anyone who is minimally informed is aware that the invention and deployment of nuclear weapons has created a condition of considerable danger.[73] There is dispute – and probably rationally unresolvable dispute – about the scale of the disaster that is now possible and about the intensity of the risk that any particular assessment of this scale will in fact be actualized over any particular span of time. There is also a miscellany of proposals as to what different political actors would be well advised to do about these risks: few, if any, of them intellectually at all compelling. One point which is clear, however, is how centrally the nature of the problem of what to do is captured by conceiving it in terms of the construction, reproduction and repair of structures of well-founded mutual trust. There are two simple reasons why this is so, perhaps individually necessary and certainly jointly sufficient to ensure that it remains so. The first is that the knowledge of how to make these instruments of destruction is ineliminable in principle except by their large-scale use. This knowledge and the possibilities which it embodies are with us for as long as anything we could sensibly think of as our way of life, or civilization itself, is going to continue. The problem is not how to rid ourselves of this knowledge. We cannot unlearn it. The problem is to stop it getting rid of us. The second reason is that the level of threat, and its erratic but rapid intensification are themselves a product of obtrusive structures of well-founded mutual mistrust.

These structures are not going to vanish into thin air in the face of moral disapprobation, more particularly of moral disapprobation on the part of those who are essentially bystanders. Building the structures of mutual trust that would be required to diminish the urgency of the risk cannot be done by burying one's head in the sand, still less by encouraging others to bury theirs. It can only be done by focusing more clearly the scale of the risk itself and establishing a clear mutual understanding of the priority of the need to reduce it over the need to diminish other – often in their own terms equally realistic and indisputably grave – anxieties.

Once such structures had been built they might in due course relapse into occasions for confidence. But until they have been built the project of erecting them will remain as perilous and as urgent an exercise in the pragmatics of trust and betrayal as any staged in the mountains of the High Atlas.[74]

4

Rights and Political Conflict

i.e, English language

In the course of the last three decades the concept of rights has come to play an increasingly prominent role in Anglo-Saxon moral philosophy. Over much the same period of time it has also come to play an increasingly prominent role in the domestic political conflicts of the United States of America and in the litany of (all too well-founded) political complaint at the governmental practices of communist states and of military and civil dictatorships throughout the world. There are clearly numerous connections between these three trajectories of discourse and understanding. In the case of some of the major recent contributions to Anglo-Saxon moral and legal theory these connections have often been made highly specific.[1] But despite the political energy and the high intelligence which has often gone into these discussions it cannot be said that our current understanding of the status and scope of claims of right in political controversy is as yet especially clear. I shall try to show why this is so. I shall also try to suggest how far it is reasonable to look to an analysis of the concept of individual and collective rights to help us to resolve political conflicts in modern capitalist democracies, and how far any such recourse is necessarily the pursuit of a forlorn hope.

Rights are standardly analysed by philosophers and jurists as bundles of distinct forms of entitlements: liberties, claim-rights (discretionary or otherwise on the part of an agent), powers and immunities.[2] Civil rights or civil liberties (such as the right to freedom of expression, movement, religious practice, physical security, and the ownership of personal property) are bundles of rights which either are, or in the judgement of the speaker ought to be, recognized by the public law of a political community and protected by the courts and law enforcement agencies of that community. It is important in modern political dispute that civil liberties should be in this way ambiguous between rights which citizens ought to possess and rights which under existing law they uncontentiously do enjoy. (It is one of the least controversial features of modern conceptions of political justice that any substantial and historically continuing body of persons living within a particular territorial state is entitled to the citizenship of that state.[3] The distinctive odium attached to the politics of the Union of South Africa has been a direct product of its refusal to acknowledge the black majority of its own population as citizens at all, a choice the normative anomaly of which was in effect acknowledged by the brazen invention of the Bantustans as ersatz states in which the subjugated majority could find themselves as citizens of at least somewhere in particular.)

There is therefore no contradiction in affirming that the civil liberties of the black population of South Africa are regularly and systematically violated, even where such liberties are in fact ascribed to them by the existing public law of the Union. What marks South Africa out from other massively right-violating states in the modern world (Uganda, Afghanistan, Iraq, and – in the Lebanon if not on the West Bank of the Jordan – the state of Israel) is not the comparative scale on which human rights are violated in practice but the explicitness with which political rights are withheld in principle. Perhaps unsurprisingly, most right-violation in the modern world is more a matter of practice than it is one of principle. The use of obviously brutal techniques of interrogation in the course of criminal investigation is well nigh universal in modern states; and the routine practice of protracted and technically sophisticated physical and mental torture is a commonplace of the domestic politics of a wide miscellany of modern states. But no state today (as far as I am aware) explicitly claims in the constitutive documents that define its sovereignty or in its formal public law the entitlement to treat its citizens (or any other human beings) in such loathsome ways. (The legal prescription of brutal punishments is not at all the same as the instrumental infliction of extreme pain without legal sanction by state functionaries in pursuit of what they take to be state interests, let alone for their personal amusement.)

Civil liberties which are formally recognized by the public law of a particular society can reasonably be spoken of as civil rights. All modern states acknowledge a wide range of civil rights on the part of those whom they acknowledge as their citizens. (Indeed all except the exuberantly barbaric overtly extend these rights to such aliens as they legally permit to enter or reside within their territories). Some modern states (the United States being the most conspicuous and historically imposing example) secure such rights in a particularly robust and thorough manner by entrenching them within the set of constitutive texts that defines their sovereignty. In the United States the civil rights of its citizens are defined in the first instance by the Bill of Rights, a series of amendments to the US constitution, and redefined in accordance with this Bill and with the presumed requirements of the original constitution itself through the decisions of the full range of domestic courts under the final jurisdiction of the Supreme Court. As a first approximation, what the disputed civil rights of American citizens at a given time really are is what the Supreme Court has tacitly or explicitly determined them to be. In the very different legal and political structure of the United Kingdom, civil rights have a decidedly less crisp texture. Here they derive from the complex amalgam of prescription and judicial precedent characteristic of the common law and from the statutory provisions of the presumptively sovereign Crown-in-Parliament. Whereas American civil rights are an historically emergent (and perhaps also in some instances a potentially historically recessive) feature of American public law, the terminology of civil rights does not apply very happily to English political debate and conflict. In Britain, consequently, the language of civil liberties has more the flavour of moral criticism of the workings of society, economy and state than of a confident appeal to existing positive or constitutional law. The fact that in a given instance there may well be no relevant law to which to make appeal is itself often part of the ground of the complaint, while the sense that there is seldom or never a relevant provision of constitutional law to appeal to serves to render the complaints markedly shriller and correspondingly less disciplined. In addition, and quite distinctly from this contrast between the legal terrain on which conflicts over civil liberties arise in the two countries, the far greater ideological salience of conflicts of class interest in British politics greatly accentuates the externality and conceptual instability of political defences of beleaguered civil liberties. The view that moral prescriptions are essentially to be analysed in terms of the emotional force for their proponents that they seek to convey and the emotional impact upon their auditors that they are intended to achieve is less fashionable than it used to be among moral philosophers.[4] But it is wise to be alert to how much better fitted such an analysis is likely to prove for capturing the character of British disputes over civil liberties in the United Kingdom than it is for doing justice to American arguments over civil rights within the United States.

To see why civil liberties that are not anchored in any determinate constitutional protection are open to such limitless and disorderly contestation it is helpful to consider one key transition in the modern understanding of rights. When Thomas Jefferson came to draft the American Declaration of Independence, he began his defence of the menaced interests of the American colonies by taking his stand on a set of truths which he claimed (optimistically) to be self-evident.[5] All men – he meant all human beings – are created equal, and all are endowed by their Creator with certain inalienable rights, the rights to life, to liberty and to the pursuit of happiness. Modern philosophers disagree vigorously over whether any human rights can reasonably be said to be inalienable.[6] Even those who in effect concede human beings all to be in some sense born equal disagree extravagantly over the implications of such equality for their subsequent legitimate entitlements.[7] Some modern philosophers still believe all men have been created; and a few, even writing outside the rubric of Catholic or Protestant dogmatics, do presume that the more fundamental rights that human beings enjoy are rights with which they have been endowed by their Creator.[8] But many citizens in all civilized states in the modern world doubt that there ever was a Creator. Even more citizens of these states doubt their capacity to infer the purposes of a Creator from the properties of the created universe; and more citizens still doubt the practical good sense of grounding their own political claims in the last instance on premises which, as they well know, many or even most of their fellow citizens confidently reject.

Most modern theorists of human rights, accordingly, whatever their personal religious predilections, ground such rights in what they take to be the relevant properties of human nature. Some, indeed, acknowledge frankly that 'rights are not plausible candidates for objective existence', though they naturally proceed to add with greater or less elaboration that neither are goods, or goals, or duties or any other organizing categories of human evaluative discourse.[9] But many, understandably, seek to blur the harsh line of division between essentially capricious human invention[10] and theocentric credulity by elaborating some more or less ingenious or evasive variety of ethical naturalism: the thesis that human goods, whatever their historical origins, are now firmly part of the furniture of the historical world that human beings inhabit.[11] And if human goods are genuinely part of the furniture of the human world, why not human rights?

There can be no doubt that the view of human goods or rights as historical inventions of the human species is metaphysically more relaxed and parsimonious than any view which grounds such goods or rights in the purposes of a Divine Creator. To believe that human goods are cultural inventions could hardly strain the credulity of even the most sceptical. It certainly does not entail the view that such goods or rights are arbitrary or whimsical in their specification.[12] But what it does do is to limit severely their externality and in particular their recalcitrance to the ebbs and flows of individual sentiment. This may seem to us admirably unsuperstitious in itself. But it does have some consequences that we might reasonably regret. John Locke, for example, constructed his entire moral and political theory – and arguably his entire philosophy[13] – around the commands and threats of a concerned Creator precisely because he judged that without such an extraterrestrial focus of authority and source of sanctions there could not be a secure rational basis on which human beings might live with one another in peace and amity.[14] It is possible, of course, that he was simply in error in so doing. But it is also possible (and in my view more likely) that he showed a sounder strategic judgement at this point than the more optimistic liberal and socialist thinkers of the last two centuries. The externality of divine authority in Locke's theory (like the putative objectivity of the Forms in Plato's *Republic*) gave to every human being the most pressing and decisive reasons for subjecting their own idiosyncratic tastes and preferences to a wholly independent range of requirements.[15] It fused together the demands of rationality and those of morality.[16] It converted the severely external reasons of the divine law of nature into reasons genuinely internal to each human agent's grounds for action.[17]

Without a comparable externality and independence of the contingent preferences of individuals or cultural communities no human value, good or right can enjoy any greater authority than the individuals or cultural communities concerned feel inclined to accord to it. 'A belief in moral prescriptivity has flourished within the tradition of moral thinking, but it cannot in the end be defended. So we are not looking for objective truth or reality in a moral system. Moral entities – values or standards or whatever they may be – belong within human thinking and practice: they are either explicitly or implicitly posited, adopted, or laid down.'[18] This is a natural enough perspective for a moral philosopher whose most urgent preoccupation in relation to morality may often (and even appropriately) be with the design of a moral system.[19] But it is a profoundly discouraging perspective for anyone who hopes that claims of right may serve not merely to capture more compellingly their own sense of their moral intuitions but also to direct political choice and political power towards ends that these would not otherwise have pursued.

In recent Anglo-Saxon moral philosophy the most important disagreement over the standing of rights has been a disagreement about their centrality to the design of an adequate moral and political theory. It is a disagreement between philosophers who suspect or hope that it may prove possible to explain the force of rights ultimately in terms of consequences (?Scanlon),[20] philosophers who see the two concepts as possessing an essentially independent weight (Scheffler, Dworkin),[21] and philosophers who either tacitly presume the priority of rights over goods

(Nozick)[22] or even hope that rights may serve to ground a comprehensive moral theory (Mackie).[23] This last view draws its attractions from the extreme deference shown by many recent philosophers to the value of autonomy. But it may well be the case that it impairs the intelligibility of autonomy as a value[24] and it certainly involves an unacceptable separation between a narrow conception of morality as a political system of uniform self-protection and a more expansive conception of morality as a theory of how to live well.

With the exception of Robert Nozick's arbitrarily specified and practically inapplicable theory of rights, none of these theories strays much beyond the bounds of a fairly confined liberalism (except perhaps in Raz?[25]). They are therefore, after their respective fashions, well enough equipped to speak to contemporary political sentiment wherever (but only wherever) this already happens to be fairly resolutely liberal in character. No doubt there are (or at any rate could be) some important conflicts of putative rights in which both sets of rights in question can be readily identified in purely liberal terms. (Abortion seems a plausible candidate.) But there can be no doubt that most major political conflicts that involve the affirmation and denial of claims of right, most cases where claims of right are keenly felt but plainly conflict with one another, stray beyond the confines of liberal values. In these instances – and especially where a liberal theory openly sanctions one set of claims and repudiates the force of the other – such a theory can add nothing but intellectual embellishment to the claims which it sponsors. All it can do is to express more elaborately a historically given political interest. Indeed, if it were to do any more than this – and to do so by any other means than the rational conversion to its own tenets[26] of the exponents of the rights that it denies – it would precisely secure that constitutional over-representation or double-counting which Dworkin regards as the major moral blemish of unrestricted utilitarian preferences.[27]

If moral tenets are merely posited, adopted and laid down, then conflicts between the moral tenets of two or more persons or social groups or political communities are fundamentally clashes of will. True, one person, group or community may be more confused or ignorant than its opponent; and one may also (and perhaps even consequently) be worse or better placed to commend to others the values that it has posited, laid down or adopted than its less coherent or more benighted opponent can hope to prove. But even after a relatively intense process of mutual persuasion or mutual abuse the clashes of will are seldom likely simply to dissipate. Behind conficts of will, individual, social or political, there stand conflicts of (at least imagined) interest. Between the conflicting wills and interests of individuals, at least in many instances, a wider community or even, *in extremis*, a legitimate state can reasonably claim to mediate. Between the conflicting wills and interests of communities or social groups, even not especially legitimate states are apt to find themselves compelled sooner or later to mediate. Between states in serious conflict the only appeal is still today, as Locke put it, the appeal to Heaven: a bleaker thought for most of us than it was for him.[28]

I have insisted that in modern political conflicts of right there are always clashes of will and interest, and that modern philosophical analysts of rights have no satisfactory basis on which to override such clashes. In many instances, indeed, they do not really possess any satisfactory basis on which to adjudicate between claims of right even from the viewpoint of their own preferred moral theory. To round out our understanding of the significance of such conflicts of right we need two further elements: a somewhat richer conception of how best to represent the character of such clashes of will and interest, and a more definite view of the similarities and discrepancies between the right-claiming units that come into conflict in these clashes. The first of these is rather less challenging than the second. The conflicting claims of right represent clashes of wills and the clashes of will in turn derive from perceived interests. But here the perception is at least as important as the interest. What comes into conflict is not just particular persons in externally specifiable social or economic locations (miners, policemen, students, blacks) but conceptions of how the social, economic or political relations of these persons or groups ought to be. Speaking only a little fancifully, what comes into conflict is the moral or political theories or systems held by individuals or groups.[29] In the uncomfortable (and not always terribly authentic) moral and political pluralism of capitalist democracies today we are all amateur moral and political theorists. To abandon our claims to be so is in effect voluntarily to disfranchise ourselves. (One vote, one amateur moral and political theory.)

Hence the overwhelming contemporary political importance of the issue of just which units really are the legitimate bearers of rights and responsibilities. In the societies which first seriously attempted to set out the rights of man it was still a central cultural assumption for the great majority of their inhabitants that individual human beings possess immortal souls. For this reason (and no doubt also for others) human rights were first articulated in a highly individualist form. This form plainly has its analytical advantages. Apart from Siamese twins, human beings all evidently are individuals. The principal point of affirming the rights of man was to make such rights more systematically and dependably available to their legitimate beneficiaries. There is nothing puzzling in the idea that every beneficiary of a human right will turn out either to be an individual or a set of individuals. (This could be equally true even if animals as well as humans were to be seen as bearers of rights.) Some rights, most notably the right to life, are individual or they are nothing. But with the disappearance of a determinate external locus of authority conceptually impervious to human whim and the concomitant evanescence of the individual soul, claims of purely individual right become markedly less imposing. It is one thing to affirm that the will of a common Creator denies to another person or group or state the right to take one's life. It is a very different matter to insist that one's own amateur moral theory disputes the same entitlement. (The notably absolutist political theory of Thomas Hobbes, for example, begins precisely from the fact that all human beings are strongly inclined to value their own opinions and judgements.[30] The more numerous and the less externally restricted the potential sources of rights, the more imperative the need to constrain them in practice: to render them compatible with peace, security and the wide range of contingently or inherently public goods[31] that a society of any merit must hope to offer its members.)

Where claims of right conflict systematically, recurrently, and on a large scale in a society, they reflect the collision of wills, of perceived interests and of moral and political theories. Liberal political theory, in so far as it centres on the value of autonomy, naturally attaches great weight to encroachments on the liberties of individuals: liberties of thought, expression, religious practice, physical security. To attach great weight to the rights of individuals is an effective prophylactic against paternalist moralism.[32] But, as Joseph Raz has insisted,[33] it does not necessarily enable one to give a very compelling account of the point (or, indeed, even the character) of many individual liberties. Perhaps more importantly, it is also poorly endowed to do justice to the significance of claims of right which cannot be clearly formulated in terms of rights of individuals to act as they happen to choose.

Modern political theory is inclined to recognize only two conceptual locations for genuine rights: the individual and the state. Even this degree of plurality is often somewhat unstable, liberal theories being inclined to collapse state rights without residue into individual entitlement,[34] while socialist theorists, notoriously, find acute difficulties in rationalizing the subsistence of any individual rights at all where these rights have plainly become rights against a socialist state.[35] It is clear why both individuals and states should be generally recognized as at least claimants of rights, however disputed their respective titles may be. What is not clear is why anyone should suppose that states and individuals are the sole legitimate bearers of rights. The view that many other human groupings intermediate between individual and state have an equally good claim to bear rights has had important defenders in European politics from the days of Althusius to those of Gierke, Maitland and G. D. H. Cole.[36] It registers much of the practical political consciousness and action of the pluralist and neocorporatist politics of capitalist democracies today.[37] Where human moral and political discourse is seen to be merely a field of cultural invention it is difficult to see how it can be justified to ignore coherently and realistically formulated claims of right that emanate from any definite human source.

What is disturbing about the plethora of groupings that advance such claims is not their ontological insubstantiality or (at least in many cases) their lack of moral dignity: it is simply their number and diversity. Theories of human rights were at first elaborated to prune drastically the sorts of valid claims that human beings can levy upon one another.[38] But once the relativity of human values to 'forms of life' has become widely acknowledged, it is no longer clear that the concept of rights retains the theoretical force to prune anything at all. True, the constraints of consistency and compatibility with fact place some restrictions on the range of right claims that possess any rational cogency. But, given consistency and compatibility with fact, it is hard to see how any authentically presented claim of right offered on behalf of a determinate human grouping can properly be simply discounted. It is not the cacophony of actually presented claims of right but the residual chaos of conflicting claims that survives even after these have been filtered for consistency, authenticity and compatibility with fact that suggests that there cannot really be a rights-based theory of modern politics that possesses any great intellectual force.[39]

I have argued that it is appropriate to see, encapsulated within any claim of right presented by a human individual or group a tacit moral and political theory espoused by that group. A natural response for modern intellectuals to the chaos of conflicting claims of right is to identify, independently of such tacitly espoused theories, a set of 'objectively existing' social and political groupings, and to interpret the theories in question as psychological mechanisms of defence instrumentally deployed by their proponents in the course of social conflict.[40] To this strategy of understanding there is one simple but fundamental objection. What constitutes a right-claiming human grouping in the course of social and political conflict is not an externally specifiable social location. Rather, it is precisely the espousal of a moral and political theory about its own identity and social extension.[41] What the interests of a given individual, group, community or even state truly are depends partially on how they conceive themselves and on what, consequently, they deem their own interests to be. (It does not, of course, depend exclusively upon such considerations. Interests are not just individual or collective fantasies.[42])

There is no Archimedean cognitive vantage point outside the space of human social and political conflict from which the latter can be validly apprehended and appraised. When it comes to the understanding of modern politics, we are all ideologues whether we like it or not (though some of us are certainly crasser and less self-aware ideologues than others). In the case of reasonably extensive conflicts of rights, accordingly, whether these rights be individual or collective, natural or cultural, there will seldom be any decisive means of intellectual adjudication on just how far any particular set of claims must be taken as valid. Even to describe a reasonably extensive conflict of rights adequately is a formidable intellectual task; and in many instances an adequate description of such a conflict would be as much of an adjudication as it is sensible to hope for.

There certainly are such things as inherently public goods: goods which if they are provided for any members of a group must be made equally available to all. The massive importance of such goods in social and political life has been strongly emphasized in recent decades.[43] The practical problems of free-riding (of drawing the benefits of a public good while actively seeking to avoid contributing to the costs of its provision) have become a central theme in the understanding of modern politics. What makes a good a public good is not that it is in fact provided by the public or that it is not enjoyed by an individual. It is simply that once it has been provided at all to the members of a given group it cannot be withheld from any of them. It is not, by analogy, clear that there really are any such entities as inherently collective rights. (If there appear verbally to be such rights this is simply because they can be generated, trivially, by adding the formula of 'a right to' to some favoured collective goods.) What, however, there certainly are is rights of agency or protection claimed by particular collectivities. These rights are valued and demanded, like the most classic of the rights of man, as rights for the individual members of the collectivity. It is these individual members (if anyone) who would enjoy them. What makes them appear to be collective rights is not the *nature* of their prospective beneficiaries but, rather, their identity. Such rights are collective in the sense (and only in the sense) that their scope and distribution explicitly mentions the collectivity of members on whose behalf they are claimed. On the beneficiary theory of rights, if not on the liberty theory,[44] there is no contradiction in insisting that the rights to act claimed by a collectivity are simply the rights of its individual members even where the actions in question are unwelcome to some of these members. As Rousseau insisted, membership in a benign political community is a peculiarly strong example of an inherent public good. It is possible, if seldom agreeable, to be forced to be free.[45]

In the case of a lengthy and anomalous industrial dispute such as the 1984/5 British miners' strike many different conceptions of right customarily come into collision. It is absurd to think of some particular subset of these as transparently valid and the remainder as evidently misplaced. An adequate description of these collisions of right would have to take the form of an adequate history of modern Britain (and perhaps not just of *modern* Britain either; and perhaps not just of *Britain* either. And so on). There are, of course, always complicated questions of positive law involved in such disputes: what state officials are obliged and permitted to do, what forms of picketing are or are not legitimate, under what conditions the leadership of a union possesses the authority to instruct its members to take strike action, and to what degree its existing legal immunities depend upon its respecting these conditions. The analysis of what the law is in relation to such questions is a matter for lawyers. But neither lawyers, nor union officials, nor industrial managers, nor professional politicians have any privileged standing in determining what the law should be. There, we are all of us simply amateur moral and political theorists strictly on a par with one another.

The most important disagreement in the case of the miners' strike – as in the case of most other major industrial disputes – was over the question of whether the law ought to be designed to favour or obstruct, to facilitate or to impede, strike action. In this instance only the very callow could hope to resolve the dispute (perhaps indeed even to express it) with anything less elaborate than a complete moral and political theory. For those who own only their own power to labour – in an economy founded on public as well as in one founded on private ownership – the right to withdraw their labour is of overwhelming importance. (How could it not be so?) The wages won by a powerful union from a monopoly employer are a clear instance of a public good for the union's own members. (They may well have a more disputable status from other points of view.) To choose to draw the benefits of union membership while refusing to incur the costs of cooperating in the threats which secure these benefits is to choose to ride freely. On the other hand a union closed shop in a monopoly employer is rather less evidently a public good from any definite point of view. It can be defended as an instrumental precondition for effective self-defence on the part of the workforce; and the occupational community to which it applies can be celebrated for its social merits. But the closed shop as such can hardly be celebrated in itself. Under full communism – as a moral ideal[46] – there will most certainly not be closed shops.

Egalitarian socialists naturally regret the obstruction of strike action within a capitalist economy. Liberal economists, by contrast, are still inclined to hanker after the Loi Le Chapelier and to regret that any combinations of employers or workers should be legally permitted (let alone protected). Both have quite important arguments for their point of view. Both, that is, can point to real and substantial costs, often costs which fall as much on others as they do on the principals, of disregarding their convictions. The present position of those inhabitants of Britain who lack market advantages is not an enviable one. But in an economy which is going to remain capitalist virtually all members of the community (including the entire working class) share with entrepreneurs and even with many *rentiers* a clear common interest in the continuing profitability of capitalist enterprise.[47] Hence the drastic importance of the strategic judgement whether or not a given economy is going to remain capitalist. Hence, too, the equally drastic importance of the probable short and long term welfare consequences of its ceasing to remain capitalist. On no possible understanding was the miners's strike a direct positive contribution to the profitability of British capitalist enterprise. But nor, for that matter, was it plausibly much of a contribution to enhancing the competing political charms of socialist enterprise.

Conflicts between classes that own the means of production and classes that are obliged to sell their labour, however they may be best described and whether or not they are ineradicable in principle, remain central to the politics of capitalist societies. (At least in imagination they also stretch far beyond these at present into the potentially eschatological conflicts between societies.) Because they are still so central, the moral and political theories to which they give rise are exceedingly complex in structure. They certainly eventuate in sharply contrasting conceptions of right; but these conceptions themselves rest upon extremely elaborate causal beliefs. At least in the case of the causal beliefs, issues of validity or error arise not just contingently and from time to time but permanently and by necessity. (Here, again, it is plainly inadequate to see the clash of wills, interests and moral and political theories simply as the collision of fantasies.)

Let us take a highly simplified interpretation of the claims of right that came into collision in the course of the miner's strike. Is it or is it not convincing to insist that where a majority of the members of a trade union have (however grudgingly or irregularly) come to take strike action, the remaining members have a right to be protected by the agents of the government in continuing to work as they choose? Is it or is it not convincing to insist that in a major industrial dispute those with only their labour to sell are fully justified in systematically menacing their reluctant fellow workers into withdrawing their labour even if this policy of systematic menace results in extensive injury and even occasional loss of life?

The first of these questions, understood as a question of moral and political entitlement and not as a question of positive law, is relatively easy to answer with confidence. There definitely are some doubts about the constitutional merit of the process through which the National Union of Mineworkers came out on strike in 1984. There are separate and at least equally pressing doubts, simply from the viewpoint of the interests of its own members as to whether it was well advised to do so. (This is a complicated question, not resolvable simply by pointing out that the strike failed. At the point at which the strike began no one could in principle have *known* that the strike would fail.) There are further – and perhaps even more pressing – doubts as to whether the success of the strike would have been in the interest of the British working class at large. (To ignore the price competitivity of a nationally subsidized energy industry within a national economy massively committed to international trade is to impose a substantial and indefinitely extensible rent on all other national producers. On any coherent economic theory, much of this rent will fall sooner or later on the rewards of labour.) But what there cannot be, waiving all these doubts, is a right on the part of members of a trade union to be assisted by the force of the state in subverting the properly arrived at decisions of their union. (The issue of the legitimacy of a closed shop is a distinct question. But here too the case against is scarcely overwhelming. It may be very difficult to become a coal miner without becoming a member of the NUM. But no one in Great Britain is *obliged* to become a coal miner.) The legal definition of picketing is a proper (and, in any society in which strike action is not simply outlawed, an inevitable) focus of public policy. But a public policy explicitly aimed at weakening the capacity of unions to impose their collective authority upon their own members is in intention a partisan intervention against the institution of trade unions as such. To assist free-riding on the part of union members just *is* to impair the capacity of unions to secure public goods for their membership.[48] It is not an appealing view that union membership should deprive a person of their major civil rights. But the 'right' of a union member to break a properly declared strike is not a civil right at all. Indeed it is a clear violation of the duties incumbent on any member of such an association. There is no *right* on the part of union members to break strikes properly declared by their own unions. It is pure hypocrisy to pretend that the use of massive police or military power to control mass picketing within a single union has anything to do with the protection of the right of other members of that union to work as they choose. The justification of its use must rest, if it is to rest anywhere at all, on the public policy grounds which motivated the legislation that made mass picketing illegal.

On the other hand, even if membership of a union implies the incurring of duties and the foregoing of liberties corresponding with these duties, it plainly does not imply the abrogation of all the civil, let alone all the human rights, of the member. The immediacy and intensity of some forms of class conflict has a somewhat corrosive impact on even such central liberal values as freedom of expression or autonomy. (The autonomous breach of a duty is not really any more beguiling than the heteronymous breach of one.) It calls into question their relevance, where it does not impair their intrinsic appeal. But it has decidedly less impact on rights to physical security. The view that mass picketing is merely a legitimate means of expressing the sentiments of fellow workers (an impeccably liberal view as far as it goes – and one much emphasized in public by union leaders in the course of strikes) can hardly be held altogether in good faith. The contempt of others does have some motivational force, though it is as apt to arouse anger as it is to evoke shame. But there is no serious question that the passion on which union leaders must rely to keep a fraying strike solid is the passion of fear. Mass picketing is a ritual of self-righteous solidarity for the pickets; but its instrumental purpose is the intimidation of those at whom it is directed. The most effective means of intimidation, both for those seeking to enforce a strike and for those seeking to break it, is the threat to life and limb. Dissident union members do not have a right to try to break a properly declared strike of their own union. But if they choose to flout their union duties in this way, they certainly do retain a legal entitlement to the civil (and, if necessary, military) protection of their rights to life and to physical security. For a trade union or a political leader to claim the entitlement to entrench on these rights is implicitly (or explicitly) to challenge the legitimacy of the state. A moral and political theory sufficient to back such a challenge is an elaborate and ambitious venture and requires the support of a great deal of well justified belief about economic, social and political causality. So too, of course, does a moral and political theory sufficient to demonstrate the legitimacy of the state.[49]

This may well seem too sceptical a note on which to close. But it is, I think, worth insisting upon it with some vehemence. The intellectual and political appeal of claims of right is that of powerful and authoritative simplification. To *claim* a right which is not simply a contingent right under positive law is to seek to cut through the tangle of conflicting sentiment and belief that prevails in any modern capitalist society[50] to something solid and unchallengeable that lies beyond it. But there is no reason to believe that anything solid and unchallengeable does lie *beyond* the heterogeneity of belief and sentiment that make up a human society.[51] Behind all human judgements of truth and falsity all there really is is forms of human life.

We can see how important such a conclusion is wherever we ourselves are inclined to reject the legitimacy of a state. Throwing petrol bombs at policemen is as natural an expression of prevailing popular sentiment on occasion in Catholic or Protestant districts of Belfast or Londonderry, or even in black areas of Toxteth or Brixton or Handsworth, as it was in Chile or Poland or is in South Africa. But since the majority of the population of the state in question takes a very different attitude towards the legitimacy of their government in the former cases than it does in the latter ones, it is natural for it to feel that the cases differ decisively from one another. (From the point of view of the majority, they *do* differ decisively.) But if anyone has human rights, individual soldiers and policemen possess them also. The right deliberately to kill simply in order to intimidate seems a bold claim in the face of riot, even in what is otherwise a state of impeccable legitimacy. (Could riots actually occur in a state that truly was of *impeccable* legitimacy?) But the right to kill in individual self-defence in the face of riot is hard to deny even to the forces of coercion of the most repressive state. Riot is a form of temporary or local civil war. Only moral imbeciles welcome the onset of civil war for its own sake. But in a state that is profoundly unjust the choice which its inhabitants face is a choice between submitting to tyranny and injustice or unleashing civil war. In those circumstances, as Locke long ago insisted, the responsibility for the exercise of force and for the harm that follows from it, rests on the unjust authorities.[52] The blood is on their hands.

Today, as in the late seventeenth century, the most important question about any political community is always the question of how far it has contrived to make itself a true civil society and how far it remains (for many or even most of its members) just a state of suppressed war. The degree to which particular claims of right are acknowledged and secured is one important criterion of where a particular society should be placed along this continuum. But this very assessment requires the tacit elaboration of an entire moral and political theory. Conflicting claims of right must be adjudicated within the theory as a whole. (Particular claims, of course, may themselves be best expressed by constructing an alternative theory of equivalent scope and then confronting the two theories systematically with one another.) What we cannot rationally hope today is that such claims should possess the power to validate themselves one by one and out of their own superior authority.

We may choose to regard human beings as equal.[53] We may build and believe and defend moral and political theories that deny that any power on earth possesses the moral authority to deprive a human being of some particular rights. We may even claim that some human rights are absolute or inalienable[54] – though it is unlikely that our claim will be entirely convincing.[55] But only the grossly ignorant or confused can any longer suppose that any human rights at all truly are self-evident.

5

Liberty as a Substantive Political Value

The saying: 'It must needs be that offences come; but woe to him by whom the offence cometh' is terrifying. What is it in us that lies, murders, steals?
George Büchner, letter March 1834[1]

There is at least one major chasm in the historical understanding of liberty as a substantive political value: a distinction drawn in the famous terms of Benjamin Constant between the liberty of the ancients and that of the moderns, between rights of public agency and rights of private enjoyment. Somewhat elusively related to this chasm, there is also a second distinction, urged most notably by Isaiah Berlin,[2] between negative liberties of non-interference and positive liberties for the development of some set of powers or potentialities held to be of overriding value for a particular agent, or perhaps for all human agents. Berlin himself firmly proposes Constant as the prime champion of negative liberty,[3] thus implicitly amalgamating the two distinctions. But it is far from clear that Constant himself would have welcomed the assimilation since it elides the principal reason which led him to wish to draw the distinction so sharply in the first place, an insistence on the impossibility in principle of realizing the ancient conceptions of political agency within the inhospitable practical organization of modern political societies, and on the murderous consequences that are likely to result from the confused attempt to realize them in this profoundly alien setting.[4] Even if Constant himself had been disposed to view the assimilation with more enthusiasm, there would in any case be a further and more pressing reason for modern theorists to adopt a more critical stance towards it. The negative conception of liberty as non-interference in the realization of an individual's own contingent desires certainly does not require an imaginative detachment from the issues of ancient or modern political and economic organization.[5] But since it is specified merely in terms of the tastes of an individual person, it readily degenerates into a reductive and plastic ideological currency for expressing political blame or commendation, with little, if any, power of sustained political illumination.

On any coherent theory of the human good the actual operations of any conceivable assemblage of political, social and economic institutions will often be open to moral criticism. Interference with the free flow of individual desire or purpose provides one of the simplest and most consistently evocative grounds for evaluative complaint in the face of the workings of human social institutions. But it does so too perfunctorily and too erratically to serve by itself as at all a sound basis for political appraisal. If the theorization of liberty as a substantive political value is confined to such meagre conceptual resources it stands no chance whatsoever of directing our judgements rationally between competing practical proposals for the institutional design of, or even for the benign operation of, economic, social and political institutions. Considered simply as a component of ethical theory, a conception of negative liberty as a systematic theoretical defence of private rights of non-interference can be constructed today on at least two very different foundations, the elevated Kantian commitment to human autonomy, and the more despondent, pragmatic, and perhaps implicitly nihilist views of human agents which go back to Thomas Hobbes.

Of these two possible foundations, the Kantian certainly furnishes a more resonant defence for beleaguered liberties, since the Hobbesian, in its author's own eyes, so brusquely discourages any practical expression by individual subjects or groups of subjects of differences of opinion between themselves and their rulers. It is not necessary to accept Hobbes's own estimate of his degree of intellectual success in constructing his theory[6] to judge that a Hobbesian stress on the practically given heterogeneity of human desire is likely to furnish a rather flimsy foundation for any conception of liberty as a substantive political value. The Kantian emphasis on autonomy has played a far more prominent role in recent American political philosophy; and it clearly possesses more of an elective affinity with the view that liberty is indeed a substantive political value. But because of its emphasis on the exercise of reason and the espousal of responsibility – on the dignity of agency as against the compulsions of sentiment – it is hard to see how it can be presented coherently as a theory of negative liberty. The Kantian approach explicitly embodies a metaphysical theory of morality, of the standing of the right and the good.[7] Its political implications are a secondary, and comparatively indeterminate, appendage to this project. The Hobbesian approach, by contrast, begins with the implications of the heterogeneity of more or less self-righteous desire for the prudent design of political order and draws the explicit conclusion that it is rational to minimize the role of moral aspiration (or self-righteousness) in constituting and sustaining the significance of this order. Hobbes, accordingly, was a bitter enemy of classical conceptions of liberty as an essentially public and politically articulated value,[8] while Kant, with more than a little debt to Jean-Jacques Rousseau, was at worst a nostalgic friend of classical republican notions of public liberty.

In what follows I shall first set out the distinction between ancient and modern conceptions of liberty as expressed by Constant and explain what he saw to be its significance. I shall next set beside it the classical republican conception of political liberty, as expressed most vividly in Machiavelli's *Discorsi*,[9] a conception grounded as Quentin Skinner has impressively shown on a *concept* of liberty as intractably negative as Hobbes's own.[10] I shall then consider the question of whether there does at present exist a coherent theory of *modern* liberty as a substantive political value in any of the extant traditions of political belief, stressing in particular the discontinuity between ancient (though of course in no sense superannuated) preoccupations with foreign subjugation and modern preoccupations with the distribution of advantage in international and domestic economic exchange. In conclusion I shall argue that the theoretical and historical setting of Constant's distinction does indeed mark a division between a historical sphere in which a political theory could be constructed (as Machiavelli's was) as a systematic defence of liberty as a substantive political value and a historical sphere (our own) in which any serious political theory must be constructed in two precariously related dimensions – an economic and a political – only one of which can be illuminatingly considered at all in the idiom of political liberty. In doing so I do not argue in any sense *against* the status of liberty as a substantive political value within a polity, however its economy may be organized. I merely deny the possibility of constructing a coherent theory of how any modern economy ought to be organized on the basis of a specification of its political order. This denial is at present politically more than a little controversial and it could hardly be of greater practical importance.

One point which follows from it, and which deserves all the emphasis that it can be given, is the prudential importance within any modern political order of sustaining a certain range of effective intellectual and political liberty – not necessarily a liberty to impugn all locally extant principles of political legitimacy, but certainly a liberty to question the

*takes a bite is/ought point
or silly.*

effectiveness of any currently applied principle of economic organization. It is in relation to the somewhat opaque dynamics of the system of production and exchange that citizen equality in the modern world is most continuously and inescapably at issue. Here the liberty to question and to judge are certainly political liberties, since in any society today there will be interests deeply ensconced in the prevailing structure of its system of production that will find such questioning deeply offensive. On a bold understanding, any such right to question and to judge is incipiently a right of insurrection, and certainly a right to cashier and replace political authorities whose performance it finds wanting. It is a major weakness of the institutionalized political legitimacy of existing socialist states that they should have such feeble ideological or political ripostes to uninstitutionalized challenge from their enraged citizenry: a weakness epitomized by the striking conjunctions between the moral economy of Polish crowds and the hasty recomposition of a decadent regime or by Brecht's mordant proposal that the government of East Germany should dissolve the people and elect a replacement. But since it is over the administration of the economy that this political void is most obtrusive, it is worth noting also that the representative system of capitalist democracies has likewise experienced, and is continuing to experience, mounting difficulties in relating punitive or optimistic changes in the tenure of political authority to well considered modifications in the functioning of its economies.[11]

I

Constant's distinction between ancient and modern liberty is drawn in the first place between a conception of liberty particularly dear to ancient peoples and one whose enjoyment is especially precious to modern nations.[12] The vain attempt to furnish France in the course of the revolution with the former had in practice ensured the withholding from her of the latter.[13] The political form which alone could furnish France with the latter, a representative government, virtually unknown to the ancient world,[14] was in effect a discovery of the moderns and one for which their condition precluded the ancient peoples from feeling the necessity or appreciating the advantages.[15] The social organization of ancient peoples led them to desire a liberty wholly different from that which the system of representative government assured to Constant's contemporaries.[16] To an Englishman, a Frenchman or an American of Constant's day the word liberty meant a number of different things: the right to be under the sole authority of the laws; to be free from arrest, detention or execution at the arbitrary will of one or more individuals; the right to express one's opinions; to choose and practise one's occupation; to dispose of one's property, however fecklessly one chose to do so; to come and go without obtaining permission from anyone or giving an account of one's motives. It was a right to consort with others, either to confer together on common interests, or to practise whatever mode of worship a believer and his associates might prefer, or simply to fill one's days or hours in the manner most suited to one's inclinations or fantasies. Finally, for each person, it was a right to exert some influence on the administration of government, whether by the nomination of some or all public officials or by representations, petitions or demands to which those in authority are obliged to pay some heed.[17]

Ancient liberty, by contrast, was a matter of exercising collectively but directly a number of aspects of sovereign power: deliberating in the public assembly on issues of war and peace, making treaties of alliance with foreign states, voting on laws, pronouncing legal verdicts, inspecting the accounts, actions and administration of magistrates, and calling upon them to explain their stewardship before the entire people, to accuse, condemn or absolve them.[18] The ancient world saw not the slightest tension between this mode of liberty and the complete subjection of the individual to the authority of the whole. All private actions were subject to a severe surveillance. No respect was accorded to individual independence, either in opinions, in occupations, or above all in religion. In the most important and intimate of human concerns the authority of the social body intervened, and obstructed the individual will.[19] Amongst the ancients, the individual, despite his habitual sovereignty in public affairs, was virtually a slave in all his private relations.[20] As an individual he was confined, watched and repressed in all his movements. As a component of the collective citizen body he could interrogate, beggar, condemn, exile or put to death his magistrates or superiors. As a subject of the collective citizen body he, in his turn, could be deprived of his dignities, banished or put to death by the discretionary authority of the whole to which he belonged. Among the moderns, by contrast, the individual, despite his independence within private life, is even in the freest of states sovereign only in appearance. His sovereignty is always restricted and almost always in practice suspended. And even if, at fixed and rare intervals in which he is still extensively constrained, he does have the opportunity to exercise this sovereignty, it is only in order to abdicate it once more.[21]

The goal of the ancients was to share social power among all the citizens of the same fatherland. That was what they termed 'liberty'. The goal of the moderns is security in private enjoyments; and what they accordingly mean by liberty is the guarantees which their institutions furnish for these enjoyments.[22] Individual independence is the prime need of the moderns and this is why they must never be asked to sacrifice it in order to establish political liberty.[23] Individual liberty is the true modern liberty. Political liberty, to be sure, is its guarantee – and for that very reason indispensable. But to ask the peoples of Constant's day to sacrifice, like the ancients, their individual liberty in its entirety to their political liberty is a reliable method of weakening their commitment to the latter and, in the event, of thereby depriving them of both.[24]

The ancients, as Condorcet has observed, had no idea of individual rights,[25] a fact reflected in the virtual enslavement of individual existence to the collective body. Only in one ancient community, the comparatively commercialized city of Athens,[26] was this subjection somewhat less complete.

The source of this essential difference between ancient and modern societies lay in a number of distinct, though interconnected, features of their respective organization. Ancient republics occupied very restricted territories. Even the largest, most powerful and most populous of them did not equal in extent the smallest of modern states.[27] One inevitable consequence of these restricted confines was an exceedingly warlike public disposition. Ancient republics lived in a condition of permanent mutual menace, purchasing their security, independence, and indeed their entire existence at the cost of the permanent willingness and capacity to make war. War was the constant interest and the well nigh habitual occupation of the free peoples of antiquity. As a natural (Constant himself says, a necessary) consequence of this mode of existence all ancient states possessed a substantial slave labour force.[28]

The modern world was very different. The least of modern states was incomparably vaster than even Rome had been for the greater part of its republican history. Even the division of Europe into a number of different states had become, thanks to the progress of enlightenment, more apparent than real. While each separate people had once constituted an isolated family which felt itself a born enemy of other families, a mass of human beings now existed which, although living under different names and within a variety of modes of social organization, was nevertheless essentially homogeneous in its nature. It was strong enough to have nothing to fear from non-European peoples (or as Constant somewhat complacently put it 'barbarian hordes'). It was also enlightened enough to see war as an expense rather than an opportunity; and its uniform tendency was therefore towards peace.[29] (It is scarcely necessary to underline the optimism of this verdict, passed so soon after the end of the revolutionary and Napoleonic wars, or to emphasize its lack of prophetic insight into the dynamics of twentieth-century history.)

But optimistic though this picture of the European social relations of his day certainly was, it was in no sense sentimental in its foundations. For Constant, commerce was quite explicitly a continuation of warfare by other (if less malign) means.[30] Both warfare and commerce are modes of securing possession of the objects of desire; and commerce is merely an act of homage to the strength of a possessor by one who aspires to possess. It is an attempt to accumulate gradually what one can no longer hope to conquer by immediate violance. A man who was always stronger would never have reason to contemplate engaging in commerce. As a gentler and more effective means of engaging the interests of others in what suits one's own interest, commerce is a product of the experience of successful resistance to more direct means of securing these interests.[31] In due course, therefore, as Constant hoped, a time must come at which commerce replaced war; and this time, so he fondly imagined, had indeed already arrived, at least for Europe, in his own day. For the ancient world a successful war would contribute handsomely to public and private wealth in the form of slaves, tribute and the seizure of agricultural land. But for modern nations even the most successful of wars cost infinitely more than it could hope to contribute in terms of economic advantage.[32] It is worth underlining the close dependence of Constant's sanguine estimates of the beneficence and stability of modern liberty on three distinct judgements: the civilizing impact and evident mutual advantage of international economic exchange, the effective military security of all relatively commercialized societies against military threats from pre-commercial societies, and the manifest absence of rational material advantage for any modern state power in pursuing either its own interests or those of its subjects by the threat or use of armed force against other modern states. (We need not consider directly in this context the possible material advantages for such states or for their own domestic subjects which might accrue from pursuing their interests by the threat or use of armed force against such forms of human society as were not as yet organized on a basis of convenience for participation in a system of international commerce.)[33]

There are four principal consequences of these contrasts between ancient and modern societies. Firstly, the sheer extent of modern states diminishes proportionally the political importance of each of their individual inhabitants. The most obscure republican citizen of Rome or Athens was, at least in Constant's eyes, a genuine power in himself, while the personal influence of an individual citizen of the Great Britain or United States of his day was a virtually imperceptible element in the collective will which imposed its direction upon their governments.[34] Secondly, the abolition of slavery (at least within Europe itself) had deprived the free population of all the leisure which their ancient predecessors had drawn from consigning the greater part of the manual labour of their society to slaves. Without their slave population twenty thousand Athenians could hardly have had the opportunity to deliberate daily on public affairs in the Assembly.[35] Thirdly, unlike war, commerce does not leave lengthy intervals of inactivity in men's lives. The perpetual exercise of political rights, the daily discussion of affairs of state, the incessant strife and deliberations of ancient factions which for the free peoples of antiquity provided a merciful relief from tedium and inactivity could in a modern nation only constitute an exhausting nuisance, since in such a nation every individual is actively engaged in his own enterprises and in the pursuit or enjoyment of his own personal pleasures and is consequently anxious to be deflected from these as seldom and as briefly as possible.[36] Above all, commerce inspires in men a lively taste for personal independence.[37] Commerce provides for their needs and satisfies their desires directly, and without the intervention of any public authority. Such intervention is virtually always a disruption and a nuisance. Whenever the public power attempts to take a hand in particular economic ventures it inconveniences their initiators. Whenever a government insists on undertaking an economic venture on behalf of its citizens it carries this out less successfully and more expensively than they could have done it for themselves.[38] (It would not be wise, plainly, to take Constant in every respect as an authority on political economy.)

In a modern society, accordingly, it is no longer possible to experience the active and constant participation in the exercise of collective power which was the essence of ancient liberty.[39] The part that every citizen in an ancient state could play in exerting national sovereignty was not, as it has since become, an abstract presumption. The will of each might carry a real influence. The exercise of this will could afford a vivid and repeated pleasure. Because this was so, ancient citizens were ready to pay a much higher price for the preservation of their political rights and for their role in the administration of the state. But in a modern society such compensations are sadly absent. Lost in the multitude, an individual citizen can seldom or never detect the traces of his own influence or even the palpable benefits of his own participation. The exercise of political rights, accordingly, offers to a modern citizen only a travesty of the enjoyment that the ancients found in it, while the progress of an increasingly commercial civilization and the spread of communication between different peoples have vastly multiplied and diversified the means of particular happiness. In consequence, modern citizens are far

more attached than their ancient predecessors to the individual independence which they can now hope to enjoy in peace.[40] When the
ancients sacrificed this independence for the exercise of political rights,
they sacrificed less to secure more. But in Constant's day it had become
necessary in such an exchange to sacrifice more in order to obtain
altogether less.[41]

For Montesquieu this contrast in commitment to political liberty and
to commercial enjoyment was attributable to the constitutional and
political distinction between republics and monarchies. But in fact the
real contrast is one between the ancient and modern worlds as a whole.[42]
In Constant's day the citizens of republics and the subjects of monarchies
were alike united in their eminently self-conscious desire for private
enjoyments. Before the French revolution, the modern nation most
deeply committed to the defence of its liberties was also the nation with
the keenest attachment to the enjoyments of life; and its commitment to
liberty was above all a commitment to what it saw as the guarantee of the
enjoyments which it cherished.[43] In the ancient world, where liberty
existed, men were willing to endure privations; but in the modern world
only slavery could compel a population to resign itself to privation. The
hope of forming a community of Spartiates through the exercise of public
liberty is, in this changed world, merely a chimera.[44]

Constant himself firmly refused to conclude from this contrast, as a
number of his contemporaries had done, that the appropriate political
order for a modern commercial society, with its severely limited citizen
commitment to, and its equally limited opportunity for, the exercise of
public liberty was a manipulative despotism based upon the scientific
exploitation of the corrupt sentiments of its subjects.[45] What was
necessary in his eyes was not to abandon the political guarantee of
private liberty but, rather, to extend the scope of private enjoyment and
civil liberty ('C'est la jouissance qu'il faut étendre '[46]). It was not that
modern individuals had lost their political rights: the right to consent to
laws, to deliberate about their interests, or to play a full part in the social
body to which they belonged. But modern governments had also
acquired quite new duties. The progress of civilization required of them a
far greater respect than their predecessors had been apt to display for the
habits, affections and independence of individuals, and demanded that
they exert on these an altogether lighter and more prudent touch.
(Constant also supposed, more optimistically, that the requirements of
commerce, the mobility of commercial property and the increased
commitment to individual liberty had made despotic arbitrariness not
merely more offensive but also far less easy to maintain.[47] 'Que le pouvoir
s'y résigne donc; il nous faut de la liberté, et nous l'aurons.')[48]

But since modern liberty differs so much from its ancient predecessor it requires a very different political articulation. In the ancient model, the more the citizens consecrated their time and energies to the exercise of their political rights, the freer they believed themselves to be. But in a modern society, the more time that the exercise of their political rights leaves available for the pursuit of their private interests, the more precious for its citizens will their liberty be.[49] Hence the necessity of the representative system.[50] What this system essentially amounts to is an institutional structure through which a nation unburdens itself on to the shoulders of a number of individuals of those tasks it cannot, or does not wish to, carry out itself. (Poor individuals, says Constant a trifle sardonically, carry out their own business; but the rich avail themselves of stewards.) The representative system constitutes an authority conferred on a certain number of men by the mass of the people who wish their interests to be defended but do not have the time to be perpetually engaged in defending these themselves. But, just as rich men keep a severe and watchful eye on the performance of their stewards to ensure against the negligence, corruption or incapacity of the latter, modern nations which adopt the representative system in order to enjoy their personal liberties must maintain an active and constant surveillance[51] upon their representatives and reserve for themselves at reasonably brief intervals the right to dismiss them if they have disappointed their wishes and to revoke their powers where these have been abused.

Modern liberty faces different dangers from those that threatened its ancient predecessor. The principal danger for ancient liberty was that its beneficiaries, in their exclusive preoccupation with participation in public power, might sacrifice too large a proportion of their individual rights and enjoyments. The danger for modern liberty, by contrast, is that in their absorption with the enjoyment of their private independence, its beneficiaries may renounce too readily their right to share in political power. The holders of public authority are naturally only too delighted at this prospect, being eager to spare their subjects every trouble save those of obeying and paying, and being all too ready to promise to provide for the happiness which is the motive for all the labours and the object of all the hopes of those over whom they rule. But to accept this offer would not merely be imprudent: it is more expedient for a government to confine itself to being just and leave its citizens to find happiness for themselves. It would also be ignoble. The exercise of political liberty is in itself a uniquely important and energizing field for the development of virtue and for the quest for human perfectibility.[52] Happiness does not exhaust the goals of human life.[53] Even within the France of Constant's own day the regular exercise of political liberty was in his eyes both an ennobling experience throughout the citizen body as a whole and an effective guarantee for the defence of their legitimate interests. The problem of modern society was how to combine modern private liberty with political liberty through the effective moral education of the citizen body and the provision of a system of public institutions which gave to each member of this body the fullest opportunity to defend his interests.[57]

II

When the latter is expressed in these terms, however, the categorical distinction between ancient and modern liberty begins appreciably to blur. For ancient liberty, too, as Machiavelli for example defended it, involved the defence of public liberty through a system of public institutions (*ordini*) which guaranteed the effective moral education of the citizen body in the virtues of courage, temperance and prudence in order to satisfy the private desires of these citizens. It is true that Machiavelli divides the citizen body into two groups of very unequal size, and with sharply distinct dispositions (*umori*).[55] On the one hand, there are the *grandi* whose principal desire is to win personal power and glory, whose characteristic vice is *ambizione*, an elite which 'desidera di essere libera per comandare'. On the other there are the decidedly more numerous *plebe* or *popolo* whose principal desire is simply to live in security 'without anxieties about the free enjoyment of their property, without any doubts about the honour of their womenfolk and children, without any fears for themselves'.[56] Their characteristic vice is the vice of *licenza*, the desire to live with as little interference as possible just as they choose to live. These, accordingly, 'desiderono la libertà per vivere sicuri'.[57]

The constrasting dispositions of these two groups naturally favours a fairly sharp division of political labour in which the *grandi* monopolize political prominence since for them the enjoyment of political prominence constitutes so much of what life is about, and the *popolo* consigns to public affairs only such energies as it is effectively badgered into giving by the effectiveness of prevailing social discipline (*ordini*). Machiavelli's massively unsentimental view of human motivation does not merely identify civic commitment as a fundamentally instrumental good: it also locates the propensity for political apathy firmly at the centre of the unedified sentiments of the majority of human beings. For him, political education is essential not because it offers most people the opportunity for the fullest development of their human potentialities but because without it most people cannot be trusted to commit to public affairs and public service anything like the degree of energy that is in fact necessary to give themselves the best possible chance of preserving their own domestic liberties or of retaining the political independence of their community as a whole. A free way of life, a *vivere libero*, in Machiavelli's eyes is not merely the fundamental precondition for the *grandi* to exercise their ambition[58] (an opportunity that, with a little mild cultural modification, they might also hope to secure at the court of a successful despot: in a politically emasculated form many of the individual cultural ideals of Machiavelli could still be pursued by Castiglione's *Courtier*). It is also the fundamental precondition even for the less energetic populace to enjoy their property without fear of having it removed from them by force. Only a free city is subject to the control of no other power and thus able to govern itself according to its own will. Only a free city whose citizens are deeply and energetically committed to defend with arms its free way of life can hope to retain its freedom against the multiplicity of external military threats to which it will inevitably be subject. Virtue and public commitment are thus preconditions for private enjoyment in Machiavelli's eyes, though the goal of human life in his eyes is just as much a matter of enjoyment of what men happen to find enjoyable as it is in those of Constant.[59]

Because for Machiavelli the most acute and permanent threat to the interests of a citizen body was the threat of external force, of foreign rapine and conquest, the most evocative and fundamental form of civic commitment was military service in a citizen militia. Despite (or perhaps because of) the drastic recent recension of such commitment in the *levée en masse*, and despite the military triumphs of the revolutionary and Napoleonic armies, Constant's conception of the principal threats to citizen interests was altogether more domestic. The commercialization of Europe had not merely done much to homogenize the cultures of different political communities and to provide their populations with a common interest in the preservation of peace, it had also bred a far less bellicose disposition in these populations. Threats to the private enjoyment of property now came, in his eyes, from the forlorn attempt to implement anachronistic political models, not from the sword of foreign conquerors (or even the shining sabres of hussars).[60] There is perhaps little reason to accept the judgements of either Machiavelli or Constant on the range and comparative intensity of hazards to which the private enjoyments of the majority of the European population were in fact subject even in their own day, let alone to adopt them as a basis on which to form more generalized estimates of such perils at a miscellany of other times and places. But the contrast between their two views will serve very adequately to bring out a number of conceptual relations.

The most important of these is simple enough. Both Machiavelli and

Constant present a system of political liberty as an instrumental good, the point of which rests in the last instance on the existence of a myriad of other given human purposes. Both see the instrumental good in question primarily as a device for averting a single dominant form of harm (a social *summum malum*). For Machiavelli, this is foreign conquest, the extermination of the political independence of a community. For Constant, however, it most emphatically is not. On his account, the grounds for ignoring such a risk are provided by the historical obsolescence of the risk itself. Modern European commercial states do not feel bellicose towards one another and hence no longer menace each other's political independence. They are on the other hand still liable, through a defective social and political self-understanding and under the influence of ideological phantasms from a remote past, to interfere massively with the private enjoyments of their citizens in a vain attempt to reshape their polities to accord better with an anachronistic aesthetic susceptibility. The commercialization of society guarantees the privatization of the concerns of the majority of the citizens (or, in Machiavelli's categories, it lends powerful cultural support to sentiments that these would have experienced in any case and thus reinforces socially a natural disposition which only its firm social suppression can keep from being corrupt). But these concerns in themselves no longer have, on Constant's analysis, any direct instrumental connection with political independence as such. (The appropriate political form for a fully commercialized world would perhaps be a world empire, with its political order arranged in the form of a representative system.) Because in its domestic politics the representative system still furnishes an essential guarantee for the protection of individual interests, political subjugation certainly involves significant risks. (Even in their domestic politics the lack of mutual animosity between modern European nations is therefore of great importance.) But because of the close relation between the extension of modes of enjoyment and the development of international commerce, and because human goods are defined theoretically and experienced existentially at the level of private enjoyments, it is easy to see how in liberal theory after Constant the extension of commercial civilization, even at the cost of the political independence of its beneficiaries, might seem to those intent on extending it a relatively clear benefit, while for Machiavelli any such claim could be little better than a contradiction in terms.

The relationship between political rights and political units, between national independence and civic membership, between constitutional structure and sovereign territoriality, has been very poorly considered in modern political theory. The cultural and political acceptance of the privatization of enjoyment in commercial society has varied considerably from country to country and from decade to decade. But it is hard – and in the end politically rather expensive – to resist it in any society of our own day; and there can by now be rather little doubt that, over any lengthy span of time, it conceptually favours a conventional and detached view of the nature of civic membership, rather than a fervent focus on the sovereign political unit as the site of ultimate human interests. (Even when accompanied with some of the accoutrements of civilization, the pleasures of direct subjugation were never in themselves very vivid from the viewpoint of the subjugated; and the geopolitics of the last four decades have caused them by now to come to be distributed on a piecemeal rather than a wholesale basis.) It would not be going too far to say that there is at present no powerful theorization of liberty as a substantive political value expressed at the level of independent political communities. Our conceptions of political independence are taken from a theory of sovereignty devised to rationalize the absolute monarchies of early modern Europe;[61] the attempt to specify theoretically just why independent political units today (Kampuchea, Chad) ought rationally to be seen as the locus of final allegiance and the site of human flourishing for their individual citizens has been left to a relatively perfunctory and tatty series of ideological improvisations.[62]

what of
nationalism?

III

Between Machiavelli and Constant there is a sharp alteration in the instrumental importance assigned to civic virtue. There is also a signifi-cant change in the ways in which the cultural ecology of a society is conceived, and particularly in the assessment of how far the cultural reality of any society can realistically be designed by political calculation and secured through political institutions and by the exercise of political will. For Machiavelli the *ordini* which shape a society, which impose order upon it, are necessarily an instance of political design: while it certainly requires luck and skill to design them with any great success, it is in the design of such *ordini* that political intelligence makes its most important contribution to human social flourishing. To repudiate the potential efficacy of such *ordini*, accordingly, is to repudiate the view that politics can be anything more than an improvisatory exercise in individual agility and fortitude.

For Constant, by contrast, commercial society certainly has its *ordini*, the assemblage of institutions which naturally favour its practical require-ments. But this assemblage in itself does extremely little to mould the culture of the society. Rather, it expresses that culture. Culturally speaking, that is to say, commercial society comes extremely close to moulding itself. In doing so it sharply constrains the range of explicitly political institutions that can be appropriate to it. At times, Constant can even write as though it uniquely prescribes at least some of their key aspects: 'il nous faut de la liberté, et nous l'aurons.'[63] But the main emphasis of his thought plainly falls upon the range of antecedent political options which the commercialization of society closes off and renders impossible, and not upon a unique political and social apparatus which any developed commercial society imperiously requires. Even here there is some ambiguity in his attitudes as to whether what commercial society in fact does is to render the options in question genuinely impossible or whether it merely makes them highly undesirable. Constant himself readily acknowledges both the practical utility and the ethical necessity of civic virtue even in a commercial society. What he denies is that such virtue can any longer be expressed satisfactorily in an idiom of public agency. Yet even here a comparison with Machiavelli brings out a certain ambivalence in his view. No one considering the earlier years of the French revolution could plausibly claim that this episode had offered insufficient scope for the exertion of *ambizione* in public agency:[64] even if many of those who contrived to exercise their ambitions most energetically were scarcely themselves *grandi* by social origin. (It is a psychologically important feature of Machiavelli's own writings that it was so plainly with the *grandi* rather than the *popolo* that he characteristically identified himself.)

When set against the social and political division of labour between *grandi* and *popolo* (a division of peculiar ideological sensitivity in the aftermath of 1789 and the triumph of the *tiers état*), it was far from easy to pick out the outlines of Constant's theory of modern liberty as a substantive political value. The Abbé Sieyès, in the first years of the revolution, had set out a powerful defence of the representative system as the sole legitimate political expression of a society founded on the division of labour, a society in which, unlike in the Estate system of the *ancien régime*, all citizens had work to do and the necessary labour of their entire society ought to be divided accordingly among all its members.[65] (In this perspective, the Athenian demos, freed for incessant participation in public affairs by the labour of its hapless slaves, was an ancient analogue of the caste prerogatives of the privileged orders.)[66] Here Constant's emphasis upon the purely arithmetical and geographical futility of political activity on the territorial scale of the modern state was a little beside the point. The representative system itself provided for at least a proportion of the modern *grandi* (very possibly for as large a proportion as the practical political realities of the Athenian assembly in the days of Pericles[67] or the

Florentine republic in Machiavelli's early manhood had succeeded in furnishing) the opportunity for a mode of public agency which was at least not necessarily any more futile than any other instance of human political practice. From the majority of the *popolo*, to be sure, it asked as little as it was in a position to offer; and it was scarcely surprising in consequence that on most occasions they should view it with pretty muted interest. But, with the sole exception of fears of foreign threats (or hopes of foreign aggrandizement), this comparative lack of interest was not a product of the cultural deformities of commercial society (which may be presumed to affect the fundamental preoccupations of the *popolo* –or most of us – rather little, however much they modify the schedule of current sources of enjoyment) but of the directness and weight with which public decisions bear upon these preoccupations. In an Italian city republic of Machiavelli's day (at least in Machiavelli's own eyes) the line between a benign and pragmatically realistic enjoyment of privacy and a corrupt privatization of personal commitments, between living the good life and succumbing to licence, was drawn not by a prissy assessment of the objects of popular desire but by appraising the relation between their personal commitments and the ways in which the collective interests of the citizenry as a whole were currently in jeopardy. Civic virtue was not a substitute for personal enjoyment (though an excessive zest for personal enjoyment could of course subvert civic virtue more or less without residue). Rather it was an indispensable complement to private enjoyments which deserved a genuine lexical priority over these, when and only when it was required to defend their future possibility. (No one who reads Machiavelli's letters can believe that civic virtue is seen by him as a substitute for personal enjoyments.) Civic virtue is in fact an analogue at the social level of the role of prudence in rationalizing the stream of individual desire. Hence the plausiblity of the judgement either for individuals or communities that at least a measure of virtue may be a precondition for the maximization of freedom.

The view that a more full-blown conception of virtue might be an acceptable substitute for freedom, or even that it may simply *be* freedom – that virtue and freedom are in the last instance identical – is at the centre of all conceptions of so-called positive freedom. It certainly demands, as Skinner says, an objective notion of what human flourishing or happiness ultimately consists in.[68] But whether such a conception in its turn genuinely requires a *concept* of liberty different from that which Machiavelli and Constant share with Berlin, or whether indeed an equation between virtue and liberty could ever be rationally sustained at the level of a real political order are altogether more questionable. It remains doubtful that a coherent concept of liberty can be clearly explicated in other terms than those set out over fifteen years ago by Gerald McCallum[69] – as the freedom of an agent or agency from a range of potential or actual restraints for a range of potential or actual projects or performances. The most robust possible conception of liberty, both morally and politically, would be one in which the range of potential or actual projects for a given agent was specified on the basis of knowledge of the objective content of what it was for that particular agent to flourish. Rousseau certainly made a spirited attempt to specify collective freedom on such a basis, within a political order of ancient liberty. But few elements of his account retain cogency even on the modest territorial scale of a city like Geneva; and the subsequent political history of the world has done nothing to diminish the force of Constant's scepticism over the wisdom of entrusting governments with the responsibility for determining the content of individual happiness. However feckless (or graceless) the *popolo* may be in picking out the objects of its desire there is no reason whatever to impute a more dependable taste through time to the evanescently triumphant vectors of *ambizione*, the *grandi* who determine the practical political commitments of modern state powers.

The theory of negative liberty, as set out by Berlin and a wide variety of subsequent commentators in Britain and North America, may have confused the analysis of the concept of liberty rather more than it has illuminated it. But what its exponents certainly have done is to underline the major purely ideological strength of modern capitalist representative democracies, their steady, and in some cases by now exceedingly strongly institutionalized,[70] refusal to accord to the members of a governing stratum any persisting right to sit in moral and cultural judgement on the deeper existential choices of the great majority of their fellow citizens. In itself this certainly is an essentially negative merit (which is very far from saying that it is no merit at all). It is negative in the sense that, on its own, it gives to the citizens of these societies only a bare minimum of concern and respect[71] and furnishes them only with a motive for not regarding their society with animosity and not with grounds for feeling towards it love, devotion, commitment or even necessarily much in the way of allegiance. More positive grounds for enthusiasm or commitment have to come, if they are to come at all, from other features of the social, political or economic order. When these latter features are in good repair it is common for the rulers of these societies to be rather sensitive[72] to the cultural uncouthness of deploying in their domestic political conflicts the hectic expedients of ancient factional struggle to which Constant took such firm exception: ostracism, censorship, exile, expropriation or detention at will. It is only when these other features of the society, polity or above all economy are in markedly less good repair that it becomes dismayingly obvious that commercial society itself in no sense precludes the protracted deployment of such expedients on behalf of values with nothing whatever of the inspirational afflatus of ancient liberty.

IV

Ancient liberty was in essence a set of insecure but inspiring rights of public agency. Modern liberty, by contrast, is in essence a set of considerably less evocative but tenaciously defended rights of private enjoyment and self-expression. Since it is defined in terms of private rights or opportunities it is far less clear than in the case of its ancient predecessor just what does constitute an appropriate political setting for it. One contrast, of course, is virtually a matter of logic: that modern liberty cannot be *defined* in terms of what is judged to be its appropriate political setting, that the relation between modern liberty and the constitutional and institutional order of the modern state is external and contingent,[73] not internal and logical. (This will be so even when the state in question constitutionally guarantees a wide range of private rights, since the provision of constitutional guarantees is merely an instrumental technique for supplying the substantial reality of such rights in practice. As the history of the United States makes especially clear, constitutionally guaranteed rights require politically effective mechanisms of enforcement. They cannot simply enforce themselves.

A second contrast, helpfully salient in Constant's account, is theoretically more discomfiting. The causal mechanisms through which modern enjoyment is furnished or withheld, unlike those which dominated the ancient world, are the largely opaque and spatially highly extended relations of an international system of production and commercial exchange. Constant's emphasis on the pacificatory impact of participation in this system has proved to be distressingly over-optimistic. More importantly still, it has proved to be so on a domestic, almost as much as on an international, level. Here the full incoherence of modern political theory begins at last to come into focus. Any modern system of production and any complex range of economic exchanges depends causally on an effectively defended range of recognized rights of property. All property rights necessarily restrict freedom;[74] what a property right is is a restriction on the freedom of potential agents other than the property-holder. (Where there is no scarcity, and hence no occasion to restrict the freedom of anyone to enjoy, there will also be no occasion for the institution of property.)[75] Any modern society, however it may be organized domestically, which chooses to participate at all in inter-

national exchange, imposes through time within its own national population a particular (though, of course, an ever-changing) distribution of
restraints on the liberty to enjoy. It does so, and has to do so, in order to
make available to its members any future range of opportunities for
enjoyment for which participation in international exchange is in fact a
necessary condition.[76] (Precisely the same problem also arises within a
domestic economy, though in this setting the theoretical presumption of
governmental omnipotence and omniscience – which no one could be
asinine enough to adopt in relation to the workings of an international
system of exchange – can be used to blur the character of the choices in
question.) Any modern government, accordingly, has to offer to its
subjects or citizens at every point a set of more or less explicit proposals
as to how the balance of advantage between restraint of present
enjoyment and opportunity for future enjoyment can be expected for
most of them to come out for the better. To do this at all, every modern
government necessarily needs to form (and to keep in working order) a
range of elaborate conditional beliefs about economic causality. But it has
to do so in a world in which not merely every other government but, with
greater or less application, a very large number of its own citizens will
also be forming a cognitively somewhat less ambitious range of beliefs on
essentially the same topic.[77] In the modern commercialized world (built
by the expansion of capitalism and the political responses to this across
the face of the globe) individuals, communities, classes, nations and
power blocs do not merely produce in decent social or political privacy.
They also exchange elaborately with one another, incessantly shifting
their mutual postures in the effort to tilt the terms on which they are
obliged to trade towards their own advantage. In the stunningly complex
game-theoretic interactions of these often exceedingly active strategies
(strategies which of course at times include such analytically alien
elements as the use of massive violence), any modern government is
obliged to trust extensively to *Fortuna*, some, naturally, with far greater
success than others.[78] In their own ideological self-representations the
governments of the modern world for the most part divide up rather
sharply between those that see themselves as *free* economies, organizations of economic relations as a system of purportedly natural liberty, and
those that see themselves as genuinely socialized economies, which,
because of the common ownership of the means of production by their
participants, are undefaced by the systematic private expropriation which
underlies the economies of their rivals. But it does not take profound
insight into political theory, or great depth of economic sophistication, to
detect major elements of prevarication in both of these self-
representations. Private 'expropriation' is of fundamental importance

where, through time and *ceteris paribus*, it gratuitously abridges the opportunities of a majority to act as they would choose to act. But since public ownership as it could conceivably be institutionalized in any modern economy must logically restrict freedom just as drastically as private ownership – they restrict the freedom of different people to do different things: but they certainly also both furnish a large range of common restrictions as well – it cannot be true that either the one or the other can simply be equated with freedom. (Nor, for that matter, can it be true that the one can be equated with negative liberty and the other with positive liberty.) And even if, as domestic distributive systems, they could be plausibly presented on the grounds of their intrinsic properties as being unequivocally and categorically beneficial at a particular time to the population of a particular society, they could hardly hope to retain the same blithe and evident superiority in the context of international economic exchange.

All modern governments, as the political custodians, managers and protectors of their domestic economies, stand in a severely contingent relation to the maximization of the opportunities of the majority of their subjects to act as the latter choose (let alone, *would* choose). What intrudes between them and the securing of this goal (a goal which it would be charitable and, in so far as it does not overlap with their own removal from power, reasonably realistic to impute to virtually every government in the world – no governments are against popular contentment as such) are the devastatingly taxing disciplines of a mixed game of skill and chance: the determination of how to participate beneficially in a world economy. It is in the skilful formulation and effective implementation of economic policy that those modern governments that do not actively massacre their subjects in substantial numbers do most to alter the opportunities of most of these subjects to act as they would choose to act. Because such powers are for most of the time their most important powers, and because they bear no direct relation whatever to constitutional order, or even to the degree of legal recognition accorded to private rights, it is not possible to appraise the merits of modern governments as sustainers of modern liberty – the liberty to act as one chooses – by inspecting the constitutional order, or even the fundamental socio-economic structure of a particular society at a particular time.

It is clearly important here how far the specification of modern liberty as a matter of essentially private enjoyment or freedom of action has in fact been extended culturally, through the commercialization of the world. And it is certainly true that there have been in the present century a number of evanescent attempts to institutionalize on the amplest scale communities of Spartiates – the Great Leap Forward, the Cultural

Revolution, the fervid nightmare of the Khmer Rouge – sometimes at the cost of many millions of lives. (There have also, of course, been attempts – perhaps with a somewhat greater potential for durability – to reverse these values still more fundamentally by the recreation of Zealot theocracies.) The exponents of modern liberty can only avert their eyes with horror from the Iran of Khomeini, whatever sympathy they can muster for the immediate sentiments that prompted its political genesis. But they may by now, if they can only contrive to ignore the louring apparatuses of mutual military menace, view with some modest complacency the history of secular socialist politics in the twentieth century as, in the last instance, a quest for the provision of essentially modern liberties by somewhat different means. Certainly, modern socialists tend to exhibit a more pained cultural fastidiousness in the face of the consequences of modern liberty than Constant showed (and thus to lay an even greater stress on the need to complement this with edification and the inculcation of civic virtue). But rather few modern socialists would now choose to proffer the rigours of compulsory participation in a putatively more expressive culture as a *substitute* for the enjoyments of a voluntarily chosen personal life.

It is not hard to see why.

V

Because of the intimate relationship between effective governmental economic policy and the liberties of personal action and enjoyment, and because of the contingent and distressingly elusive relationship between such efficacy and the constitutional framework of socio-economic structure of a modern state there cannot at present be a clear and compelling theory of the political prerequisites for the practical realization of modern liberty. This is most transparently the case in the domain of international economic exchange. But it is in fact apparent also, on reasonably close inspection, in the design of systems of domestic representation. Since modern liberty is not *defined* in terms of a constitutional or political order it can be fully expressed at the level of a state only by a cognitively and politically trustworthy link between the system of production and exchange and the state power, or by a decisive fissure between state power and productive system which guarantees that the latter can and will furnish by itself the essential material components for modern liberty without intervention by the holders of state power. All the liberal and socialist political thinking of the last two centuries – or all of it that does not dissolve the issue in mere verbiage – has wrestled with the attempt to identify a dependable link or an acceptable fissure of this kind.

None has come anywhere near succeeding. By now it seems clear that none has contrived to do so precisely because no linkage or fissure of the appropriate kind does in fact exist.[79] The reasons for this increasingly resonant absence are not difficult to detect. One early and recurrent hope was set out powerfully by the Abbé Sièyes in the preliminary stages of the Revolution, in what Marx took to be a paradigmatic expression of revolutionary consciousness.[80] Within the French nation there were only two genuinely discrete interests, the interests of the parasitic privileged castes, grounded in superstition and feudal oppression, and the common interest of the Third Estate, provider of all the real goods and services which the population of France either needed or enjoyed.[81] Under its natural political leaders, chosen through a system of national representation, the essentially political tasks which faced the national society could and would be discharged by elected representatives exercising their own judgement on behalf of their fellow citizens and taking a natural role within that national division of labour to which every genuine citizen made their active contribution. Such a view could hardly survive the perception of a society as divided, however much else might still unite it, into structurally opposed class interests. A second view, resting on the confident identification of the system of natural liberty as the most effective path towards the opulence of all, still defended today in essence by economists like Hayek and political leaders like Mrs Thatcher, has foundered and will continue to founder on the massive implausibility of this allegation to many citizens at any particular time, and on the consequent difficulty of backing it on particular occasions with effective political protection, of institutionalizing a constitutional order propitious for its protracted realization, and of combining it at all convincingly with a full range of public guarantees for private freedom of enjoyment and expression.

A third view, repeatedly explored in the socialist tradition, presents a full system of common ownership of the means of production, under the custody of national representatives (or operating with splendid automatism under the serial impulses of the entire citizenry) as providing a still more effective path towards the opulence of all but that relatively trivial number of individual property holders who must first be expropriated for it to come into operation at all. The political articulation of this proposal has never been one of its stronger suits. (One can hardly in good faith proffer Marx's *The Civil War in France* or Lenin's *What is to be Done?* as a socialist *advance* on the constitutional conceptions of *Qu'est-ce que le Tiers Etat?*) but even if it were to be presented in a more convincing institutional and constitutional format, it can no longer expect to receive

much in the way of credence.[82] To operate a socialist economy successfully may not be impossible in principle; but it has certainly proved
extremely difficult in practice. The presumption of effective prowess in
such operation is not one which a necessarily inexperienced, and a
democratically unrestrained, political équipe can any longer defensibly
claim. The protagonists of such political enterprises do not merely make
excessive – even overweening – demands on the trust of those over whom
they presume to rule. They also deliberately close their eyes to what are
by now exceedingly clear causal features of the projects they propose to
undertake. For the socialization of an economy by itself to furnish an
answer to the problem of institutionalizing modern liberty, it would have
to be true that economic causality within an administered economy was
transparent and relatively simple. But, by induction from the history of
economic thought between 1776 and 1984, and of economic policy in
capitalist or socialist economies in the twentieth century, it is fairly clear
by now that economic causality is extremely opaque and perhaps
unimaginably, as well as unmanageably, complex.

There is every reason to suppose that the game-theoretic dilemmas of
interacting rational strategies at the level of individual economic agents,
of communities, of classes, of national populations, of states and of power
blocs demand (and, at least formally, in many instances permit) political
or moral solutions.[83] But there is very much less reason to suppose that
anyone today has a very cogent conception of how to identify potential
solutions in practice, let alone of how to contrive actually to provide them
in reality. (To take the most powerful recent construction of the
implications of such problems in moral theory, it seems unlikely that even
intense and protracted individual encounters across an entire population,
with the revisionist conception of personal identity offered by Derek
Parfit, would do much to furnish *political* solutions. At least, the close
parallels between Parfit's views and those of the Buddha on this question,
taken with the recent experience of a politically energized Buddhism[84] do
not offer much encouragement on this score.)

VI

One should not, of course, exaggerate the pathos of this predicament.
Some aspects of modern liberty are recognised as entitlements, at least by
overt profession, in the vast majority of societies in the modern world.[85]
Few modern states continue to display on a permanent basis explicitly
citizen-excluding systems of rights of public agency. (The Union of South
Africa and the Kingdom of Saudi Arabia are perhaps the most important

remaining instances.) Most modern constitutions formally recognize a large proportion of the rights of personal security and freedom of private action defended by Constant, even if this recognition in many countries is often more honoured in the breach than in the observance. (The opacity and the overwhelming practical importance of the workings of economies has certainly imparted a sharper edge to his insistence on the incompatibility of censorship, arbitrary arrest and the apparatus of modern as well as ancient political persecution with the effective enjoyment of modern liberty.)

Most recent western political philosophy of any distinction is either utilitarian (and hence specified ultimately in terms of opportunities for personal enjoyment and free agency) or else presents itself as an attempt to systematize social, economic and political rights, opportunities and duties in terms of some conception of liberty.[86] It would be a fair criticism of some of these writers that they deploy, as Herbert Hart says, a 'blindingly general use of concepts like "interference with liberty".'[87] It would be a fair criticism of others that they place quite unwarrantable and arbitrary restrictions on what aspects of organized social life they take to constitute restrictions on liberty.[88] It would be an important reservation to make in the case of virtually all of them that they take their stand ultimately on epistemically questionable, and very actively questioned, conceptions of human value.[89] But even if today we still lack (and are unlikely soon to acquire) any very cogent conception of how to institutionalize modern liberty, we do at least have reason to be grateful at the comparative paucity of articulated defences which are now offered for servitude as such as a political order permanently and deeply appropriate to the nature of the great majority of human beings.[90]

Yet it remains the case that we understand very poorly indeed how a regime of modern liberty can be institutionalized successfully for any length of time. We have little, if any, idea of where civic virtue can reasonably be expected to come from in a regime devoted to the extension of personal enjoyment. And we have no idea at all of how to subject our awesome powers of destruction to the service of those enjoyments which they were supposedly developed to protect.[91]

Offences will certainly continue to come. We can only hope that none of them will in the event prove grave enough to pronounce an older doom upon the entire project of modern liberty and do our several best in the meantime to prevent them coming too directly and massively from the collective imprudence with which (individual by individual, class by class, nation by nation) we so determinedly pursue our personal enjoyments.

less 'recentta' to mean 'votian'

6

Revolution

Hannah Arendt

The imaginative setting of the concept of revolution was initially provided by the development of theoretical astronomy. But its modern political force has come principally from the massive historical impact of two great political convulsions, the French revolution of 1789–94 and the second Russian revolution of 1917, the October revolution, which founded the modern Soviet state.

The tension between the distanced and plainly suprahuman necessitarian frame of its initial meaning and the vividly agonistic political turmoil of its most important modern instances has left the modern conception of revolution in a sorry state. Partly its present analytical *epigraph to Dunn's essays* debility has been a simple product of the struggle to impose intellectual order through too few ideas upon too vast and heterogeneous a range of experience. But it has also partly derived from the centrality to modern politics of dispute over the character and significance of twentieth-century revolutionary struggles. In addition to this combination of conceptual fatigue and ideological provocation, one further feature of the concept itself renders it even less stable and even more problematic than most other prominent modern categories of political understanding.[1]

In contrast with democracy or justice or equality or liberty, revolution is not in the first place a normative standard which human beings hold up against social and political reality and to which they attempt to induce the latter to conform – to mould it. Rather, revolution is itself in the first place a feature of the real historical world at particular times and places:

I am extremely grateful to Terence Ball, James Farr and Russell Hanson, and to G. A. Cohen and Quentin Skinner for their helpful comments on the first draft of this essay.

something which, for example, occurred in France between 1789 and 1794, in Russia between 1917 and a date indeterminately much later, in China between 1911 and at least 1949. Even in the case of the concepts of practical reason it is difficult to fashion and sustain clear and rationally shared understandings of politically important and vexed values. But where a concept is standardly employed both to characterize real historical episodes and to express demanding political values there cannot, even in principle, be any decisive intellectual strategy for making and keeping it analytically clear; and there are in addition bound to be overwhelming practical pressures to render those who use it more than a little confused about what they are saying. Modern politics is indeed more than a little confusing, not to say spiritually somewhat dismaying. The concept of revolution epitomizes both its cognitive opacity and its limited human charms. But, since revolution is defined in the first instance by real historical happenings, it also serves handily to remind us that politics is here to stay for just as long as we are. (For most of its past the human species on the whole lived extremely local and culturally segregated lives. But from now on it will pull through as a species – or go under together.)

Modern conceptions of revolution assemble precariously together a variety of distinct ideas: the destruction of old and putatively obsolete political, social and economic orders; the purposeful political creation of new political, social and economic orders which are proclaimed by their architects to be decisively superior to their predecessors; a view of modern world history which renders the collapse of the old regimes and the emergence of the new regimes evidently desirable, causally unsurprising and perhaps even causally ineluctable; the existential value and causal importance of human lives lived in the endeavour to speed the collapse of the old and the reconstruction of the new. Except to impressionable readers of Hegel not all these elements are plausibly compatible with one another and every single one of them is open to (and encounters) the most vigorous dispute. No understanding of the historical development of the concept of revolution will (or should) resolve such disputes. What it may do is to help to explain why these elements are now assembled precariously together under the umbrella of a single vaguely specified but highly emotive concept.

It is helpful to begin by asking why the concept of revolution has no clear ancient antecedent, why in a sense it emerges suddenly and fully formed with the collapse of the French *ancien régime*. Before 1789 there was no word in any world language which carries the meaning of the modern word 'revolutionary' (the intentional agent of revolution);[2] and the word 'revolution' (which figured in a variety of European languages) was, in no sense an important instrument of political understanding.[3] Yet many of the elements which go to make up the modern conception of revolution were clearly present independently in the political thinking of the ancient world. Major ancient political thinkers, notably Plato and Aristotle, reflected at length on the stability of forms of regime and on the conditions which caused one form of regime to mutate into another. The hectic politics of the Greek *polis* centred for at least two centuries on the often violent conflict between domestic social groups and the contrasting regime forms (democracy, oligarchy, tyranny) these favoured. Both ideologically and practically the political fate of any one *polis* was linked intimately with those of many others.[4] With the transition of Greek political theory to Rome (in the person of the hostage Polybius),[5] the intellectual residue of this experience was transposed (in an admittedly not enormously impressive form) into the most influential framework for understanding the triumphant course of Roman military conquest and the more ambiguous trajectory of Rome's domestic politics. It was Polybius' explanation of Rome's majestic recovery from the disaster of Cannae to dominate the Mediterranean world and destroy its rival Carthage, transmitted through the Augustan historian Livy to the Florentine Niccolò Machiavelli, that furnished the most ambitious theory for interpreting the trajectory of modern state forms in the century and a half that preceded the French revolution.[6]

The missing element in the ancient understandings of politics which precluded the appearance of the modern conception of revolution was a secular understanding of the history of the world as a single frame of human meaning with a determinate direction of internal development. (This absence, plainly, was not necessarily a deficiency in ancient understandings of politics.) There is good reason to attribute the impact of a linear and unitary conception of world history on the modern imagination largely to the theoretical structure of the Christian religion and to its extension to virtually the entire population of Europe over many centuries. But although linear Christian conceptions of history did enter powerfully into the making and interpretation of history in major political crises over at least a millennium,[7] it has been a firmly secular descendant of this frame of understanding that features in the modern conception of revolution. And this secular form itself registered not only a complicated array of domestic changes in social and economic relations and in their ideological assessment but also a vision of the remainder of the world from a continent well on the way towards dominating this. By 1789 a linear conception of history did not merely embody an imaginative perspective enforced by centuries of exposure to the idiosyncrasies of the Christian religion, it also captured one decisive and entirely objective feature of the relations between communities across the face of the globe.

Few modern analysts of politics genuinely believe it to be intellectually prudent to rest their understanding of what is occurring politically on explicitly Christian categories. (Modern Christianity may appraise politics confidently enough; but only in its most uncouth embodiments does it still regard itself as an independent apparatus for comprehending political reality.) Yet no coherent understanding of modern politics is possible which does not put a recognition of global economic and strategic relations at its very centre. Both liberal and Marxist interpreters of modern politics share this emphasis on the overwhelming importance of the world economy and its political armature. But neither, perhaps, any longer has much idea how to disentangle the evident cogency of this viewpoint from the very different frame of meaning within which the historical trajectory itself first appeared unambiguously desirable.[8]

The term 'revolution' derives from a medieval Latin noun.[9] Its primary meaning is well caught by the modern English verb 'to revolve'. Revolution, like the celestial spheres in Ptolemaic astronomy or the earth and the planets in Copernican astronomy, goes round and round. Such a term applied with little effort to ancient conceptions of political experience. But it very obviously does not apply felicitously to major historical convulsions like the French or Russian revolutions.

Speculation about the trajectory of regime forms (sometimes, as with Polybius in *The Histories*, centred on the imagery of the revolving wheel) was prominent in the political theory of ancient Greece, as was speculation about the consequences of the conflicting interests of rich and poor, landowners and endebted peasants, and about the stability of political orders. But it was not until the seventeenth-century mechanization of the world picture and the central imaginative role of astronomy in its promotion that the term 'revolution' was first applied to major political changes within a framework of any real explanatory ambition. Even then, in the contrasting idioms of thinkers such as Harrington and Locke, it had no very determinate political implication, applying as readily to the restoration of a violated order of natural or historical right[10] as it did to a shift in the social or ethnic basis of political power,[11] and usually in fact signify little more than a minor political disturbance.

What transformed 'revolution' into a central term in the interpretation and practice of modern politics was the combined intellectual and political impact of the French revolution. Since 1789 (and because of the historically experienced character of the French revolution) it has always been difficult to separate clearly the choice of explanatory and analytical models for interpreting major episodes of violent political conflict within particular societies from political appraisals of their desirability.

Neither the causation of the French revolution itself nor the reasons for its dynamic impact on the categories of political understanding are as yet at all well understood. But what is clear is how drastic a rupture it did mark with the prior categories of political interpretation. In this respect it stands in sharp contrast not merely with the English Great Rebellion (first described as the English revolution in the aftermath of the French revolution)[12] but also with the Glorious Revolution in 1688 (a self-conscious and ideologically nervous restoration in its eventual political outcome)[13] and even the American revolution, which appealed to the accepted theoretical premises of British constitutionalism against the practices of British colonial administration.[14] Even the vigorous revival of the European republican tradition (Machiavelli, Harrington, Hume, Montesquieu) in designing a federal constitutional order appropriate for the independent United States did not markedly extend the political imagination of England or continental Europe.[15]

The classical Marxist vision of the French revolution as the rising of a vigorously productive and proudly self-conscious bourgeoisie against a parasitic nobility tenaciously fettering the expanding forces of production has been buried irretrievably by the historical scholarship of the last few decades.[16] But a number of features of the concepts of revolution that had taken shape by 1794 were plainly present in the consciousness of some in the course of the half century which preceded its outbreak. The example of the English Great Rebellion, with its devout ideologues, convulsive struggles for popular liberty and memorable climax in the judicial execution of an anointed monarch, had been considered at length by David Hume. Both the episode itself and Hume's sceptical analysis of its causes and consequences received close attention within the highest circles of the *ancien régime* state and among the ideologists who mourned its passing and strove to speed its restoration.[17]

Some decades before the revolution there is evidence, both among leading royal officials and among dissident *philosophes*, of an acute sense of emerging political tension between an isolated and poorly articulated royal government and state structure and an increasingly confident and irritated public opinion.[18] In a few isolated cases there was even some awareness of how far such tensions might in the end lead.[19] In addition, in the sophisticated Scottish reworking of Harrington's political theory by Hume, Smith and Millar,[20] there was available a conception of the relations between economic and political organization and a vision of the historical trajectory of Europe into which the French revolution, as this actually occurred, could be fitted with little analytical discomfort.[21]

The revolution began, in the eyes of its protagonists, as a political project to enact the rights of man in the form of a renovated political

order of full citizen equality, capable of furnishing a genuine representation of all legitimate national interests.[22] Its political dependence upon
the revolutionary *journées*, the insurrectionary crowd action of the
Parisian *Sansculottes*,[23] and eventually upon the state-administered terror
of the Jacobin dictatorship, was a regrettable necessity enforced on its
protagonists by the barbarous obstruction of the partisans of the old
regime and by the persistent dissensions and intermittent treacheries
within their own ranks. The lesson which partisans of the revolution
drew from this conjunction was not that there must be a measure of
inadequacy in their understanding of their own goals but, rather, that the
self-protecting and self-enforcing power of enlightenment and equality
could not hope to operate until the political resistance of the deeply
obscurantist and inegalitarian *ancien régime* had been crushed utterly.[24]
Foes of the revolution naturally drew the very different lesson that the
political and social conceptions which inspired the revolutionaries were
profoundly incoherent, the motives which impelled them ugly and the
odious means which they had employed a luminous token of their confusion and malignity.[25] The initial explanatory problem raised by the revolution (which was also its principal stimulus to subsequent political
action) arose from its apparently unanticipated and uncoordinated political trajectory and its impressive recalcitrance to the shaping political will
of its participants,[26] an impact that consorted comfortably enough with
the imagery of mechanical determination associated with Newtonian
physics, as it did, at least after Thermidor, with an older providentialist
theodicy.

The boldest practical lesson drawn from this feature of the revolution
was the historical invention of the role of professional revolutionary,
synthesizing assurance in the mechanical guarantee of revolution's
recurrence with optimism about the opportunities for personal political
contribution which this recurrence might in due course offer to the
vigorous, convinced and politically alert.[27] A number of less adventurous
lessons were also drawn from the intimate conjunction of violent struggle
with the civilizing project of political and social demystification and
democratization. In the face of these lessons less intrepid political
responses to the revolution divided into three principal groupings. One,
which may be helpfully described as Utopian, resigned itself austerely to
segregating the project of social and political enlightenment from violent
competition for political power and authority, restricting itself instead to
education and to exemplary social experiments on a modest scale.[28] A
second, epitomized by the Whiggism of early nineteenth-century Britain,
focused determinedly on the imperative to confine political struggle
within a constitutional order capable of adapting itself to the practical

needs of an expanding commercial society. A third, firmly in the ascendant in continental Europe after the final defeat of Napoleon, set itself instead to the solemn attempt to extirpate enlightenment as such.[29]

In the century following the restoration of the Bourbons the absolute monarchies that had existed in many parts of Europe in the late eighteenth century were duly modified by the creation of national representative institutions and national markets and by the extension of legal equality throughout their subject populations. Many European countries saw their reigning dynasties overthrown by popular uprisings and in some cases replaced temporarily or permanently by republican governments. These abrupt transitions were universally described as revolutions; and their recurrence helped to sustain the optimism of self-conscious professional revolutionaries from Buonarroti to Auguste Blanqui.[30] But no nineteenth-century revolution was in fact initiated or *Italy?* politically controlled for much of its course by self-conscious revolutionaries. None established revolutionary governments with the dynamism and international impact of the Jacobin regime; and almost all in fact terminated in the reestablishment of monarchical institutions.

By the beginning of the twentieth century in western Europe – and despite the rise of mass political parties dedicated to the eventual establishment of socialist or communist republics – the role of professional revolutionary had come to seem something of a romantic anachronism. Only within the more archaic state form and economy of Tsarist Russia was it still genuinely cogent to see the dedicated pursuit of violent political subversion as a clear precondition for civilizing and democratizing an entire society. One principal ground for this shift in political perception was the greatly increased repressive capacity of western European states, with their civil police forces and heavily armed professional soldiery. In Paris in 1830, and in Paris, Berlin, and Vienna in 1848, monarchical government had in effect collapsed almost instantaneously in the face of revolutions *journées* unleashed by the hungry *menu peuple* of the capital cities. In the aftermath of 1848 the governments of western Europe were naturally at some pains to prevent a repetition of these indignities; and in peacetime conditions they proved themselves for over half a century well able to do so.[31] It was the cataclysm of the First World War which brought the direct experience of revolution back to western Europe; and it was its political outcome in Russia which ensured that the category of revolution would remain for the imaginable future at the centre of political understanding.

The role of Marxist political theory in inspiring the political leadership of the second Russian revolution, in October 1917, and the bold explanatory ambitions of Marxism as a system of historical and social analysis, taken in conjunction, render it no longer possible to separate assessments of the character and causation of revolutions from assessments of the political merits and the intellectual coherence and validity of marxism itself. Liberal and marxist interpretations of the causes of the collapse of the French *ancien régime* shared an explanatory perspective which inserted political power firmly into a history of changing social and economic organization, a history which liberal thinkers and statesmen hoped had essentially reached its destination but which the followers of Karl Marx confidently expected would in due course be compelled (mechanically) to move at least one vital stage further.[32] Since the middle of the nineteenth century this fundamental disagreement in explanatory perspective has grounded the two most moralistic and ideologically dynamic understandings of modern politics. (In the course of the present century, dramatically, these two vividly inimical ideologies have come to roost in the two major world powers.)

For liberal thinkers the principal political implication of the French revolution was the long-term inevitability and the permanent desirability of eliminating arbitrary historical privilege and domination from human social relations. What was to hold modern societies together, following this purgation, was a national and international system of free market exchange and the minimal coercive force required to guarantee the property rights of its participants. For Marxists, by contast, a market in labour was itself a form of arbitrary domination, as well as a consequence of arbitrary historical privilege and coercion. The indispensable further stage of social evolution, accordingly, was the abolition of private property rights in the means of production and the concomitant organization of production, allocation of labour and distribution of its product on the basis of common ownership. What made this transformation not merely morally imperative but also historically imminent was the ineradicable instability and the growing internal contradictions of market economies organized on the basis of private ownership.[33] Marx himself never succeeded either in working out to his own satisfaction a full analysis of the internal contradictions of the capitalist mode of production or in linking these contradictions convincingly with the instabilities of the trade cycle. Subsequent Marxist economists cannot plausibly be said to have triumphed where he failed. But they have continued to regard the capitalist world economy with scepticism as well as animosity, cultivating a sensitivity to its indisputably erratic movements and inspecting it hopefully for signs of incipient disintegration. Thus far, despite the fearsome destructiveness of two world wars, these more extreme hopes have been disappointed.

More importantly, however, the instabilities and contradictions of market economies can now be compared in some detail with analogous features in supposedly rationally planned economies organized on the basis of common ownership.[34] Such comparisons, if conducted fairly,[35] are not necessarily overwhelmingly flattering to either camp, though each has naturally by now had considerable practice in explaining away their more embarrassing features. No form of modern economy has had marked success over long periods of time in combining such simple desiderata as full employment for its labour force, rising productivity and increasing provision of goods keenly desired by consumers.[36] Whatever else may be true about it, socialist production has failed as yet to prove itself productively superior to capitalist production; and there is no imminent prospect of its coming to do so. Nor, as yet, has any modern state contrived to combine an entire economy organized on the basis of common ownership with a form of government even minimally responsible to the governed or with a range of effectively guaranteed civil rights which remotely matches that of the major capitalist democracies. (None has in fact made the least attempt to do so.) There is, accordingly, no ground whatever for resting an analysis of the modern conception of revolution directly upon the self-understandings of the lineal political heirs of the major twentieth-century revolutions.

How, then, is it now most illuminating to envisage the concept of revolution? To answer this question it is necessary to consider carefully just what we might most urgently require the concept to assist us to understand. One perfectly defensible way of envisaging the concept is to treat it as specified by the full range of historical instances to which it has in practice been intelligibly applied by any human beings at all. This nominalist strategy of understanding has the advantage of simplicity; and, if clearly announced, it could hardly mislead anyone. But it has the massive disadvantage of trivializing the concept beyond hope of recall. Since 1789, and in part because of the impressive historical resonance of the French revolution, the term 'revolution' has been applied with increasing abandon to an immense variety of political episodes.[37] Some of these have involved the economic, political and social transformation of vast societies like Russia and China. Some have involved little more than the unconstitutional exchange of personnel at the summit of existing states. Others have involved a substantial degree of social and economic change orchestrated through an essentially unchanged state apparatus, with drastic consequences for the character of the resulting state.[38] Others still have combined the threat and use of violence from outside the state with a constitutional succession to power and an equally drastic use of the power thus acquired. (The most important example of this pattern was provided by the Nazi regime.) No term used to designate such a huge miscellany of political episodes could hope to serve as an effective instrument of anaysis. If revolution is left simply as a term of common speech the extreme promiscuity of its modern usage now precludes its being judged to express a single clear concept.

This would be a matter of no consequence if there were in modern political experience no distinctive and massively important phenomena which the term 'revolution' is uniquely equipped to pick out and assist us to understand. But not even their most vituperative foes are reluctant to acknowledge that the communist revolutions of the twentieth century form a distinctive and a prodigiously important type of political happening. The geopolitical and ideological conflicts of the late twentieth century certainly cannot be fully understood simply by an analysis of the nature of the major revolutions of this century. But they cannot even be coherently considered without such an analysis. This fact in itself underlines the most important single consideration about the revolutions of the twentieth century. There are a number of examples in earlier European history (most importantly the Revolt of the Netherlands) in which revolutionary action led to the fission of a dynastic empire and to the establishment of an independent national political unit. But no major social upheaval within a single political unit did in fact produce directly the permanent establishment of a new state form professedly dedicated to consolidating the social purposes of the insurgents. Before the twentieth century, domestic revolutions (revolutions occurring within a single country and directed against their own ruling groups and political orders) invariably terminated in restorations, however dramatic the intervening upheavals and however deeply the restored order was marked by these in its political culture and expectations.

What has been novel about the revolutions of the twentieth century is the proven capacity of revolutionary action not merely to overthrow for a time an *ancien* or a comparatively *parvenu* regime but also to establish a new regime capable of protecting itself effectively and more or less indefinitely. It is this trajectory from collapse to re-creation, for better or worse, which has placed the revolutions of the twentieth century at the centre of modern world history. The principal purpose for which a concept of revolution is now required is to focus the character and explain the occurrence of such historical episodes. In facing this task the promiscuity and mental indolence of the term's modern application are not of much assistance.

Since it has been principally the Russian and Chinese revolutions that have thrust this task of comprehension upon us it may be helpful to lay out the main problems in applying the concept in relation to these. In both countries an ancient (and comparatively economically backward) dynastic empire disintegrated in the early twentieth century; and in each, in due course, an effective new government was established by the military and political efforts of a communist party. In each the collapse of the old order and the establishment of the new were chronologically and politically distinct processes, separated in the Russian case by some eight months and the Chinese case, more strikingly, by almost forty years.[39] In neither case was the initial collapse of the ancien regime attributable to the agency of the party which was in due course to construct the new order. (In the Chinese case the party itself did not even come into existence until a full decade after the demise of the imperial state.) It is still extremely unclear how the relations between the collapse of the old and the construction of the new can best be understood. But one important question to press is whether it is in fact appropriate to consider the first and the second in precisely the same terms. It is on the answer given to this question that the basic understanding of revolution as a concept must now depend. (It is important to emphasize that this is a matter of the choice of a cognitive strategy – and perhaps of political identification. It is not a matter of extrahuman necessity – constraint by the laws of logic or even the indefeasible current meaning of a word.)

Each of the two victorious political parties, despite their somewhat heretical status by the canons of international marxism at the time when they made their decisive bid for power, now possesses a relatively firm frame for understanding the relevant revolution in its entirety. Even the most idiosyncratic of communist parties still profess belief in some interpretation of the framework of historical and political analysis initially devised by Karl Marx. This framework explains the collapse of antique structures of political, economic and social relations by their productive feebleness in comparison with competing societies and by the political fragility in the face of domestic class forces of their existing state powers. It also explains (with rather more sleight of hand) the establishment of communist political authority in these comparatively retarded economic settings as a particularly dramatic example of the advantages of combining the most advanced understanding of world history and its political implications with the comparatively feeble political resistance afforded by an archaic economy and the state which this supports. (The politics of internal class relations and the world-historical role of the proletariat in revolutionary praxis have to be glossed with rather more circumspection.) This explanatory focus on the advantages of backwardness harks back to Marx's own early political writings, with their emphasis on the discreditable political torpor of Germany,[40] and to the leading themes of Russian revolutionary populism in the second half of the nineteenth century (with which Marx himself also flirted for a time in his last years[41]). In the early twentieth century this stress on the political advantages of backwardness (which in the Russian case after 1917 was essentially an involuntary retrospective accommodation to revolutionary success within a single vast country) was supplemented by Trotsky's insistence on the 'law of uneven and combined development' and the resulting political vulnerability of capitalism, considered as a worldwide system of production and exchange, at its weakest link.[42]

This expansive, if not very tightly coordinated, framework of understanding has the merit of inclusiveness and it does offer a helpful explanatory orientation towards the pattern and timing of the incidence of collapsing anciens regimes in the twentieth century.[43] How helpful an approach it can offer towards the legitimation of communist regimes even in the longest run is a rather different question and will probably prove to turn principally (barring thermonuclear war) on whether or not the marxist premise of the productive superiority of socialism is in the end vindicated,[44] a prospect over which even communist regimes at present appear increasingly diffident. But even if a reworked marxist approach were to succeed in combining an explanation of the collapse of anciens regimes with a more convincing legitimation of whatever communist regimes replace these, only those of the most unblinking credulity need conclude that it offers any special assistance in explaining the political establishment of any communist regime that has thus far emerged.[45]

The destruction of an old regime and the construction of a new social and economic order with a state power effectively capable of protecting this is certainly a sufficient condition for a revolution. On any assessment of their present political merits, accordingly, what took place in both Russia and China in this century was appropriately identified as a revolution. If the self-understanding of the political agencies of revolution were comprehensively veridical, or even if there was sufficient reason to see a socialist organization of production as plainly economically and socially superior to a capitalist organization, it would be reasonable to specify the character and seek to explain the causation of revolutions through the categories of Marx's theory of history.[46] As matters now stand, however, it is absurd to accord Marxism any automatic cognitive authority in the explanation of revolutions. And once a marxist categorization is no longer privileged it is no longer clear how far it is reasonable to expect there to be a unitary causal explanation of revolutions at all.

Both Marx and Engels, in their explanation of the French revolution and in their anticipation of future revolutions, were at pains to insist that revolutions are a product of profound structural contradictions within a society and not of the political machinations of professional revolutionaries, the 'alchemists of revolution' with their exaggeration of the role of human will and calculation and their 'police-spy' conceptions of the precipitants of revolution.[47] A revolution, Engels observed, 'is a pure phenomenon of nature',[48] echoing the imagery of mechanical determination which the French revolution had rendered imaginatively so natural. Like other pure phenomena of nature, its future occurrence could be anticipated with as much assurance as any other instance of causal determination.[49] As Wendell Phillips more recently put it: 'Revolutions are not made. They come.'[50]

But while the imagery of mechanical causal determination does sometimes fit rather well the political collapse of an *ancien* (or even a *parvenu*) regime, particularly in the face of popular upheavals in city or countryside,[51] it emphatically does not fit the purposeful, strategic, and energetically concerted political agency of a modern revolutionary party in arms, even before the final collapse of the old order. (The Long March was not an avalanche.) Nor, even more clearly, does it at all fit the struggle of a revolutionary party that has once succeeded in taking state power to retain this power and to mould a new society and economy through its exercise. The political prospects for armed insurgency certainly depend upon domestic class relations and the structural strength or weakness of an incumbent state. But the decision to unleash armed insurgency, and the political and military skill with which this is conducted, all play an eminently causal role in determining which states do collapse.[52] There is no logical or conceptual relation between the fragility of modern state forms and the competitive prowess of modern revolutionary agencies. Because there is no such necessary link between the two, there cannot be a single and coherently unified modern explanatory theory of even the most important and distinctive form of modern revolution, either in the idiom of mechanical causal determination at the level of a complete society or in the idiom of intentional strategic practice. (There of course can, should, and will be systematic inquiry into the determinants of regime vulnerability and into the destructive and constructive effectiveness of varieties of strategic practice by revolutionaries and by counter-revolutionaries. But these two distinct components must be assembled together in each instance and cannot ever be jointly derived from a single, overarching, analysis.)

One important conclusion of the most impressive modern study of the determinants of regime vulnerability, the major impact of interstate military relations,[53] still further underlines the causal weight of human judgement and strategic calculation. It also calls sharply into question the essentially endogenous and intranational conception of the nature and causation of revolutions that emerged from the French revolution (at

least as this was perceived from within France itself). Whether or not this
has been true in earlier centuries,[54] in the twentieth century it is inappropriate to see the collapse of even the most decrepit and offensive
anciens regimes, as Marx (following its liberal historians) saw the French
revolution, simply as the internal overthrow of an increasingly anachronistic and parasitic political order by the vigorous exertions of its thriving
and productive subjects. The repressive capacities of almost all modern
states depend extensively on tight and complex linkages with numerous
foreign powers; and the revolutionary potency of modern insurgents and
the constructive efficacy of modern revolutionary governments likewise
depend elaborately on directly comparable linkages of material aid, on
imported ideas and on the modification of strategic expedients pioneered
elsewhere.[55] As in any other fiercely competitive political process the
causal role of human learning in modern revolution is extremely hard to
exaggerate.[56]

It is not surprising that the concept of revolution should have sagged
heavily under these conflicting pressures. Nor should it appear surprising
that the same pressures have blighted the intellectual cogency of those
social scientific theories of revolution that aspire to the scope and
generality of theories in the sciences of nature.[57] Short of a lexically
dictatorial world government there is no way of hauling the concept itself
back into a neat and definite form. But it is of course open to any user of it
to establish a precise grip of their own upon the understanding that they
will choose to give to it.

In so choosing there are at least two points that it is wise to bear in
mind. One is that the most important of twentieth-century revolutions
have gained their importance not from the undeniable drama of their
commencement but from the scale of their long-term consequences. It is
the durability and the institutionalized political determinacy of their
outcomes which distinguishes modern revolutions so sharply from their
predecessors. The key feature of these outcomes in the case of
communist revolutions[58] is the union between a particular structure of
government (usually under 'normal' conditions a ruling revolutionary
party on the Leninist model) and the reconstruction of an economy on
the basis of public ownership of at least the major means of production.
In thinking about revolution it is essential to distinguish sharply between
the political decomposition of an existing state form (however spontaneous or externally assisted this decomposition may have been) and the
political construction of a new society through a transformed structure of
ownership and production. It cannot be appropriate to confine the use of
the term 'revolution' to instances of this second process, since by this
criterion there had never been a revolution until the twentieth century.

A second point to bear in mind is that the key experience which turned the term 'revolution' into a central category of modern political discourse was the unexpected collapse of an absolutist political order of some longevity in the face of the angry political energy of its subjects. By that criterion the French revolution of 1789 has not merely had a considerable array of successors (not all of which have proved in ideological terms its more or less legitimate progeny);[59] but it also had fairly clear predecessors, most notably in the English Great Rebellion.[60] The Great Rebellion no more changed the basic system of ownership and production in mid-seventeenth-century England than the French revolution changed this in late eighteenth-century France. But in the case of each there was a close relation between the popular insurgency and long-drawn-out political struggle and the appearance of drastic doctrines of social and even economic equality.[61] Between the continuing emotional charge of these remarkably exigent ideologies and the more grubby practical consequences of twentieth-century revolutionary state-building the concept of revolution faces uneasily in two very different directions. In doing so it comes close to condensing within a single term the full instability of modern political understanding.

You'd learn as much listening to John Lennon.

7

Country Risk: Social and Cultural Aspects

Mr Macquedy Then, sir, I presume you set no value on the right
   principles of rent, profit, wages, and currency?
The Rev. Dr Folliott My principles, sir, in these things are, to take as much
   as I can get, and to pay no more than I can help. These are every man's
   principles, whether they be the right principles or no. There, sir, is
   political economy in a nutshell.
Mr Macquedy The principles, sir, which regulate production and consumption, are independent of the will of any individual as to giving or
   taking, and do not lie in a nutshell by any means.
   Thomas Love Peacock, *Crotchet Castle*, ch. 2, 'The March of Mind'

The growing importance of country risk

Among the components of what bankers and corporate investors now
analyze as 'country risk', the categories of political and social or cultural
risk are of special interest for any social or political theorist. Country risk
in the first instance may be seen simply as a type of risk faced by an international capital investment, loan, or export sale, not because of the
properties of the factor markets concerned or the capacity to pay or
repay of the foreign borrower or buyer, but because of the character of
social and political relations in the country in question and because of the
implications this character may have for the possibility of the expropria-

I am very grateful to Richard Herring and to Michael Cook, Geoffrey Hawthorn,
Michael Ignatieff and Quentin Skinner for their generous help in emending the
first draft of this chapter.

tion of the investment, default on the loan, or more or less protracted failure to pay for the export.[1] Social and cultural risk may be contrasted with economic or political risk as representing that set of hazards for lenders, investors, or exporters that arises from the fact that human beings are not merely economic agents in institutionalized political settings but also social and cultural creatures.

The growing salience of country risk in the thinking of bankers and businesspeople is a product of the drastic changes in the shape of the world economy since the end of World War II and of the particularly turbulent conditions that have prevailed since the OPEC price increases of 1973. These changes can be traced in virtually any measure of the degree of foreign trade exposure of the advanced capitalist economies[2] and come out particularly vividly, for example, in the growth of the proportion of the US domestic market in manufactures accounted for by large-scale firms (now virtually all multinational in scope) from 17 per cent in 1950 to 42 per cent in 1967 and 62 per cent in 1974[3] or in the increase in the percentage of patents issued to foreigners, for example, from 13 per cent in 1955 in the United States to over 30 per cent in 1972.[4] The rapidity of modern communications, the rapid growth in the scale of international exchanges, and the greatly increased complexity and instability of the environment in which investment decisions are made have compelled a more explicit awareness of political and social factors. The growing importance, especially since 1973, of the less-developed countries in sustaining the export industries of Europe, the United States, and Japan in conditions of recession[5] and the greatly increased loan exposure of international banks in these countries,[6] which has been necessary to sustain this pattern of exports,[7] have focused attention especially on the non-oil exporters among the less-developed countries. (The impact of the recession on the growth rates of these countries appear to have been less than in the case of either the industrialized countries or the members of OPEC itself.[8]) In response to this experience, and perhaps especially in response to the Iranian revolution,[9] it now seems quite natural to a banker to recommend in assessing longer-term risks, particularly of default on a loan, the use of a country risk matrix that allocates almost half the numerical assessment of risk to political or strategic factors.[10]

Distinguishing political from social and cultural risk

The division between political risk and social or cultural risk is arbitrary. The distinction, that is to say, may be clumsy or illuminating. It cannot be true or false. For analytical purposes, it is useful to take it as the distinction between hazards that follow directly from the purposes of an incumbent government and any reasonably predictable constitutional successor and hazards that follow, by a necessarily less direct path, from the beliefs, values and attitudes of a population at large. Social and cultural risk is risk threatened by the as yet politically inefficacious, that is, the political risk of the temporarily politically impotent – a form of involuntarily delayed gratification. (Where social and cultural risk is effectively actualized, as, for example, in extralegal interventions by factory workforces in Chile during the presidency of Allende[11] or in the occupation of foreign-owned farms or factories in Portugal, it becomes effective essentially because it is accepted and protected by the forces of coercion of an incumbent government and ceases to be so as soon as these forces intervene to reverse it.) The analytical distinction between political and social risk is thus partly one of time horizon. (Imminent social and cultural risk is risk on the very point of becoming political risk.) It is also partly one of organizational specificity and hence of practical tractability. The assessment of political risk falls within the field of what Jon Elster refers to as 'routine politics'.[12] In effect, it can be seen essentially as a competitive game played by an investor, lender, or (less plausibly) exporter against a single rationally acting other player, namely, the foreign state in question; and calculation of advantage within it would be strongly analogous to market calculations.

Social and cultural risk, by contrast, is necessarily organizationally diffuse. It consists in a set of actual and potential responses that have not yet been synthesized (and that may well never become synthesized) into a single rational actor and that, in consequence, permit neither the eliciting of common interests through negotiation nor the securing of firm instrumental advantage through skilful competitive play. Political risk is no doubt increasingly an investor's or banker's headache. But social or cultural risk is closer to being their nightmare. (Because social and cultural risk is less immediate than political risk, it is unlikely to apply to export payments and it is particularly likely to apply to long-term investments, though present levels of international indebtedness of less-developed countries may well in due course cause it to apply equally obviously also to international loans.)[13]

This contrast as it stands is obviously over-simple. In practice, the transition from social or cultural risk is neither neat nor sudden. Given the political circumstances that have prevailed and the political traditions that have developed since World War II, social or cultural risk in even the most effectively repressive of capitalist societies is unlikely to remain entirely organizationally inchoate for very long.[14] We know much less, at least outside Poland and Czechoslovakia, about the form that social and cultural risk takes within communist countries. The Polish case certainly suggests that an accurate assessment of such risk may be of urgent importance for western bankers and businesspeople.[15]

Semi-organized social and cultural risks, in the form of small-scale terrorist organizations or, still more, in the form of an organized revolutionary movement, are more elusive competitors than an incumbent government. (They are so, not least, because incumbent governments necessarily have such strong views of the types of contact or relations that foreign interests may have with them.) But in the case, for example, of the kidnapping of corporation executives for ransom, the nature of the competitive game is extremely clear. An instructive example of the transfer of (*economic*) risk in such cases is the insuring of executives against the risk of ransom payments. In reported instances, where premiums per year per executive insured amount to one-tenth of the maximum ransom sum for which they are insured, the level of social and cultural risk would appear to be high.[16] Where terrorists are especially gifted and committed to their activities, as in West Germany some years ago, they can no doubt, at least for a time, impose insurance hazards of this scale even where they are themselves socially rather isolated. But most effective terrorist activity over long periods of time is restricted to settings in which there is strong communal solidarity: the Catholic population of Northern Ireland, the Palestinian diaspora, incipiently the black communities in the Union of South Africa. An intermediate case, at present largely confined to domestic personnel, would be the activities of the Red Brigades in Italy.

Other forms of 'social' or 'cultural' risk sometimes mentioned include ethnic, tribal or communal animosities and particular local traditions of organized labour. Communal riots and, more extremely, civil war[17] can hardly expedite most business transactions (though they no doubt gratify manufacturers of arms and police apparatus), and it is no doubt exceedingly trying to have to deal with labour organizations that are culturally more militant or workforces less cooperative than those to be found in one's home market.[18] But it is analytically uneconomical to consider the control and costing of labour as an external and political element in determining a productive investment, and it is hard, outside Uganda and Ruanda, and perhaps Nigeria, to believe that tribal or communal strife has yet made a large difference over several years to the profitability of many foreign investments or even to the repayment of many loans.

On the whole it is likely to be more illuminating not to attempt a shapeless but exhaustive inventory of all the social or cultural factors that

may possibly already have given or should, in future, give bankers or
businesspeople a sleepless night or two, but to try instead to bring into
focus just what in a society or culture is likely to menace the property
rights of foreign lenders or investors. If political risk, at its simplest, is the
more or less effective encroachment by foreign governments on the profit
margins of an investor, social or cultural risk is perhaps, prototypically,
the rising impatience of a population in the face of a government that it
perceives to be serving not its interests but rather those of foreign
investors or foreign governments.

Response to political risk: intellectual and practical

There has been some recent study of how investors do in fact respond to
what political scientists believe to be semi-behavioural measures of
political risk. The results are predictably inconclusive (Thunell)[19] and
even if they were clearer and the measures themselves were more
convincing it is not obvious what implications they would have for how
investors have good reason to respond to such indexes. In fact, one of the
main theses I wish to advance is that investors would be unwise to waste
their time in inspecting such indexes at all. Contrast, for example, Jodice[20]
or, more cautiously, Rummell and Heenan.[21]

   There have also been some distinctly more illuminating studies of the
incidence of forced divestment of American investment in foreign countries.[22] These confirm, unsurprisingly, that forced divestment, more
generally, and expropriation, in particular, both actions that can only be
performed by governments, have in fact been implemented in a rational
and discriminating manner. Following the logic of the 'obsolescing
bargain', the terms on which it initially appears attractive to a host
country to acquire a foreign investment, together with its organizational
linkages and technological knowledge, become in many cases steadily
less attractive to the recipient,[23] producing a 'shift in power from multinationals to home countries which is cumulative, irreversible and
speeding up all the time'.[24] Forced divestment has markedly accelerated
over the period from 1960 to 1976.[25] In the case of most countries it has
concentrated especially on extractive, utility, banking and insurance
sectors,[26] though in the five countries that between 1970 and 1976 took
over an especially large number of foreign firms (Algeria, Chile, Peru,
Ethiopia and Tanzania) the largest portion of the takeovers came in the
manufacturing and trading sectors. The industries in which forced
divestment has been least frequent – drugs, chemicals, and plastics[27] – all
tend to have very high research and development expenditures and to be

globally integrated, whereas those in which it has been most frequent tend to have low research and development expenditures and to display low international integration. Forced divestment has increased in frequency and scale, and it has been selective, even at the level of firms. What this pattern reflects is a change in the balance of power, following a change in the balance of perceived advantage in a competitive game.[28] There is some residual vagueness as to how to model each of the players in this game. Partly this reflects awareness of what each player is like in actuality. Governments are plural entities and their members have many purposes besides that of maximizing the gross national product of the countries they govern. Multinational corporations are at least equally plural entities, the components of which baffle academic analysts as to the real objects of their allegiance[29] and which, like governments, certainly act as they do partly because of their organizational character-istics. If what was in question here was the historical explanation of particular investment decisions it might be appropriate to apply, as Thunell does, the contrasting models of Graham Allison – rational actor, organizational process, and bureaucratic politics – to see which best captures the historical *explicandum*.[30] But risk analysis is part of the theory of rational choice, and in order to appear within that theory at all investors and lenders must be represented as rational actors. The question is not what they are like or what, consequently, they are likely in practice to do, but rather what they have good reason to do. And, in effect, the first thing they have good reason to do in confronting political risk is to get themselves together as rational actors, to identify goals, and to get their organizational processes and bureaucratic politics sufficiently under control to enable themselves to operate as though they in fact are rational actors.

Because social and cultural risk is organizationally diffuse in its form and necessarily holistic in its consequential impact, it is impossible in principle to calculate its probability with any accuracy. But, if it cannot be accurately predicted, and if the pragmatics of what to do about it are thus, in theory, rather simple, this does not imply any necessary obstruction to an understanding of its nature. All that can be done about it, offsetting loss of profit by 'insurance', is to pass on as much as possible of the expected risk to a third party or set of parties, while passing on as little as possible of the expected profit. (If the analysis offered here is valid, it follows that actuarially sound insurance cannot in principle be written for such risks, though governments may nevertheless elect to provide cover against them.) This, of course, is a familiar and intricate competitive game, and all its interest lies in a type of detailed knowledge of particular cases that, at least outside business schools, academic commentators virtually never possess, except in severely retrospective circumstances. And since the expected risk cannot in principle be predicted with any accuracy, the only additional clear consideration (one of sophomoric simplicity) is that in international transactions there are no countries at all in which social and cultural country risk is zero. Any countries of standardly high profitability are especially unlikely to display zero social and cultural risk.

The desirability of transferring risk was already apparent to a (deservedly) politically vulnerable American copper company in Chile as early as the mid-1960s.[31] The arrangements under which the Kennecott Copper Corporation sold a 51 per cent interest in its huge El Teniente mine to the Chilean government in return for $80 million, a management contract, and a cut in its tax rate, financed a vast expansion of the mine through loans from the Export–Import Bank and the Chilean Copper Corporation, secured an insurance guarantee of the sale price from the American Agency for International Development (together with a Chilean government guarantee of both sale price and Export–Import Bank loan, justiciable under the law of the state of New York), and raised additional funds for the mine expansion by writing long-term contracts for its output with European and Asian customers and selling collection rights on these to consortia of European and Japanese banks, were impressively complex and single-minded.[32] As Robert Haldeman, the executive vice-president of Kennecott's Chilean operations, put it: 'The aim of these arrangements is to insure that nobody expropriates Kennecott without upsetting relations to customers, creditors and governments on three continents.' The aim was successfully realized and Kennecott was handsomely rewarded for its interim stewardship and very adequately compensated, despite prior pledges – 'Ni un centavo'[33] – when President Allende expropriated the mine. Unsurprisingly, these arrangements set a fashion.[34]

Understanding the nature of social and cultural risk

The transferring of political risk is a relatively urgent objective for a prudent investor or banker. But, since the time scale of social or cultural risk is in general less importunate, in its case there is much to be said for the attempt to minimize the risk in the first place. The attempt to understand the nature of social and cultural risk should be a helpful prelude to this attempt. Two reasonably well-demarcated problems in academic social and political theory bear directly on the understanding of social and cultural risk. The first is the problem of explaining the incidence of revolution. (This is unsurprising since, on the analysis offered here, the completed trajectory of a revolution is the quintessence of actualized social and cultural risk.) The second is the less well-defined problem of identifying just what in social, cultural and political terms makes capitalist production and the patterns of exchange it generates viable at all.

Explaining revolutions: problems of method

The explanation of revolution is instructive because it has proved so elusive, and because in recent years some of the main obstacles to it have become distinctly clearer. The most influential American approaches to the explanation of revolution, the Parsonian structural functionalist analysis, with its strong emphasis on cultural factors, associated particularly with the work of Chalmers Johnson[35] and the more explicitly psychological approach of Ted Gurr, centring on the concept of relative deprivation,[36] have made an extremely unimpressive contribution to the understanding of the phenomena with which they have been concerned. The broader school of comparative politics with which Gurr's work is associated, which seeks to construct indexes of the political vulnerability of societies by the increasingly grandiose computation of social and political indicators, has continued to thrive.[37] It would be silly to deny that graphic presentation even of the inherently vague information deployed in these calculations may be of some help in focusing the judgement of potential investors who initially know nothing of the political and social relations of a particular country,[38] though, as with the more comprehensive assessments of country risk favoured by some bankers,[39] the interpretation of the implications of the results is best left to someone who already knows a great deal about the particular country in question.[40]

But the 'induction by brute force' approach adopted, with its quasi-magical aping of the routines of natural science and its innocent faith that the deficiencies of the information handled will come out in the wash, through the vigour of the computational techniques employed, has highly insecure theoretical foundations. There are a number of different objections to such 'kitchen blender' approaches to social and political analysis. The most important of these, the objection to the implied natural science ontology of human beings, is far more important in relation to social and political scientists than it is likely to prove in relation to bankers or corporate investors. For example, bankers (unlike social scientists) are no doubt rather well aware when they construct models of country risk that they are attempting to improve and clarify their judgement, not playing at natural science on especially refractory materials. One basis of the natural science paradigm is a very soggy conception of the relations between the categories of action and those of behaviour and a wholly inadequate grasp of the obstruction that cultural differentiation poses for any accurate translation from the former into the latter.[41] The unpredictability of political action (which is what is especially crucial in explaining the incidence of revolution) is probably only a blatant instance of what is true of virtually any human performance of much interest.[42] But in the context of revolutions it is an eminently pragmatic, and not merely a logical, consideration. The most impressive explanatory study of revolutions has been holistic and structural in ambition,[43] but even this has so far been explanatory within rather strict limits and has neither shown, nor perhaps could in principle show, much capacity to integrate cultural factors or strategic skill and nerve into its explanations.[44] (Culture is perhaps an unwisely broad term to employ. In this context it certainly should not be read in the idiom of 1960s 'modernization' theory, as the infliction of Western conceptions of existential and practical rationality on the hapless inhabitants of the less-developed countries.)

In the explanation of revolutions, the key cultural consideration resides in the evaluative, and still more, the causal, beliefs of candidates for political leadership.[45] Because of the intrinsically competitive character of political action (the prevalence of opponents, not the absence of authentically shared interests and commitments), the causal beliefs both of potential revolutionaries and of incumbent governments play a strongly dynamic role in revolutionary process and guarantee a persisting gap between inductive extrapolation from past conflict and the character and outcome of future conflicts. Equally importantly – and usually some-what in advance of changes in the causal beliefs of agents – shifts in the ecological context of revolutionary or counter-revolutionary action alter the prospective outcomes of identical initiatives or responses.[46] This point has a direct relevance to the assessment of political risk (and a somewhat more tangential bearing on the assessment of social and cultural risk also). Precisely because of the ecological changes in international trade that have shifted the balance of advantage from multinationals towards host countries in the exploitation of natural resources over the last two decades any assessment of political risk inferred by induction from the levels prevailing in the early 1960s to levels likely to prevail in the early 1970s would have sharply underestimated the anticipated extent of expropriation.

A further consideration, this time drawn from the structural analysis of revolutionary potentiality,[47] is the degree to which the weight of social and cultural risk will depend not simply on the characteristics of class relations within a particular national society but at least equally crucially on the precise character and organizational structure of the nation state concerned and on the balance of external pressures and supports – economic, political, ideological and military – to which this is subjected. At either of these levels of specificity, assessment by induction from episodes of behaviour will necessarily be far less illuminating than assessment founded on the attempt to grasp the internal and external dynamics to which a particular national society is exposed.

Why is capitalist production possible?: a key question, feebly answered

The second main problem in social and political theory directly relevant to the assessment of social and cultural risk is the analysis of the social, cultural and political preconditions for capitalist production and the patterns of exchange this generates. There has been much recent writing on the political aspects of this topic,[48] but it has yet to make an explanatory contribution of much power. In relation to social and cultural risk it is likely to be more helpful to focus explicitly on the intrinsic moral vulnerability of capitalism. Moreover, it is worth emphasizing that, in terms of social visibility, this is a genuine perceptual property of capitalist relations of production, which certainly does *not* depend on the (hazardous) judgement that a superior socio-economic order, 'socialism', is waiting everywhere (or anywhere) in the wings to replace it on stage. There is some evidence, too, that this property is especially hard for Americans (in contrast with the inhabitants of most countries in the world) to perceive. To a degree thus far unique in world history, and one clearly dependent on distinctive geographical and historical endowments, the United States has been a society ideologically integrated in the endorsement of capitalist relations of production.[49] By contrast, Great Britain, for example, as Professor Hayek has long complained,[50] has historically responded to capitalist production relations with what (in Hayek's eyes) are essentially primitive moral sentiments, evoked by perceptions of distributive injustice, that, when they enter into democratic politics, devastate the capacity of the market to maximize economic welfare. (Hayek himself, appropriately, draws the conclusion that majoritarian democracy based on universal adult suffrage is, against Engels, a somewhat unsuitable political shell for the reproduction of capitalist relations of production, though in the United States he would

Lenin

presumably be compelled to admit that it is still not doing too badly.) The significance of the moral vulnerability of capitalism, in the end of decisively *political* importance, is still very poorly understood and its implications are still being actively explored in practice.[51] The potential range of these political implications is, of course, restricted by the vulnerabilities of pre-capitalist production relations and, more crucially, by those of other existing states that entitle themselves 'socialist'. But it is unlikely to be necessary, to an American audience, to emphasize these latter vulnerabilities, even if the intricate politics of the Polish crisis serve to underline the point that social and cultural risk as a practical concern for bankers and investors is far from being a prerogative of capitalist societies.

What is probably the most sustained, imaginative and illuminating consideration of the construction and reconstruction, over the last three centuries, of a culture capable of facilitating capitalist production relations has been produced in recent decades by socialist (and, in many cases, marxist) historians of the British Isles.[52] But, in part, because of its political orientation, this historiography has failed to show at all clearly the interrelations between the political construction, through a legal order and public apparatus of coercion, of the space within which this culture evolved and the evolution of the culture itself. In some ways the relation appears more clearly, if more abstractly, in the powerful account of the preconditions for the flourishing of what they called a 'commercial society' set out by the great Scottish social theorists of the eighteenth century and most particularly by David Hume and Adam Smith.[53] The relations between effective governmental power, the predictable guarantee of private property, and the dynamic productivity of the 'system of natural liberty' and justice sketched in the *Wealth of Nations* were strongly emphasized by Hume and Smith themselves and the contrasts drawn, as they had been by Montesquieu, with the disincentive effects of arbitrary or despotic rule. Neither Hume nor Smith understood very well the potential ideological fragility of the new order,[54] but they did see with exemplary precision the direct dependence of this order on both secure rights of property and a government with the capacity to defend these effectively against challenge.

Comparable historical studies of the cultural incorporation of the industrial working class in Western European countries other than Great Britain for the most part have been less illuminating.[55] But the political implications of the structural and temporal differences in such incorporation have recently been emphasized by sociologists[56] and ought perhaps to be apparent to any reader of regular newspaper reports on the politics of, for example, France, Italy, Spain, West Germany, Holland, or Portugal.

It is because of how they are educated, by their experiences domestically and at work, to see and feel about their position in society – because of the culture into which they are inducted – that groups of workers or voters adopt and sustain the political tastes and allegiances they hold.

Extranational guarantees for property rights

The creation and maintenance of effective guarantees for the forms of private property required by capitalist production has proved historically to be difficult enough even within a given national society. But it is, naturally, a decidedly harder task internationally than it is domestically.[57] The quite conscious equation of extending nineteenth-century Western European conceptions of property with the prerequisites for expanding international commerce and spreading civilization itself has been effectively emphasized by recent economic historians.[58] As the British consul, Brand, put it in April 1860, in a letter to Lord John Russell, not long before the annexation of Lagos: 'The increase of trade and civilised ideas and European interests and habits demand that there should be such an administration of Government as to give efficient protection to property', while at this point in Lagos there was 'no effective protection of property, no mode of enforcing the payment of debts applicable to Europeans').[59] A month later, he wrote again: 'Year after year a feeling of insecurity is raised in the minds of those who have property exposed here, and their plans for turning that property to best account are upset by doubts as to the amount and certainty of the protection they have to expect.'[60] The issue of the sanctity of contracts[61] and the absence of effective guarantees for the payment of debts or the protection of property held by Americans in foreign countries remains an urgent preoccupation for the American government[62] as it does for American multinational corporations. The clear relation between this preoccupation in 1860 and the establishment of formal colonial rule over Lagos brings out very well how colonial rule was a natural and, for a time, an economical successor to the more erratic techniques epitomized in Lord Palmerston's slogan: 'Half-civilised governments require a dressing down every eight to ten years.'[63] The ending of colonial rule in the aftermath of World War II, an uneven and in some cases a painful process, was a product of the discovery, both by colonial powers and by political entrepreneurs in colonial territories that the balance of economic advantage in policing a congenial property law within an alien society had always been extremely narrow and that in the geopolitical context after 1945, it could be dependably reversed by political and military action.[64] Marxist theories of imperialism have not been very cogent in detail,[65] but they have certainly focused on a political phenomenon of massive dimensions – the expansion and contraction of formal and informal empire by capitalist powers – and there is no reason to believe their central explanatory intuition to be mistaken. The ebb of colonial power has created much, though not of course all, of the political frame in which the more politically vulnerable components of modern international trade occur. It certainly[66] offers part of the explanation of why expropriation of foreign enterprises is more frequent than it used to be. But, seen in broader perspective, what it principally highlights is the underlying continuity across the entire era of colonial rule and the direct connections beween the preoccupations of Palmerston and those, for example, of President Nixon.

It is worth emphasizing how much easier it proved in colonial territories to devise and extend a congenial set of property rights[67] than it was to establish a culture that fully endorsed the legitimacy of these rights[68] in the case of indigenes, let alone in the case of foreign corporate interests. Indeed, in any society the blend of voluntary choice and experienced constraint that is central to capitalist production will be perceived and understood as it is, in part because of the objective character of the exchange relations in question, but also in part because of the beliefs and attitudes – the culture – of the population. Even in the ideological haven of the United States there exist, at least among the intelligentsia, the most profound and irresolvable clashes of intuition on the relation between property entitlements and social justice.[69] The cultural attitude broadly christened 'economic nationalism'[70] may well often misdirect its holders as to which economic arrangements do and do not maximize the welfare of a given national population. But it is best understood in itself not as a belief about the causal preconditions for maximizing domestic welfare but rather as a resolute refusal to regard particular internationally extended property rights as compatible with the requirements of distributive justice and a consequent refusal to regard them as genuine rights, *entitlements*, at all.

The incidence of expropriation

In this perspective we may consider briefly the record of large-scale expropriations of American or European assets in the present century and attempt to draw a broad moral. It would not be easy to compile a reasonably full list of such expropriations,[71] let alone one that showed the relative scale of each instance in constant prices. But some of the major instances can be located readily enough: Russia after 1917, Mexico in the late 1930s, Eastern Europe and China after 1945, Vietnam, Algeria, Cuba, Chile under the presidency of Salvador Allende, Angola, and perhaps now, Iran. A number of features stand out in any such list. One is the close connection between large-scale expropriation (and more particularly of explicit confiscation with no compensation at all) and the occurrence of anti-capitalist or anti-colonial revolution. Three factors loom especially large in this particular set of revolutions: world war, decolonization, and an intimate and acute hostility toward the United States on the part of a number of countries on its more or less immediate periphery. (Iran, of course, stands at some distance from all three.) The relation of world war and a coerced decolonization to revolution is not particularly puzzling.[72] But the contrasts between Mexico, Cuba, and Chile, on the one hand,[73] and much of the rest of Latin America, on the other, may be a good deal harder to draw persuasively, though in the case of Mexico[74] and still more of Cuba[75] the intensity of the hostility at least is far from puzzling. A government that gives its subjects less reason to see it as representing their interests than as protecting the property rights of foreigners (colonial governments are an extreme example) can expect little allegiance from its subjects.[76] What is especially important in the instance of Iran is its demonstration of the capacity of a government to cast itself in this way as a catspaw of foreign interests on the basis of an altogether more distant and historically shallower relationship and of the devastating impact of this identification on its viability as a government.

The changing ecology of international capitalist enterprise

The morals to be drawn from these considerations can be summarized crudely in five points. First, the ecology within which domestic governmental power is exercised and foreign property rights are or are not protected has been changed sharply by the outward geographical pressure of capital from the most advanced industrial societies. This may yet prove to be of major importance for the security of foreign property rights even within some parts of Western Europe. Second, the same ecology has been altered in addition by a real shift of mutual advantage within investment bargaining.[77] Third, it has been further altered by the political apprehension of this shift in advantage within incumbent governments and among the ranks of immediate contenders for governmental power. (It is an important qualification to the second and third points that an unintended consequence of poor country government action that is rational in relation to each individual investment may be an increasing subsequent exclusion from international capital markets.[78] Fourth, it has been altered still further by the changing pattern of international conflict, the sharp shift in external aid and coercive threat produced by the Russian and Chinese revolutions, and the intricate competitive fields that have emerged from these changes. A clear example of the consequences of this shift is the increasing difficulty faced by the US government in resisting the expropriation of American assets and in enforcing the payment of prompt, effective, and adequate compensation where this has already taken place. This weakness is neatly epitomized by the fact that the famous Hickenlooper amendment has virtually never in fact been applied in the case of an expropriated American investment.[79] (Of course, as the fate of President Allende showed, the United States government and even individual American multinational corporations do have the capacity on occasion to intervene quite effectively by less formal means on the political margin.) Fifth, and more speculatively, there is perhaps also reason to regard this ecology as being changed still further by present (and, prospectively, by future) levels of popular political participation and response. Even the least politically sophisticated of populations in the last quarter of the twentieth century can expect to encounter a variety of agencies competing to interpret to them the political possibilities open to them. Some of these agencies may be a little surprising to western social scientists (mullahs, for example). But their cultural idiosyncrasies will not necessarily preclude their exercising dramatic power, at least of a negative kind.

This is a very simple picture. In so far as it is accurate, it should certainly discourage the attempt to predict the course of future political struggles by simple induction from past political struggles. But it should also, in compensation, help to bring out the logic through which these struggles have been and are being transformed. In terms of this logic, it seems likely that social and cultural risk will be maximized in the face of repressive governments (correctly) perceived by their subjects as tied to the protection of foreign economic interests; lands, for example, too fit for American investors to do business in. Such societies are societies of standing social and cultural risk, even if the risk happens for a time to be kept under control by skilful and ruthless repression and capable management of the economy. A tentative list of such societies might include South Africa, Indonesia, Chile today, South Korea, perhaps Argentina and Brazil, possibly in the end, Egypt.

Iran: a case study in social and cultural risk

The case of Iran is illuminating in this context not because of the direct damage it has inflicted on western economic interests (which, at least until the release of the American embassy hostages, must in comparative terms have been decisively less than the damage it inflicted on Iranian economic interests), but because of the drastic reversal of any rational assessment of the political risks of dealing with the Pahlavi monarchy that its occurrence represented.[80] What exactly made this reversal possible, and how far does it support or impugn the preceding character-ization of social and cultural risk?

Two points in particular stand out. The first is the astonishing extent to which the Shah's regime in its last eighteen months contrived to unite against itself the most heterogeneous social and political forces,[81] casting itself as the deadly enemy of Iranians of every class and ethnic grouping, across virtually the entire continuum of cultural and political allegiance in a highly differentiated and segmented society. Such patterns of projective identification, positive and negative, have long been identified as the essence of revolutionary process.[82] The second point, more distinctively, is the very close link that the Iranian revolutionaries (and the Ayatollah Khomeini, in particular) have seen throughout between their hostility to the Shah and their hostility to the United States of America. When in late June 1981[83] the headquarters of the Islamic Republican Party was bombed in Tehran with heavy loss of life in the course of the persistent internecine feuds that have dogged the country since the Shah's over-throw, the party's response took the form of yet another broadcast attack on the United States, the 'Great Satan', presenting the attack as the opening of 'a new chapter in the history of struggles by the Islamic nation against the criminal America', warning America and Israel that the Iranian revolution would not lose heart in the face of the assassination and assuring its putative followers that 'you, revolutionary people, have already identified yours and God's friends and enemies and have already declared, within the framework of this revolutionary recognition, your war on the side of the oppressed people.' To be identified so crisply as the enemies of God and to be incorporated into what is on occasion an authentically paranoid vision, in a setting where the practical political implications are so disastrous for American interests, is perhaps at present the epitome of cultural risk for Americans.[84] More domestically, of course, it had possessed very similar resonances for the Shah himself, who attributed the demonstrations scornfully, as late as June 1978, to 'a lot of mullahs pining for the seventh century'.[85]

America as the Great Satan

The first of these points, in retrospect, is not especially difficult to explain, though there do not appear to have been any publicly announced assessments of Iran that to any degree foresaw it. Indeed, there is ample evidence that neither American intelligence analysts[86] nor even Russian strategists[87] had much inkling of its likelihood. The second point is in some ways more intricate and, for present purposes, perhaps also more important. The extent of hatred for the United States felt by urban Iranians is quite remarkable, and the cultural style of Khomeini's version of Twelver Shi'ite Islam is sufficiently startling to western eyes to be readily mistaken for a form of collective derangement. But it would be an error to see the hatred as a simple product of misinformation and the religious sensibility as a medium of learning that virtually guarantees that the benign intentions of the United States will fail to secure accurate understanding. It is, for instance, exceedingly unlikely that the sentiments of the majority of the Tehran or Shiraz population would be much mollified if they were more extensively and precisely informed about the conflicts prevailing within the US administration in the years of the Shah's fall.[88] Nor is it likely that they would share the Shah's view (and that of some of the tougher American participants or academic analysts) that his eventual fall is to be attributed, first, to the vagaries of President Carter's enthusiasm for human rights, and second, to the President's incapacity to make up his mind and act firmly in situations of crisis. The American involvement with the Shah's regime was as busy and intimate as ever in these years, though it was certainly also strikingly ineffective. Throughout his reign the Shah had owed much to the United States, first for persuading the Russians at the end of World War II to return the entire territory of Iran to his rule and to withdraw their support from the left-wing regimes that had been established under their aegis in northern parts of the country, and later in 1953 for aiding the coup that brought down the nationalist government of Dr Mossadegh and enabled the Shah to return from a humiliating exile. For the last decade of his reign, and most decisively after the OPEC price increases of 1973, the Shah had become a very important ally indeed, the world's largest purchaser of American armaments, a formidable military force in the troubled Persian Gulf area, and a key bulwark against Russian advance toward the Gulf oil fields.

To be sure, this is not to say that the Shah was simply an American puppet. The leading role he played in the early stages of the OPEC cartel in forcing up the price of oil, for example, was strongly opposed to

American interests. But the directness of the links between Iran and the Pahlavi regime in 1977 was apparent enough in the country itself, with 40,000 American military and air force personnel or engineers and businesspeople permanently stationed in a small number of centres in the country and making their presence very blatantly felt.[89] It was thus a very natural assumption in the crisis of 1978-9 that the Iranian army, with its extensive American training and massive endowment of American matériel, could be trusted to serve as an instrument for implementing American purposes in the country. One does not have to be a Twelver Shi'ite waiting for the Hidden Imam, or even a militant member of Solidarity, to find this sort of calm expectation that a national army will serve as the agency for another nation's purposes[90] startlingly offensive.

Cultural risk incarnate: the role of the ulama

One way of seeing the vulnerability of the Shah's situation in 1978-9 is thus in terms of a widening gap between a state very weakly articulated with the remainder of Iranian society[91] and very closely tied to a foreign power, and a society with very little temptation to see this state as serving its own interests and with strong reasons, even in terms of day-to-day experience, for viewing it as the tool of a foreign power. The eventual mechanics of this state's breakdown appear to have been fairly simple: massive street demonstrations in the face of an increasingly irresolute army, many of the units of which were composed largely of conscripts, followed by sharp and well-coordinated strikes by the modern industrial labour force, especially in the oilfields.[92] The missing link between the fairly palpable odiousness of the Shah's regime by 1977 and the scale of popular action, culminating in the largest urban demonstration in history in Tehran, was the very practical and historically tenacious union between the urban merchants and artisans of the bazaar and the Shi'ite ulama.[93]

This alliance was an old one, older by far than the Pahlavi dynasty itself. The relations between its two partners (and their subordinate components) and the two Pahlavi monarchs changed through time. But over the decade and a half since the early 1960s, they had both simplified and deteriorated.[94] The bazaar communities had benefited rather little from the grandiose ventures of the oil boom, and in Tehran they had suffered in some respects from the urban property boom and redevelopment plans this promoted. At least since 1963, the ulama had been treated by the Shah with a mixture of hostility and contempt, despite the very real services some of them had rendered him in his coup of 1953,[95] and their economic position and cultural influence had been frontally attacked in a number of ways. In 1964, Richard Cottam estimated that it was 'most unlikely that religious influence in Iranian nationalism will ever again reach the proportions it exercised in 1951–52'.[96] In the late 1960s, Professor Nikki Keddie offered an equally low assessment of their political prospects: 'Given the continued growth of government power, and the expansion of the army, the bureaucracy, and of secular education, even in the villages, it appears probable that the political power of the ulama will continue to decline as it has in the past century . . . They now appear at most able to modify or delay certain government policies and not strongly to influence their basic thrust and direction.'[97] Writing in the same volume, Hamid Algar, the leading historian of the nineteenth-century ulama,[98] observed more forcefully that 'it would be rash to predict the progressive disintegration of the political role of the ulama. Despite all the inroads of the modern age, the Iranian national consciousness still remains wedded to Shi'i Islam, and when the integrity of the nation is held to be threatened by internal autocracy and foreign hegemony, protests in religious terms will continue to be voiced, and the appeals of men such as Āyatullah Khumaynī to be widely heeded.'[99]

The position the ulama hold in Iran differs markedly from that which they occupy in most Islamic societies.[100] Under the Qajar monarchy it involved a relatively clear separation both of functions and of powers, made possible by the possession of an independent economic base. Most of the major elements of this base were removed from the ulama's control through the Shah's land reform of the 1960s and the secularization of education and assumption of control over religious endowments and the judicial process by both of the Pahlavis. But, although this certainly had the effect of counterposing the ulama sharply to the Shah's regime, the enforced independence was sustained by the final source of economic support open to the ulama, namely, the receipt of voluntary taxes on behalf of the Hidden Imam. In the comparative affluence induced by petrodollars, this autonomous source of funds proved to be quite hand-some.[101] The combination of independence from the state and existing organizational capacity has in several instances enabled Islamic religious groupings in other settings in recent decades to act as effective agencies for political representation in societies that are largely devoid of other forms of politically effective representation (a particularly striking instance is the Mouride brotherhood in Senegal[102]). In Iran the links with the bazaar, the possession of an external linkage with the Shi'ite centre in Iraq at Najaf, and above all, in the demographic avalanche of the late 1960s and 1970s in Tehran, the vast proliferation of local religious associations among the urban population, old and new[103] made the mullahs uniquely capable of organizing and sustaining effective political opposition in the face of a savage, but by 1977, increasingly irresolute, autocracy.

It is clear, too, that the struggle against the Shah evoked some of the deepest themes in Iranian religious culture and that it resonated compellingly with the idiosyncratic emotional tone of Twelver Shi'ism, with its intense feeling for the pathos of suffering and the dignity of the struggle against tyranny and injustice even – or perhaps especially – when the struggle was beyond hope.[104] The dramas of the 1960s and 1970s were interpreted with as much assurance and effect by the ulama to their audiences through scriptural types (the martyrdom at Karbalā of the Imam Husayn and the tyranny of the Umayyad caliph Yazid) as they might have been by the Puritan giants in seventeenth-century New England. The affective dynamics of this vivid religiosity, with its sadomasochistic obsession with pain, certainly has more potential for mustering crowds to serve as machine gun fodder than a short course in the theory of surplus value. But its instrumental political utility in 1978 and 1979 should not be allowed to obscure its true nature. Weirdly, in our time, it was quite literally the stuff of which martyrs are made, and it was the glad acceptance of martyrdom, the eagerness to die on the machine guns of a heavily armed modern army, that, for the first time since the revolutions of 1848,[105] saw the army of a modern state in peacetime and without effective external threats crumble before the uprising of the *menu peuple* of the cities. Twelver Shi'ism is not likely to thrive as a late twentieth-century doctrine of state. But, even in the 1960s, at the time when opposition to the Shah's regime was at its most desperate and least effective, it gave a memorable depth of purpose to the resistance against oppression. 'We cry today because we don't want to give up to tyranny. We beat our heads and our chests because we don't want to go under the pressure of dictatorship or accept coercion ... We have been crying for 1,000 years, it doesn't matter if we cry for another 10 million in order to bring justice against tyranny. I cannot laugh so long as tyranny *is* ruling. I cry in order to resist ... We [ulama] are trying to make justice popular among society, and to prevent cruelty and tyranny ... We are crying because justice is gone.'[106]

Cultural risk actualized: the fall of the Pahlavi dynasty

It is clear, too, that the Shah's regime was a singularly felicitous object for this particular brand of odium. The chaos unleashed in the petrodollar boom of the mid-1970s was indisputably a product of *folie de grandeur*.[107]

The intimate links with the United States gave rich support to the perennial ulama claim, from the Tobacco Protest of 1891–2 to the struggle against Anglo-Iranian in the early 1950s, to defend the economic interests as well as the cultural integrity of Iran against the foreign infidel. The capitulatory regime that governed the legal status of American servicemen in Iran[108] was one of the main targets of Khomeini's 1963 attacks on the Shah,[109] and the links between American and Israeli advisers and the secret police (SAVAK) aroused particular hatred. In the face of the misery of urban Tehran by 1977, with its millions of uprooted peasants scrabbling for a place in the slackening construction boom, its soaring inflation and inexorably rising sewage levels, the antics of the tiny band of favoured beneficiaries of the oil money were egregiously obtrusive. A 15 million dollar exact reproduction of the Versailles Petit Trianon in downtown Tehran[110] and the 100 million dollar Gulf playground island of Kish, bewilderingly owned largely by SAVAK,[111] when set beside the savage repressions of the preceding decade and a half, signified a regime and social order bizarrely compounded of folly and vice. No doubt the Shah need not have fallen. He might have spent the first flood of petrodollars altogether more prudently. He might have been far less brutal in earlier years or more decisively brutal in 1977, more inhibited by concern for human rights in the 1960s and less harried by Carter's State Department at the beginning of the latter's presidency. The Shah might certainly have been retired more gracefully and replaced by a regime that initially gave better protection to American interests.[112] But what is certain is the rich abundance of reasons why he stood in danger of falling, the sheer volume of social and cultural risk that he had succeeded in amassing.

Social and cultural risk as deserved odium

At the centre of social and cultural risk is deserved odium.[113] This insight will not necessarily enable an investor over a particular time span to guess the risks of expropriation with much accuracy. The width of the gap beween rich and poor in a society, for example, may not prove a good predictor of the probability of unheaval over a given period.[114] What this would show, if it were definitely true, is that over that time span, social and cultural risk would be something investors could have afforded to ignore. It certainly does not and cannot show that they will be well advised to ignore such risk in the future over any equivalent length of time, let alone forever. Inductive political science on a scientistic model is a more or less amusing academic game. But history goes on.

It is difficult in principle to integrate assessments of social and cultural risk into the decision-making processes of lenders or investors. Apart from avoiding foreign investment and taking very low profits – to be enviable it is necessary to be successful – there is probably nothing that can be done literally to *minimize* exposure to social and cultural risk. And even this strategy would not necessarily minimize the risks of, for example, British or Italian investors. Any country from which there occurs a massive flight of capital in the face of political crisis is judged by some of its inhabitants to be decidedly riskier[115] than some other countries of which they are not nationals. Country risk begins at home.

But what can be done, and what, in the longer run at least, banks and the more ambitious internationally investing institutions have every reason to try to do is to understand the nature of social and cultural risk. Once this has been understood it can be assessed casually through regular reading of good newspapers and, less casually, by the protracted and culturally attentive study of particular countries.

The appropriate response of an investor, exporter, or even, in some cases, a lender to the social and cultural risk that their action will be perceived (and responded to) as odious by some large portion of the population of the country with which they are dealing is not the construction of a numerical model but, rather, the choice of an idiom of prudence. At the most morally disabused level, the rational response is to extract profits over a very short time horizon (to operate on a 'get it while you can' basis, as many American firms quite explicitly did in Iran).[116] This style is against the long-term interest of capitalist producers as a whole (and, more distressingly, it may well imperil many features that have been closely associated hitherto in fortunate countries with capitalist production: constitutionally elected representative governments, civil rights, cultural freedoms, etc.). But there is no reason why it should not often be economically optimal for an individual firm. A less short-term and morally crass idiom of prudence would require looking at an investment area, borrower or trading partner as elements of a real society and noting the broad incidence of foreign economic relations upon that society through time.

All economic transactions take place in real social settings. High profitability in a corrupt, repressive and disorganized society signifies high cultural and social risk though, of course, high profitability in a particular investment that is simply the outcome of the application of high intelligence does not necessarily imply high social risk. Low profitability is an honest, efficient and free society (where such are to be found) may not represent an enticing investment opportunity, but it does signal very low social and cultural risk. The essence of the relation is far from mysterious.

Very broadly, investors, lenders and exporters can expect to face the risks they *collectively* deserve. The best recipe for assessing the social and cultural risks you will face (or are facing) is to ascertain what in practice you will be (or are already) doing, that is, what the loan you make or the production in which you engage will bring about (or has already brought about) in the setting for which it is destined. It is advisable, too, to keep a weather eye open for what your compatriots are doing, since the attribution of responsibility is so likely to be collective.

Culture is not the superstitious beliefs and attitudes of alien populations. It is the medium through which men and women interpret and respond to what is done to them. What social and cultural risk means for bankers or investors is that in the end they may have to pay a price for not knowing (or not caring) what they are doing.

8

Responsibility without Power: States and the Incoherence of the Modern Conception of the Political Good

Whatever else they may be thought to constitute, and whatever causal role they should be judged to play in the shaping of modern human existence, states today are certainly entities in an endlessly reiterated system of international legal relations. Much of what happens in the world today plainly does not conform to the explicit requirements of this system (consider the vicissitudes of the hapless inhabitants of Afghanistan, El Salvador or Nicaragua). Most of what happens in the world cannot be economically and deftly understood as a direct causal product of explicit features of this system: the deliberate permissions, voluntary acts or continuing purposes of notionally sovereign states. But however far one may be from conceiving the universe as a single causal system, however disaggregated a conception one may favour of natural causality in general or social, economic or political causality in particular, it is clear enough that much of human life today is heavily affected by – bears the deep impress of – the operations of state powers. How are these operations in the last instance to be understood? How should we think about the modern state?

This is, to be sure, not intellectually a very prudent question to address. No answer to it runs the least risk of proving intellectually impressive. No answer to it offered in good faith could have the least hope of combining clarity with brevity and neatness. No doubt it is true of the operations of modern states, as of all other aspects of human affairs (and perhaps of nature more generally),[1] that we are in practice to understand them as best we can, *in situ* and with a boldly improvisatory and tactical opportunism. But political theory cannot so readily evade the task of strategic understanding. However groggy and confused its comprehension is likely in fact to prove, it has no honourable option but to strive for a form of understanding, a perspective, which is in intention synthetic, inclusive and final. (The finality is, of course, a particularly comical aspect of this commitment: a cognitive goal which bears its own absurdity boldly on its face. But given the natural possibility of the imminent extinction of the species itself, of a Last Judgement directly initiated through historically created human powers and by particular human actions, the comedy has a harsh undertone. The relaxed and elegant modesty of well-considered modern thought has been massively overtaken in the domain of politics – the domain where we may yet all end – by the accumulated immodesty of collective human performance.)

In order to consider the operations of modern states at all it is necessary first – and somewhat arbitrarily – to pin down the phenomena that we need to consider. To situate the state today in the first instance in the field of international law does not involve any special deference to the political importance or intellectual dignity of legal thinking as such. Still less does it involve a presumption that the political ambitions or substantive socio-political reality of the dizzy heterogeneity of modern states can be trimmed to a Procrustean uniformity. (States are no more a natural kind than are, for example, buildings or meals.) To achieve a sound sociological grasp of the variety of modern states it is certainly necessary to study them comparatively, and to separate them out, on the basis of such study, into a complex and empirically sensitive typology. In specifying this typology it may for some purposes prove illuminating – perhaps even indispensable – to insist on a substantial cultural component in differentiating types of state.[2] It may even be illuminating to distinguish the state proper as a culturally *sui generis* product of an extremely restricted range of historical experiences, a model which has not merely failed to extend itself from its historical birthplace in western Europe to the domains of the Asiatic mode of production[3] but which never in fact established a firm beachhead across the English Channel.[4] But it is not in this instance the state proper that we need to consider, but rather the cosmopolitanly promiscuous state of modern international law: the state for the purposes of the United Nations, IATA, the General Agreement on Trade and Tariffs, the Red Cross, the Law of the Sea. Today, as in the more or less recent past, there are always some states in the process of coming into being or passing away. (It is still relatively easy in the current ecology of international relations for a state to lose a province by secession – Bangladesh already, perhaps in future Northern Ireland, the West Bank, Eritrea. But it is now, unlike in earlier centuries, quite difficult for a state fully to pass away: consider Kampuchea.) How we choose to apply the concept of a state is a matter of (fairly) arbitrary stipulation. But under any given choice on the criteria for its application there will be only one *broadly* correct application of it to the real world at a particular time. Simply in order to obtain a bounded domain to consider, let us say that there are at present in the world just as many, but only just as many, states as the United Nations recognizes there to be. How then should we think about the mere existence of this particular array of political entities? How should we think about their several performances? (Anyone who supposes that the mere existence of this particular array represents a self-authenticating political good should take the trouble to travel a little more widely and should also think carefully about the apologetics of territorial expansion and imperial rule as a civilizing mission: Rome, China, Tokugawa Japan, Inca Peru; Thomas Jefferson (within the USA), Napoleon (within France), Fitzjames Stephen (in relation to India),[5] Lenin (within the USSR). They should also reflect briefly on how the larger of contemporary states achieved their present size and remind themselves that small can be squalid too.)

In considering these questions it is helpful to bear in mind one key distinction and to focus on one crucial disjunction. The distinction is a distinction in cognitive perspective: between the standpoints of theoretical and practical reason. The disjunction is a disjunction within historical experience; the disjunction between the notional domain of political authority and the causal processes of the production, distribution and exchange of goods and services. One reason why the concept of the state is such a vexed concept today is because it is predominantly at the level of state operations that intellectually and morally ambitious conceptions of the political good intersect with the consecutive, and sometimes quite drastic, shaping of social life. They do not on the whole, of course, do so through the former dominating the latter. Modern states are hardly a practical articulation of the Form of the Political Good. But for those who feel querulous about the trajectory of modern history (and what self-respecting modern academic or intellectual does not?) it is the failure of the operations of the state to exemplify a preferred conception of the political good that provides the principal target for immediate political complaint. It is a commonplace of modern political reason (and still more a commonplace of contemporary political sentiment) that it is those who exercise state power who bear the responsibility for setting human social and economic life to rights. The perspective of theoretical reason is analytical, explanatory and detached. Such a perspective is unlikely to find much use for a concept like responsibility. From the perspective of theoretical reason what we wish to know is what is actually happening and why is it happening, what has actually happened and why it has actually happened. From this viewpoint the past is essentially so much blood under the bridge. But, more strikingly, from this viewpoint the future also may just as well be in due course blood under the bridge too. Certainly it is not best envisaged as an object of anxious manipulative attention. From the viewpoint of theoretical reason it will not be an imperfection of any theory of human history which is sound from other points of view if it happens confidently to predict (and robustly fails to rescue us from) an exceedingly imminent Last Judgement.

The viewpoint of practical reason, by contrast, can scarcely pretend to such bland detachment.[6] It is obsessed, and rightly obsessed, by a sense of the potential imminence of disaster. This is not, of course, to say that it can afford to exhaust itself in the identification of a single political *summum malum*, or that its implications are best represented, as Hobbes perhaps envisaged them as being, as the rational systematization of the single emotion of fear. (There is more to human life than being rationally nervous.) But it is to insist that the orientation of practical reason must always be primarily an orientation towards the future; that it lives in the face of the future. (However, inadequate utilitarianism may be as a theory of human good, much of its continuing imaginative appeal, for those to whom it has appealed, has come from its steady effort to register this feature of practical reason.[7] Whatever is the point of lashing the past?[8])

In the perspective of theoretical reason there is no very taxing intellectual difficulty in deciding how the state today should best be conceived. States today are best conceived as precisely as possible just as they are; certainly sharing some features of professed self-conceptualization (largely derived from the idiom of international law), certainly divided up into a series of ideologically inimical blocs with relatively stable political cores if somewhat shifting peripheries, and, above all, stunningly variegated in their actual character. (Whatever the authenticity of either's ideological credentials, Burkina Fasso is not at all like the Soviet Union, any more than Norway is like Kuwait or India.) From the viewpoint of theoretical reason it is only as a category within international law that states in the world today can be sensibly considered to belong to, indeed to exemplify, a single theoretical category. Within any other reasonably determinate theoretical idiom it will be the overwhelming hetereogeneity of states which first needs to be registered. A radical nominalism, and a clear grasp of whatever range of questions one wishes to pursue on a particular occasion, will be a quite sufficient basis on which to analyse states and their roles at that time. Within the perspective of theoretical reason it is the factual heterogeneity of states at any point, and the far more intractably bemusing historical complexity from which they have emerged, that alone makes it *intellectually* difficult to analyse the character and contribution of state powers. No political scientist with a sophisticated knowledge of world history and a sound grasp of everything politically relevant happening in the world at the time could be seriously intellectually puzzled as to the nature of states. In the perspective of theoretical reason, let us say, it is only our ignorance and our stupidity which prevent us understanding states perfectly. And our ignorance and our stupidity are to be thought of in the first instance, in the most *passé* or positivist terms, as ignorance of fact and deficiencies in our capacity to calculate the logical consequences of propositions. Of course our ignorance and our stupidity are not going to blow over; and from the viewpoint of practical reason they are crippling enough to provoke acute and deeply rational dismay. But within the viewpoint of theoretical reason itself, the intellectual moral they pose is as simple as it is banal: inform yourself.

(I should acknowledge that it is *just* possible that the evaluatively detached conception of theoretical reason suggested here is, as many of the greatest western philosophers from Plato and Aristotle to Kant and Hegel have insisted, in the last instance unsound. But no recent western philosopher has had the least success in suggesting how they can have been right in holding this belief. It is more likely (and at present intellectually more fashionable to suppose) that there does not in fact exist any determinate perspective of theoretical reason, since all human cognitive capacities are simply the applications of biologically given and culturally nurtured powers, and the only ultimate criterion for their application must be practical.[9]

Once we shift to the perspective of practical reason, however, this orderly and plain cognitive field blurs helplessly. It is apparent enough why. While the viewpoint in theoretical reason is presumptively unified and stable in the last instance, presenting us with a universe independent of our selves and our own tastes and judgemental idiosyncrasies, the viewpoint of practical reason is extravagantly plural; and the universe it presents to us is the universe just as we see it and feel it and need both to accept it and to watch out for it. In contrast with theoretical reason where the 'us' to whom the universe is presented is a powerfully convergent and universalizing entity (at the limits the entire human race conceived as a single cognitive community or even a Divine Creator credited with cognitive perfection), the 'us' of practical reason is miserably fissile, enjoying few, if any, facilities for sustaining cognitive community on any scale at all and unravelling not merely civilizations, language groupings or presump-

tive political communities of biological universality, nationality, locality
or class but even individual lives.[10] Not only is it almost indefinitely fissile;
in addition the units into which it divides are intensely and necessarily
game-theoretically interactive. (Whatever else may or may not be
rescued from marxism as a tradition of political understanding, it is quite
impossible to believe that it possesses the resources to do justice to this
feature of human experience.) This last point is particularly important
because it in effect precludes from any possibility of ultimate success the
intellectual strategy, strongly favoured in the West over the last few
centuries, of seeking to reconnect the perspective of practical reason
neatly and stably with that of theoretical reason by individuating the
former (and thus relativizing it) to the point where it meets theoretically
determinate elements of the universe as represented by theoretical
reason (for example bundles of sensations or subjective motivational
sets).[11]

There is nothing intellectually wrong about conceiving the occupants
of the perspective of practical reason as the *loci* of an assemblage of
internal reasons, any more than there is in registering that these assemblages sum up to familial or local or national or civilizational, possibly in
some respects even to universal, viewpoints. Nor is there anything intellectually wrong about presuming that the assemblages of internal reasons
which individuals figure as within the theory of practical reason are
themselves causal products of (among other things) familial, local,
national and civilizational factors. But what is disastrous is the failure to
recognize the dizzily proliferating indeterminacies which result from the
interaction of these several viewpoints, indeterminacies that are a
product of cognitive prowess not an index of cognitive failure, and which
cannot in principle be eradicated. (Extended instruction in game theory
may or may not improve one's nerve and one's judgement in the face of
indeterminacy: in at least one crucial political domain at present we can
only hope to God that it does do so. What it cannot do is to remove
massive and pressing indeterminacy from the centre of practical reason.
Politics as a practical activity – the deployment of arms, persuasion,
energy and wealth by human beings to get what they suppose they want
– is only the most blatant expression of this indeterminacy.)

In the perspective of theoretical reason states in all their variety may
be difficult to find out about; but they are at least – once you have found
out enough – delightfully easy to understand. In the viewpoint of practical
reason the difficulties of finding out about them do not disappear from
the picture. Indeed many obvious causes for such difficulty force themselves upon the attention. (No state genuinely likes to be investigated,
sniffed over, impertinently and intimately. Even the most derelict of

states has beliefs which it would prefer its potential friends or enemies to hold about it and items which it keenly desires the former or the latter not to know. And real states are arcane, too, not simply out of a proud consciousness of public responsibility but also out of a furtive instinct of self-protection and even a modicum of shame.) What does disappear beyond hope of recall is the potential ease of ultimate understanding. In a sense indeed what disappears – since the perspective of practical reason is necessarily so deeply time-bound – is the very conception of ultimate understanding itself. The importance of this is apparent enough for those who spend their lives in the study of political science. For however persistently (and pompously) they may proclaim their commitment to the perspective of theoretical reason and however devotedly they may in fact seek to discipline their own inquiries by an image of natural science which they identify with the perspective of theoretical reason, no real living political scientist over lengthy periods of time could in fact remain consistently indifferent to the perspective of practical reason. This is certainly not, in my view, a matter for complaint: as we say in England, 'Join the human race'. What sane reason could there be for spending a lifetime studying a political subject-matter within which one's own personal political preoccupations failed to figure at all?[12]

The history of serious political thinking – to use an outmoded and coat-trailing phrase – is largely the history of the attempt to understand the implications of this instability in the perspective of practical reason and the indeterminacies that proliferate from it. No one could mistake it for a history of triumphant cognitive accumulation; but even the most sceptical of modern auditors should have little difficulty in drawing some lessons from it. If we take the perspective of practical reason as historically given to us at present by the beliefs we now happen to have, and by the desires, hopes, fears and commitments which we also at present happen to have – as individuals, as families, as local communities, as classes, as nations – then at least one important lesson can certainly be drawn from the history of serious political thought. It is that virtually every human being or assemblage of human beings at any time has good reason, often overwhelmingly good reason, not merely to check carefully whether some of their current factual beliefs are in fact valid but also to reconsider whether all their current desires, hopes, fears and commitments are in fact well-advised or morally decent.[13] The cognitively appropriate way for human beings to understand the nature and significance of states is in the first instance from where and when (and who) they are. That is the perspective in which we need to understand them. It is also a perspective in which they are certainly there to be understood. (Whatever may in the long run be decided about the status of the perspective of theoretical reason, as long as there are any human beings at all capable of choosing their own actions the perspective of practical reason is here to stay.) But it does not follow from this that the perspective of practical reason is committed willy nilly to the full folly and vice of our own current individual or communal or national or ideological self-understandings.

From the perspective of practical reason states are to be understood as they have affected, or do or may affect, us. But it is not just piety towards an antique tradition of didactic moralism to insist that we in our turn are also to be understood in part as we have affected, or do or may affect, them.[14] The causality runs firmly in both directions. The perspective of practical reason is the perspective of organized groupings of human beings just as much as of individuals. (Further indeterminacies or instabilities intrude at this point.) An additional, and quite distinct, dimension of indeterminacy is furnished by the extreme unclarity in modern thinking about the conceptual relations between some of the principal components of practical reason: most particularly between the directives of egoistic prudence and the dictates (or supposed dictates) of morality.[15]

The principal weakness in modern understandings of the significance of the operations of state powers does not come from the failure to grasp particular assemblages of factual properties in modern states. Nor does it come from the failure to register the factual properties of the miscellany of other types of organized human agency, intranational or transnational, that are also doing so much to shape our world. Rather it comes from our more or less panic-stricken imaginative incapacity to face up to the stunning cognitive intricacy of the political universe that we need to grasp. No one who listens at any length today to the public political reflections of even the most intelligent and scrupulous of the world's statesmen and stateswomen can doubt that this panic-stricken imaginative incapacity is of immense practical importance. Each of us, academic inquirers just as much as political actors, clutches more or less helplessly to us the sense of a vastly simpler world, in which we live for much of the time and know what we would keenly prefer to live for almost all of it. Is there really good reason to hope that any act of analytical simplification that we offer each other will prove to be more than a more or less cunning example of this overwhelming mechanism of denial: the transposition of personal or political evasion into a glib idiom of intellectual self-regard? (It is not altogether agreeable to belong to a trade that can turn assessing the imminence of the end of the world into a bland display of professional virtuosity.)

But, of course, a mere acknowledgement of the scale – the raw cognitive intricacy – of modern state powers, as viewed from the perspective of practical reason is of little use to anyone; briefly sobering, but enduringly, perhaps terminally, depressing. Whatever we may need political theory for, we assuredly do not need it to assist us in reducing ourselves to catatonia. What I should like to offer in conclusion is not some stupidly jaunty résumé of what state powers today do really mean for us and how, accordingly, we have good reason to conceive them. Rather I shall try briefly to summarize some of their features which appear to me to keep their shape rather well, despite the relentless fission of the perspective of practical reason, and which also seem to me of evident importance. It will not be a list of *the* important features of the contemporary (let alone the future) state: a list which only the deity has the cognitive facilities to draw up. It is not intended to be balanced, let alone exhaustive. All I would claim for it is that these features *at least* of modern states deserve our close attention, and deserve it both as political theorists and as ordinary political agents.

Let us turn briefly to the disjunction, within modern historical experience, between the notional scope of political authority and the causal process of the production, distribution and exchange of goods and services. It is, to be sure, scarcely a matter for surprise that there should exist a disjunction between an ideological conception and a causal process; and it is even less surprising when the ideological conception in question does not expressly even mention the causal process involved. But it is not going too far to say that the normative political theory of the modern world has disintegrated in the face of this disjunction. What has caused it to disintegrate, in my view, is its incapacity to abandon the state as a framework of notional political authority and responsibility and its more narrowly intellectual inability to combine the continuing acceptance of this framework with a coherent and realistic understanding of the causal character of economic production, distribution and exchange. The disintegration can of course be resisted by abandoning either component; by dissolving the state as an (all too feeble) domain of political authority and responsibility in fantasies of unconcerted mutual beneficence, or by truncating an international nexus of production and exchange to the borders of a single state; by coerced autarky. The first of these forms of resistance is the silliest of self-deceptions; but the second, as we know, can be pursued for a time as a real policy by a real state and its rulers. Recent experience of such a pursuit certainly suggests that it is a hazardous way (at least from the viewpoint of its subjects) for any modern state to seek to equate its powers with its responsibilities. One of the main errors that lies behind it is a misunderstanding of what the powers of a state in relation to economic production really are.

Here the dominance of legal and moral categories in the state's self-representation is principally to blame. A state is defined in the first instance territorially through a domain of internationally exclusive property rights. (It is redefined, of course, very elaborately in the modern world, by treaty and commercial practice, in ways that modify this assemblage of exclusive property rights quite sharply; but the modification in its turn depends on the recognition of the prior domain of exclusion.) The legal power of a state to define who owns what within its borders is today one of its most unequivocal characteristics. It is this characteristic, rendered plastic by greed and hope and usually somewhat vicarious generosity, that makes the direction of state policy today the imaginatively most natural idiom for putting the world to rights. But while any state at any time is notionally in a position to reallocate all its domestic assets to taste on the basis of some Rawlsian or utilitarian standard of distributive propriety, no actual state at any time could act quite as drastically on its own fleeting whim and from its own coercive resources. Real states are systems of power as well as structures of entitlements. Moreover even domestically the legal power to reallocate is not the same as a causal power to create. And since no state has a legal power to reallocate extensively beyond its own borders, any element of the economy over which it presides which is causally modified from beyond its borders ought not even in principle to be *wholly* subject to its powers. There have been at least two heroic attempts to bring these anomalies to order: the socialist attempt to replace the opacity of unorganized market exchange by the putative transparency of rationally planned production and allocation, and the liberal attempt to restrict the content of governmental economic policy to a tasteful handful of principles of rational abstention. But no one inspecting the morning newspaper today could suppose either of these attempts to be still intellectually in working order: two beautiful images of totality, slain by quite simple analytical weaknesses in each and then buried full fathom five by the relentless game-theoretic fission of the perspective of practical reason – trade wars, debt and currency crises, the disintegration of international economic regimes.

What inaugurates international economic regimes in the first place is a combination of power and complementarity of advantage.[16] Without some initial dominance no such regime could be established at all. Without some complementarity of advantage no such regime could be sustained for any length of time.[17] An international trade regime which genuinely was a system of expropriation to the exclusive advantage of a single party could only be established and protected by overwhelming coercive power, a power which no state in the modern world has possessed for more than a decade, except over relatively confined areas. At any particular point in time one or more international economic regimes acts as a clear causal frame, limiting the freedom of action, for better or for worse, of the vast majority of state powers in the modern world. The combination of notional legal autonomy and real causal constraint is ideologically discomfiting to modern state powers but does not necessarily cast much direct light on the interests of their subjects. Multinational corporations (notorious beneficiaries of the most recent international economic regime of any scale) certainly present an elusive fiscal target to the weakly organized governments of poor countries; and some of them – and not only chemical manufacturers – have certainly done considerable damage here and there. But not much of modern human suffering can be confidently laid exclusively at their door. It is not just the absence of omnipotence – or of economic omnipotence more particularly – that precludes most or perhaps all modern state powers from doing their subjects massive economic favours. The category that links the excess of state political responsibility (no sovereignty without responsibility) with the state's severely restricted causal powers most uncomfortably and persistently today is the category of governmental economic policy.

Even on the trusting premise that every modern state power wishes well to each and all of its subjects, its capacity to affect the welfare of most of these subjects for the better may often not be at all impressive. No multinational corporation operating in Ghana, for example, since independence – and no imperialist power leaning upon it from the out-side – has done anything like the degree of damage to the welfare of the vast majority of the Ghanaian population that has been inflicted by a succession of the country's governments: most particularly the National Redemption Council of General Acheampong.[18] Governmental economic policy is an exceedingly murky mixed game of skill and luck; but the harm that genuinely feckless policies can inflict can often be devastating. The ideologically natural way in which to think about governmental economic policy in a given state at a given time is as an attempt (authentic or feigned) to employ the governmental apparatus of that state to modify its economy to the best advantage of at least the clear majority of its own population, then or in the *relatively* near future. But of course this ideologically natural perspective is often very much at odds with the material character of the governmental apparatus itself, the personnel that compose it, its actual powers of agency and the political forces that act effectively upon it. To think of a given state as a potentially passive instrument of the welfare interests of a given population, however imaginatively natural it may be from the perspective of practical reason, is likely to involve a fairly drastic denial of many properties of the state apparatus in question – and that quite apart from the adequacy of its (or one's own) assessment of what forms of governmental action (tariffs, internal fiscal arrangements, market interventions or exclusions) would in fact be likely to serve these interests.

From the viewpoint of theoretical reason (call it 'interpreting the world') there is nothing especially puzzling about all this. There simply is the variety of state powers that happen to exist in the world today. They pursue the economic policies that they pursue because of a combination of determinate social interests, current causal belief and sheer vagaries of judgement, within the causal purlieus left open to them by their own practical make-up. The dimensions of these causal purlieus are determined not only by domestic economic and governmental organization and class composition (and the history of political perception and sentiment) but also by the performance of a wide variety of other agencies – states, large and small, regulators of the current world economic regime (OECD, the IMF, the World Bank, GATT, Comecon), transnational producing and trading agencies. Except by intermittent accident, there is nothing true and simple to be said about the resulting causal interconnections: except that these must be understood just as they are, in all their exotic heterogeneity. The role of the state within them will vary extravagantly, all the way from the helpless passivity of a country like contemporary Uganda to the purposeful managing of the process of industrial innovation at the centre of post-war Japan. Simply because of this extraordinary range in state efficacy, it is extremely unlikely that the perspective of theoretical reason establishes anything at all general about the prospective benefits or disadvantages of state ventures in concerting or modifying production, distribution or exchange. (At any particular time those that can, probably in some measure do; and those that do not, probably in large measure can't.) What is clear, however, is that a deep understanding of modern politics will definitely require a very much deeper understanding of economic processes than any we dispose of at present.

But this is, in any case, not the perspective in which any of us actually needs a deep understanding of modern politics. The perspective in which we need such an understanding is the perspective of practical reason. (Call it 'changing the world'.) Here the main problem of understanding is not raised simply by the immense factual intricacy and heterogeneity of state institutions. It is not even raised predominantly by the alarming nebulousness of contemporary conceptions of the causal dynamics of economies. Rather it stems from the extraordinary difficulty, moral and psychological as much as purely cognitive, of keeping a firm grip on our own points of view. It is natural to see any moderately teleological institution (and most public institutions in the modern world are, as Weber pointed out, rather openly teleological) as suffused with intentionality, awash with judgements of fact and value and seething with the will to bring about intended outcomes. In actual fact, of course, as social scientists have painstakingly documented of every sort of contemporary society, this teleological semblance is largely a facade. Real institutions are extremely unlike this: congeries of routines and pragmatic accommodations, small groups nesting in inaccessible niches and deploying the teleological ideologies of their habitat in studied defence of a quiet life or in the bolder quest for institutional aggrandizement, a world of standard operating procedures or bureaucratic politics,[19] but also sometimes of sustained and purposeful torpor. In the perspective of theoretical reason the full reality of these institutions – their boundless capacity for resistance to any shaping external will – can be acknowledged without imaginative distress, even perhaps with a certain unholy glee: the world of Erving Goffman. But in the perspective of practical reason they readily appear instead as exhilaratingly plastic; and the diffuse intentionality out of which they are in part quite genuinely composed seems beckoningly as though it might be (become, be made) our own. This *is* the perspective of modern politics (and not, of course, only of *modern* politics either), of incoming governments, newly crowned monarchs, legislators, political intellectuals. Its self-deceptions are familiar to us all. Of course, today, as in the past, professional politicians (and political scientists drawing on their resources) know quite well for most of the time that politics is not really like this, that most of it is an altogether less ambitious and more modest affair, as tedious as it is ignoble. But even those politicians most over-educated to the realities of their station cannot openly acknowledge their understanding all the time. And most politicians, it seems clear, now as in the past, deceive themselves about the potential scale of their contributions quite deeply and quite often. It would be as silly to sneer or mourn over this state of affairs in general as it would be to rejoice over it in general. That's just what the world is like.

There are two different respects in which we have good reason to seek to understand states in the perspective of practical reason. One is in the first instance eminently external – in their capacity as sources of potential hope or hazard. The second is less external even in the first instance – in their capacity as potential objects of modification by our own intentional actions. In the first respect we need to understand them as, and in so far as, they may affect us. In the second, we need to understand them as, and in so far as, we may or might affect them. Of course we would only be likely to have strong reasons to wish to affect them because of their capacity to affect us, so the second respect is largely parasitic on the first. But it is in fact principally the second respect which does make states genuinely difficult for us to understand. We would certainly have good

reason to study closely, and do our best to understand, anything capable
of doing us great good or great harm: even if the history of religious belief
systems suggests that we would probably find it hard to carry on our
study in a consistently calm and detached manner and might indeed find
it quite difficult to credit our incapacity to affect the source of hope or
hazard. But where it is clear from the beginning that there is at least
some possibility of our being able to affect them, then a fully detached
understanding is not even appropriate. Indeed it would be a sign either of
cognitive confusion or of mental imbalance. In this respect there is an
extremely strong pressure to represent states (or indeed subordinate
institutions or international agencies) as they would be if they behaved as
we would most wish them to behave. In so representing them, we apply
our wills and understandings to what we take to be their causal powers, in
the fond hope of admiring the products of our political craftsmanship.
And of course in so representing them we almost certainly also represent
them not merely as other than they are but as other than they could
possibly become or be made. But this approach is only the most extreme
version – the far end – of a continuum of would-be political action which
stretches from the most ambitious and rationalist exercises in political or
economic planning to the most inert accommodation to existing structures of power and to prevailing bureaucratic routines. The idea that
there might be just one point along this continuum that it was cognitively
(or for that matter morally) appropriate to occupy is not a compelling
one. Heuristically the continuum is merely the weakly constrained space
of political deliberation. Many of the instabilities of viewpoint within it at
the individual level come from familiar trade-off structures between, for
example, moral ambition and political prudence or between discrete
valued features of possible political outcomes. In so far as states figure
unstably within it they do so on the whole not because of obscurities
intrinsic to their own causal properties but rather because of obscurities
as to how we ourselves, severally or collectively, have good reason politically to act.[20]

Obviously such obscurities are sometimes of great practical importance: to say nothing of their being of the most pressing existential
significance. They may even on occasion be of great intellectual significance. But they are hardly likely in general to occur to us in a form which
does possess much strictly intellectual significance. The most insistent
guise in which these obscurities force themselves on our attention within
contemporary politics is the organization of production, distribution and
exchange. There have perhaps been a handful of passages in modern
intellectual history – the triumphant decades of Adam Smith or Ricardo,
or perhaps even of Marx or Maynard Keynes – when it seemed briefly

that structures of thought had at last been fashioned that could impose an authoritative order from the outside on this busy disorder, compelling states and individual economic agents alike to accommodate themselves to its stern requirements or to pay prohibitively for the failure to do so. But in retrospect what is most striking about even these episodes is their extreme brevity. In any modern economy production and exchange will in fact be vigorously concerted in a huge miscellany of settings by a great variety of types of agency. Choice and strategy are always in fact distributed very widely in any modern economy; and it is neither politically nor economically intelligent to attempt to reconceive the political world so that this will no longer in fact be so. In the perspective of practical reason, even for candidates for the personal assumption of state power, states are not accordingly best conceived as potentially omnipotent even in relation to the economies for which they hold responsibility. The benign conduct of economic policy requires the deft accommodation of chosen actions to available powers. Nor is the absence of omnipotence in general obviously an occasion for regret.[21] The boldest of personal candidates for state power can readily fail to secure it; and there are not many human beings (and no organized political groupings of any real historical depth) whose exclusion from omnipotence one could honestly (or sanely) regret. In endowing ourselves (or our political friends) in imagination with omnipotence, within the perspective of practical reason, we do not necessarily equip ourselves to understand much about anything.

In the domain of economics the disjunction between the national scope of governmental responsibility and the international scope of economic causality makes it extremely difficult at present to develop a coherent conception of domestic political good. (Perhaps it also makes the absence of such a conception somewhat less alarming than it might otherwise have been?) Certainly the absence itself neither discloses a distressing hiatus in our understanding of what states are nor suggests any very definite hazard or hope which they hold open to us. Economic experience is not an agreeable dimension of the experience of most human beings now alive. But its very real pains are not for the most part a consequence of instabilities in the perspective of practical reason or wholly gratuitous weaknesses in our understanding of the character of states.

It would be nice to be as confident that the same holds true of the military and strategic relations between states. In relation to economics, I have argued, we neither need to, nor should, envisage states as unified rational actors (though there is at least one context – the conduct of economic policy – in which they are under *some* pressure to attempt to operate as though they were such). In relation to military power – and to nuclear strategy still more – we certainly have equally little experiential prompting to regard them as unified rational actors; and from the viewpoint of theoretical reason we would be equally ill-advised to do so. But from the viewpoint of practical reason things are very different. Here it is quite unclear, however deep our instinctive incredulity, that we have any other option but to regard them, with the most unbending determination, as though they were indeed unitary rational wills, and to do our several best to make them as much like unitary rational wills as they can in principle be made. Even then, of course, we cannot reasonably hope to find acceptable whatever they may, as unitary rational wills, choose in fact to do. The Iraqi decision to make war on Iran has not proved wise in practice; but there is every reason to suppose that it was taken on the basis of the most attentive *realpolitik* assessment. So too, at least equally disastrously, Operation Peace in Galilee. There is nothing about conventional military power and, it seems, distressingly little about chemical or germ warfare to rationally discipline those with the opportunity and will to use them into a rigorous prudential abstention from so doing. But with nuclear weapons, we must still hope, at some level the structures genuinely must be different. (Nuclear winter would be more perturbing than liberal disapproval.) At the very least the risk of prompting the extermination of human life is a very different sort of risk from that of bringing down a regime or even decimating a particular population. It is the level of destructive possibility – the capacity for obliterating order and meaning – in which the difference resides.

The view that the primary role of states is the protection of their own subjects (against each other, but also against the rest of the world) goes back a long way, particularly in the natural law tradition of the West. The pooling of rights or powers, the entitlement to act and the capacity to act more effectively, as both Hobbes and Locke saw it, supplemented whatever services it could hope to offer in a domestic setting with even more handsome contributions in external defence. Or so for a long time it seemed. On slightly more careful consideration, costs as well as gains became apparent. The propinquity of a really impressive capacity for self-defence in another state was almost always also the propinquity of a fairly impressive capacity for aggression, suggesting at once the need to enhance capacities for self-defence in a variety of surrounding settings. And so on. The difficulty of combining stable trust over lengthy periods of time with profound disparities in vulnerability is scarcely surprising in itself; and it has certainly not been rendered any easier by the intermittent infliction of extremely severe wounds. After the experience of two world wars the prospects for avoiding a third with a massive thermonuclear component cannot be said to look good.

Despite much discussion, and despite in some countries (the USSR, Switzerland) a fair degree of investment, the prospect of effective defence against thermonuclear attack appears thus far to be over-optimistic. As long as it continues to do so it will leave states whose potential enemies happen to possess thermonuclear weapons with the unenviable choice between a defenceless trust in their benign intentions and a plausible capacity for retaliation even in the aftermath of thermonuclear attack. The firm preference for the second of these alternatives is the foundation of the strategy of deterrence, particularly in its most robust form of mutual assured destruction. Here the frenzy of the will to thrust rationality on at least all nuclear states other than one's own is almost audible. No state, surely, could risk *that* in the hope of any possible gain whatever. But there have proved to be many difficulties in this strategy.[22] One difficulty is an intellectual difficulty (analogous to the instability of theories of generally beneficial international economic regimes):[23] the tendency of the most carefully theorized and apparently robust structures of mutual deterrence to sag and decompose under the weight of intensive reconsideration. This tendency is quite rationally and objectively terrifying. It is certainly not the fault of states as such. Indeed it is not really even in itself a direct consequence of human defects, but rather of the irresistible dynamism of human inventiveness. And it is quite unclear in principle that anything can be done directly about it. What could be done about it, indirectly, would be to buffer the balance of threat self-consciously against the potentially destabilizing cognitive advances of either side, to attempt to construct dependable mutual guarantees of deterrent stability rather than persist in manoeuvring for relative advantage in technical innovation.

Dependable mutual guarantees of deterrent stability are intellectually hard (perhaps impossible) to devise. But even if they were devised, there is a second difficulty, more intimately related to the nature of states, which would militate sharply against their provision in practice. Actual states, like all other large assemblages of heterogeneous organizations, do not in fact possess a single rational (or irrational) will. It is not some readily rectifiable defect but what they are most fundamentally like that precludes their possessing anything of the kind. They do, of course, possess sovereign decision procedures, and titular rulers, and commanders-in-chief of their armed forces. But only at intervals and only by immense exertions in concerting their diffuse activities – and only then with considerable good fortune – can they really act as centres of discrete rational will. Studies of comparatively open public bureaucracies and their decision making, as in the United States, even studies of large-scale private economic organizations, cast grave doubt on the capacity of a modern state apparatus to get itself into a condition and keep itself in a condition to give and sustain trustworthy mutual guarantees of nuclear balance. There are many other aspects of the life of states in which the inability to reach and sustain such a level of unitary rational resolution need not be any more disturbing than its analogue in the economic domain. But the creation and preservation of international rationality in the deployment of thermonuclear weapons is not one of them. It is a matter of pressing interest whether states like those we have at present with us even possess the capacity to halt the proliferation of nuclear weapons: weapons, one should remember, which the Republic of Iraq might quite well be in control of at this moment.

Even more disturbing is the possibility that the two principal modern state powers – those that live most permanently in the face of the possibility of unleashing thermonuclear weapons – may not in fact under all circumstances be in final control of their own forces. This possibility has long been the stuff of paranoid fantasy. But technical developments in the weapons and deployment systems of the main nuclear arsenals have made it in the last decade and a half alarmingly more plausible. A combination of very short reaction times produced by the speed and propinquity of potential firings, the massive worldwide processing of information by both sides in the attempt to minimize this source of hazard, and the tight coupling between the respective information-processing systems and force deployments of the two sides, together with the extreme difficulty of retaining central control over worldwide military deployment in conditions of high alert (let alone actual combat) has made the image of the state as final chooser of war or peace seem distressingly fictive.[24] The interaction between the military and intelligence apparatuses of the two powers in conditions of acute tension is not merely likely to exacerbate these tensions (as it has of course done in the prelude to other wars in the past); it would also initiate a process of almost neurological degeneration in the decision-taking integration and reach of the two powers, localizing control over combat forces at a terrifying rate and in a pattern that only great good fortune would necessarily offer the opportunity to reverse.[25]

Human beings have always had to live with a great deal of disorder. Throughout its history the modern state has played a complicated and ambivalent but on balance (thus far) also a benign role in bringing this disorder under some measure of restraint. The strongest ideological claim that has been advanced on its behalf (still a strong claim in violent and anarchic societies) is that the creation of effective sovereign power, as Bodin or Hobbes conceived this, does within the territory subjected to it diminish the scale of interpersonal conflict by restricting the scope for the violent exercise of individual or group will. It is not plausible that states are playing a less prominent role in the shaping of human life today, though many other sorts of agencies, international, transnational and domestic (including we ourselves) are playing active roles also. On balance it still seems likely – despite the appalling record of organized violence in the twentieth century – that states today do *somewhat* more good than harm. But what is unnerving about the world we live in now is the sense of a challenge, a new challenge which some states face already and which can hardly without catastrophe ever disappear again from human history.[26] It is hard to see how we can hope to address this challenge except, in the end, through the responses of state powers. But whether states themselves could in principle display the causal capacity to face this challenge successfully for us is at best as yet quite unclear.

Personally, I doubt it.

9

The Politics of Representation
and Good Government in
Post-colonial Africa

Lorsque les hommes qui disposent des destinées de la terre se trompent sur
ce qui est possible, c'est un grand mal.
                    Benjamin Constant, *De l'Esprit de Conquête et de l'Usurpation*

There are at least two perspectives in which it is both natural and appropriate to consider the political character of African states. The first is the
retrospective perspective of causal explanation. The second is the
partially retrospective, but always also at least partly forward-looking,
perspective of political appraisal. The former is firmly a perspective of
theoretical reason; the latter, equally firmly, a perspective of practical
reason.[1] Much of the history of western philosophy has been devoted to
the more or less forlorn effort to establish quite how in the last instance
the two relate to one another.[2] Unsurprisingly, understanding of the
politics of modern Africa, like understanding of the politics of virtually
everywhere else at virtually all times, has been bedevilled by a failure to
distinguish these two perspectives and to retain a clear grasp of the
distinction.
    It is scarcely open to serious dispute any longer that the bulk of the
political history of post-war Africa has been profoundly discouraging. It
has been discouraging to those who favour democracy, or any system of
robustly institutionalized political accountability. But it has been little, if
any, more encouraging to those who would be more than content, in the
absence of such a system, with simply a steady and dependable improve-
ment in the living conditions of the great majority of Africa's populations.
With the notable exception of Zaire (which has clung with some tenacity
to its historical role within the European imagination of epitomizing the
heart of darkness), the moment of political independence was one of real

optimism in almost all African countries. The subsequent descent into gloom and fear was anticipated with any confidence only by the more unblinkingly reactionary defenders of colonial rule. Much academic energy has accordingly been devoted in recent years to efforts to explain just why these earlier hopes have in the event been disappointed. Still more energy, of a more practical character, has naturally also been devoted in most of the countries in question to emphasizing the need to do better and to exploring a miscellany of suggestions on how it might be possible to succeed in this. Thus far, however, the explanations of failure and decay have proved overwhelmingly more cogent than the quest to synthesize new and more effective strategies for political, social and economic betterment.

What the accumulated weight of these explanations has made clear is how deeply ill-placed was the initial optimism of independence. It has indicated, for example, and beyond the possibility of rational doubt, how hard it is in principle for the populations of African states to hold their governments responsible to them over lengthy periods of time. It has also underlined how hard it necessarily is for any African government to manage its domestic economy effectively and to affect its relations with the world market in a way which dependably benefits the majority of its own citizens. And it has shown unmistakably also just why it has proved more attractive to African political leaders, and to the far larger ranges of subordinates who have protected and sustained their leadership, to act as they have acted and to refrain from acting in other and potentially less destructive ways. A natural response to this growing comprehension, for political leaders and academic interpreters but also for the populace at large, is a mood of growing despair or its psychologically linked anti-thesis, the espousal of an extreme and very poorly characterized alternative political project. Whether on metaphysical grounds or purely on grounds of intellectual strategy the theoretical project of retrospective causal explanation is explicitly determinist. But the perspective of practical reason cannot coherently be explicitly determinist. Determinism may or may not, in some version or other, be true. But from the perspective of practical reason it has no determinate sense, and hence no determinate practical relevance. To confuse retrospective causal explanation with prospective political appraisal is the political vice of fatalism. Too much explanation is not only bad for the will; it is also bad for the political intelligence. But, of course, too much will is at least equally bad for the political intelligence.

Neither fatalism, nor voluntarism: political understanding.

At the centre of political understanding lies the very simple thought that in explaining the past it is necessary to take all past acts as given, but that in choosing and making the future, however constrained the circumstances in which men and women must act and however imperious the grounds they may sometimes possess for acting in one way rather than another, there simply are as yet no human actions at all to take as given. One reason, at least, why African governments have for the most part done so badly since 1957 is the excess of optimism in which they began. In 1951, exceedingly few African political leaders, north of the Union and outside Ethiopia and Liberia, possessed any direct personal understanding of how easy it is to do unintended harm through the exercise of governmental power. Today in Africa only the wilfully blind or deaf or the genuinely imbecile can be unaware of this any longer. It would be foolish to assume that the habitual motives or political dexterity of African political leaders in the future will be notably superior to those of recent decades, and even more foolish to assume that the conditions in which they will have to act are likely to offer them greater ease and calm or more freedom of manoeuvre. But it is certainly not foolish to suppose that the decades since independence have provided, for those who choose to take it, an excellent opportunity to learn many political lessons and to develop an altogether more sober and more profound conception of the nature of prudent government in modern Africa.

It is perhaps important to emphasize that there is no quarter of the world where ample evidence of imprudent government cannot be identified, and nowhere where those who have governed imprudently have lacked their own, more or less vivid and importunate, reasons for acting as they did. What particularly marks Africa out among the areas of the modern world is not the turpitude or clumsiness of its rulers. It is the combination of its historical economic weakness (and its consequently painful susceptibility to misgovernment within the modern international political economy)[3] with the comparatively weak institutionalization of its civil society at the level of the territorial state.[4] (The economies of African countries are substantially easier to bring to real ruin by misgovernment than, for example, those of the United States of America or Italy or the Soviet Union or Saudi Arabia, though Great Britain and Poland would offer close competition.) While those who rule, in Africa as elsewhere,[5] are better placed than most to find their own consolations, it should not therefore be assumed that the exercise of rule there is often a particularly simple and comfortable task.

When Richard Sklar tells us that what Africa needs is 'a democracy without tears'[6] – don't we all? – it is scarcely the perspective of causal explanation which he is choosing to adopt. It is easy enough to see why he should elect to escape from this perspective, at least for a brief interlude, and even easier to see why he should wish to deny most of the claims which he assails. Like the rest of the world, Africa indisputably does not *need* the combination of autocracy and tears. But in political understanding there is always real danger in straying too far from causal explanation: the danger in particular of ceasing to talk about politics at all. The theory of what is intrinsically desirable is an important component of political theory, but it is only one of the important components of political theory.[7] To proffer it as a sufficient basis for political understanding is to be, in the most pejorative of senses, utopian. The political error directly complementary to utopianism, a genuinely consistent fatalism, is rather seldom encountered, although the intellectual grounds for rejecting it are difficult to state with much precision.[8] A more common analytical and political vice is the combination of a despondently and uniformly causal representation of past political failure with a more or less discreet or incoherent presentation of the putatively superior properties of a present political regime or candidate regime; fatalism mitigated by evasion or sheer confusion. On the whole the concept of democracy is not much help in clarifying these issues, having in modern political usage everywhere a very substantial measure of evasion or confusion (or both) firmly built into it.[9] A more promising, if less stirring, pair of conceptions are those of representation and good government.

Virtually all serious modern political theory which is in any sense directed at issues of practical reason (which aspires to guide political conduct and not solely to explain past circumstance) is concerned with the relations between representation and good government. The two principal modern secular ideologies of political understanding, the liberal and the socialist, both tend to present these relations in suspiciously anodyne terms. But there is in fact no coherent and realistic theory within any modern tradition of political understanding of why this linkage should in general be expected to operate satisfactorily in any institution. The unhappy relations between theory and practice in the politics of modern Africa are simply a special case of the unstable and contradictory character of the modern understanding of politics in general. And the latter in turn is not an index of some modern falling away from more ancient levels of wisdom and adeptness but rather the outcome of several centuries of a more pertinacious and less mystified struggle to comprehend the relevant practical considerations.[10]

It is not difficult to explain why political representation in Africa has for the most part been both intermittent and a trifle perfunctory; nor is it difficult to explain why good government, even on the part of the best intentioned of African governors, has been relatively infrequent in post-war Africa.[11] Good government is, of course, to be interpreted not in terms of the intentions of the rulers, which tend (at least professedly) to be excellent in most societies at most times, but rather in terms of the consequences of their rule for those over whom they rule.[12] But easy though it is to explain each of these two political deficiencies in modern African states, it is important to recognize how weak in some ways are the connections between the two. Both in liberal and in socialist understanding the provision of a genuinely valid structure for the representation of legitimate social interests comes close to guaranteeing that government will be on balance good. But, in fact, since the initial establishment of predominantly capitalist economies, the representation of legitimate interests is neither a necessary nor a sufficient condition for the beneficent exercise of governmental power. Neither in a representative democracy presiding over a predominantly capitalist economy, nor in any form of socialist state yet experienced or even described with any clarity,[13] can the most exquisite level of political accountability furnish any guarantee at all of governmental skill. The massively extraverted character of all but the most derelict of African economies north of the Union renders them intensely vulnerable to the pursuit of maladroit economic policies by their governors. Some aspects of the policies pursued can certainly be explained in part by the perceived interests of comparatively small ruling groups, or by the broader class interests of those recruited directly into the proliferating governmental apparatus or of those employed on a rapidly expanded public sector payroll. But many aspects of these policies (as of the economic policies of most governments in the modern world) are better explained by purely cognitive errors, misjudgements of the internal causal dynamics of a domestic economy[14] and of the prospectively even less readily transparent causal dynamics of the world economy, the rhythms of which massively affect the interests of the great majority of the populations of all African countries. It is reasonable (though not necessarily always correct) to see the interests of governments and their pensionaries as systematically set against the interests of the remainder of a national population. And the distorting policy effects of such self-interested choices might indeed be offset by improving the degree to which governments are rendered accountable to those whom they govern. (In so far as the relations between rulers and ruled are correctly seen as a zero–sum competitive game of material appropriation, any increase in accountability will necessarily amount to a diminution in the comparative extractive power of the rulers and a corresponding gain in the retained assets of the remainder of the population.) By contrast it would be quite unreasonable to anticipate that the cognitive grasp of the dynamics of the world or domestic economy enjoyed by the populace at large will prove systematically superior to that of their past or present African rulers, and correspondingly unreasonable to expect formulations of economic policy in African states to improve merely because of a strengthening of the system of political representation.

The degree to which the representation of social interests is effectively institutionalized both in the fundamental form of a state and in its more intimate political processes is certainly affected by political will and artifice. Departing colonial administrators, incoming military rulers or nationalist victors, all dismantle some structures of interest representation and establish others. In no instances, however, do they necessarily succeed either in dismantling or in establishing protection for quite the range of interests they initially had in mind. The representation of interests is a murky and heuristic competitive enterprise in which those who can, get themselves represented, and those who cannot, seldom discover that even the most generous provisions of enlightened despots or revolutionary parties quite succeed in furnishing representation on their behalf. On balance, and in notable contrast to the optimism of late eighteenth- and early nineteenth-century liberal thinkers like Sieyès and James Mill[15] (to say nothing of early twentieth-century socialist thinkers) the constructive attempt of political ingenuity and energy at the centre of modern states to guarantee political representation has been dismayingly ineffective. What does furnish and sustain political representation, it appears, is something which lies deeper and less self-consciously in the texture of social organization: the capacity for protracted and confident self-organization of the bearers of different social interests. It is quite unclear that this capacity, a capacity for incessant, costly and inevitably contested agency, can be discerned at all at the level of a state's structure. The marxist insistence that capitalist democracy (or autocracy) is structurally committed, in the last instance, to the defence of the interests of capital, within the ebulliently representative politics of the western world (with their endless flurry of interest group exertion), does underline something which is relatively easy to miss and which is definitely of the greatest importance.[16] But in relation to African countries such insistence is just an airy tautology that does little to clarify the character and contours of class membership or the dimensions of political agency within African states. Nor does it explain the outcome of political agency in the individual state at any particular time.

Because the capacity to secure political representation depends on the capacity for self-organization and on the coherent and accurate understanding of interests (individual, group, class, national), it can be assessed only by a highly specific and ethnographically delicate investigation of particular examples (an activity which in any society, and certainly in most African countries today, is difficult to distinguish sharply from social espionage). Such investigation of modern social organization in Africa has seldom been carried through with much success. Indeed, with the possible exception of Kenya and perhaps incipiently of the Union of South Africa (where the invidiousness of social espionage would be particularly blatant), it has not really been attempted with much energy at the level of a modern territorial state. But it is a safe presumption that it has been carried through most successfully for relatively small-scale rural localities where the structure of social interests is cognitively less elusive. (Note the tendency, to which no modern social theorist can be immune, to keep the literally unimaginable social, political and economic complexity of any modern society firmly in its place by adopting and manipulating a more and more determinedly abstract vocabulary. Modern social theory is literally a sustained pretence to comprehend the necessarily large unintelligible: an intellectual equivalent of whistling to keep our courage up.)[17] But if it is probably true today that no one understands the process of interest representation in any African country particularly well, some features of this process are now definitely better understood than they were a quarter of a century ago.

On the evidence of the last twenty-five years it seems a dependable conclusion that those best placed to represent themselves in African countries are the denizens of the higher reaches, civil and still more military, of its state apparatuses. They are better placed even in the weakest of African states because, although they can and of course do not infrequently choose to impede each other, it is exceptionally difficult for their fellow citizens to impede them from collectively representing themselves. In relatively prosperous and fiscally sound states (Nigeria in the aftermath of 1973, the Ivory Coast until 1980, Ghana up to about 1960) they can dispose directly of large and locally derived revenues, garnered through the rents on foreign extractive activities or from the control of the marketing of remunerative export crops.[18] Even in the poorest of African states, where a large part of the state budget is funded by foreign aid transfers, it is to them that the transfers are made.[19] Despite the efforts and hopes of Nyerere and Cabral,[20] it is unsurprising that they should have elected to employ this allocative discretion in some measure on their own behalf, rather than committing class suicide. Nor are the state structures within which they exercise this discretion at all responsive in general to initiatives emanating from elsewhere in their own domestic societies. Partly, this is simply a consequence of the manner in which these states were initially constructed and kept in working order (often with increasing difficulty) until the termination of colonial rule.

Built first to subjugate from the outside and adapted primarily to represent external interests,[21] their initiation into local representative politics was brief, superficial[22] and essentially involuntary. Even when their institutional structures were devised with some care to guarantee at least the representation of localities in the post-colonial order, the protective linkages between local society and political order were in any case still too recent and too flimsy to impel local society to make much effort to defend the political order against disruptive internal reconstruction; and the self-organizing political capacities of local society were in any case still too inexperienced and improvisatory to enable it to defend its own conception of state legitimacy with much effect.[23]

Liberal democratic theory prescribes in the first instance the representation of individuals. But except at the most heroically abstract levels it is hard to see how individuals can in fact be represented effectively at the centre of a modern state.[24] More determinate conceptions of representation prescribe the representation of broad social categories (including social classes) or of localities of varying scales. The one social category in Africa which is by common consent rather successful in representing itself is the membership of the higher echelons of the state apparatus: career politicians, senior civil servants (particularly when involved in the regulation of international trade or the award of major public contracts), senior army officers and managers of state sector economic enterprises. In early nineteenth-century utilitarian theories of representation, the problem which was seen as central to designing political institutions was how to guarantee that the representatives of the people (individuals as axiomatically self-interested as those whom they volunteered to represent) should have at least as much to fear on returning to private life as they had to gain from abusing their power while in office.[25] Even within utilitarian theory this perspective was not sustained very consistently;[26] and it never won much applause from utilitarianism's Whig critics.[27] Nor were the remedies proposed especially compelling: elections for periods so brief that no representative could hope to exact as much from the theft of public funds as they could expect to lose on their return to private life from the institutionalized practice of such theft by their successors. But crude and equivocal though this aspect of utilitarian theory certainly was, the political vicissitudes of modern Africa have at least established its relevance to the political design of benign capitalist (or *soi-distant* socialist) orders.

As yet the practice of public sector self-representation has not been depicted very fully and sensitively for any African country (an omission which is scarcely surprising in view of the blatantly illegal form which much of it takes and the severe penalties sometimes meted out in vengeance by enraged successor regimes).[28] Even the most intimate and ethnographically vivid portrait of an African state elite at work and play which we possess, Abner Cohen's study of the Creole community of Freetown,[29] skirts such problems with undue discretion and, in any case, makes too little attempt to characterize the structure of the state that furnishes their habitat. Even in Nigeria, where public sector self-representation has much of the abrasive élan of Ben Jonson's London (or Venice), and where the scale of economic interest and political significance effortlessly dwarfs the rest of West Africa, we still lack a systematic and powerful analysis of the key processes involved.[30] But what we definitely do know by now, on the basis of West African experience, is that the somewhat shop-worn categories of national and comprador bourgeoisies neither depict current social and economic configurations at all clearly nor explain much of either their formation or their mode of operation. In any of the more prosperous African countries of the last fifteen years there certainly are national bourgeoisies, sometimes with considerable genealogical and cultural depth behind them.[31] But it is clear that neither their economic prospects nor their power to mould national political processes to their advantage have been a function predominantly of their initial position within a domestic socio-economic order. Rather, over time both have been determined predominantly by the fiscal lien of the national government on receipts from international trade, in the Nigerian case especially from the spectacular rent transferred after 1973 from multinational oil extraction.

Seen from West Africa the switchback of the world trading system often reduces national political independence to something of a phantasm (as it is apt to do on occasion even in wealthier parts of the world or in the eyes of socialist incumbents of 10 Downing Street or the Elysée palace). For substantial periods of time, however, many African governments have in fact retained a substantial measure of allocative discretion; and it is only the hopelessly indigent or the relentlessly feckless that retain no allocative discretion at all. In so far as governmental allocative discretion has been exercised, inside and outside the law, to establish and sustain a local bourgeoisie by the allocation of discriminatory rents or privileges or by the individual and illegal sale of public assets at well below cost, it is reasonable to see the resulting bourgeoisie as a state client, just as it is correct to discern relations of patronage, not necessarily running in the same direction, between its individual members and particular state officials. The economic basis for the foundation of such bourgeoisies remains the exploitation of comparative advantage within international trade. The scale of their formation, accordingly, has been less a function of their own will to independence from or servility towards foreign capital than it has of the fluctuating levels of comparative advantage in different fields of production and of the vulnerability of the more profitable of these to governmental exactions. The most important impact of African governments on the formation of local client bourgeoisies has therefore come not in their overt or covert enthusiasm for private capital accumulation, but in the degree to which the economic policies they have pursued have fostered, diminished or, in the extreme cases, eliminated local comparative advantage.[32]

Normative theories of representation, of course, seldom explicitly applaud either public sector self-representation or the establishment and protection of state powers which serve merely as executive committees of local (or foreign) bourgeoisies. On the whole the 'middling ranks' in Africa have yet to find effective ideological defenders, though in the more prosperous of African countries, and particularly outside the national political process, they too have often had some success in defending themselves. But the two largest and normatively best-accredited social categories in modern Africa, the industrial proletariat and the peasantry, have had singularly little success in securing effective political representation. The view that peasants are ill-positioned to secure, and neither diligent nor proficient in seeking to secure, their collective interests as a social category within national politics has distinguished authority behind it.[33] Marx's initial assessment of the revolutionary potential of the French smallholding peasantry in the mid nineteenth century has proved an inadequate basis for understanding the subsequent political experience of the majority of the world's population.[34] But however prominent the role played by peasants in twentieth-century revolutions, and however remarkable the political (and, still more, the military) achievements of some peasant representative agencies over the last three-quarters of a century, it remains hard to doubt that Marx's estimate of the capacity of the peasantry to act coherently in national politics to ensure the representation of its own collective interests was essentially correct. Considered in the round and over its entire lifespan, not even the Chinese Communist Party, the most dramatic and distinguished twentieth-century political agency of peasant representation, furnishes much ground for questioning this judgement.

Similar doubts certainly obtain about the degree to which the industrial proletariat has contrived to secure effective political representation in African countries. Some of these doubts, to be sure, are essentially ideological and turn on a fundamental scepticism as to whether this class has ever secured lasting and effective political representation anywhere.[35] (This scepticism is at least in part a product of the acute ambivalence of the intellectual and political tradition that emphasizes the necessity for such representation over the issue of whether the proletariat can or cannot be expected and trusted adequately to represent itself. It is also the consequence of the exceedingly hazy suggestions which this tradition offers as to how, if it genuinely can do so, its capacity to represent itself can hope to be embodied in enduring political institutions.)[36] But more important doubts, for our purposes, follow simply from the relative demographic insubstantiality of the proletariat in the vast majority of African countries north of the Union, and from the direct economic dependence of much of this proletariat on the disbursements of the state.[37] It is hardly surprising that in Africa, as elsewhere, a proletariat should prove less well placed to represent itself than the political masters of the state and the higher echelons of its employees. But it is of some importance that in Africa such representative efficacy as the proletariat has achieved has come predominantly from its location on the public sector payroll and from its capacity to motivate African governments to distort rural–urban terms of trade by the threat of civil and political disruption in the immediate vicinity of the seats of government.[38] At different points in modern African history the national labour movements of particular countries (Guinea, Nigeria, Zambia) have exerted considerable, if somewhat fleeting, political pressure. But their limited demographic weight and the fundamental economic weakness that follows from a more or less permanently slack urban labour market has meant that more enduring representative efficacy has necessarily been confined to individual industries or localities. Where, as on the railways or in the mines,[39] there exist relatively stable and enduring (essentially single class) occupational communities, however petty bourgeois the ultimate social ambitions of the more prosperous members of the wage labour force,[40] there can and sometimes do arise levels of solidarity and industrial self-discipline which can make the workforce of a single industry not only a formidable partner in the operation of its own plant but a formidable potential opponent even to a national government still in full control of its own forces of coercion. At least at the level of the locality, it seems a fair judgement that African proletarians have on occasion come closer to representing their own interests than any other comparably extended social category.

In so doing they have in effect aligned themselves, perhaps not altogether wittingly, with the aspect of authentic political representation that has been most successfully (and least coercively) institutionalized in African societies since independence: the representation of place and local community. There is deep disagreement within European political reason how far the representation of locality as such is to be applauded.

On the whole the judgement that it is to be applauded is a judgement of the political right, going back to Justus Möser's acute appreciation of *Lokalvernunft*.[41] The view entailed by the imposed universality of the world market that only universality merits (and in the end only it will be able to secure) effective self-representation is set out memorably by Marx and Engels as early as *The German Ideology*.[42] Disputes of this character tend to the irascible reiteration of tautologies; but it is not difficult in this instance to see some merit in both points of view.[43] It would certainly be a happy accident if the representation of universal classes and the representation of localities as such coincided, especially where the localities in question (like most localities) are some way from being single class occupational communities. But whereas universal classes are a little thin on the ground in Africa, localities are certainly in plentiful supply; and whereas the authentic universality of universal classes (proletariat or bourgeois or peasant) is readily open to question, the most sceptical can hardly dispute that localities are genuinely there.

On the whole the study on a local scale of electoral competition and political development in Africa has handsomely confirmed the ideological substance of localities.[44] Village, town, chiefdom and region – perhaps, to speak loosely, even tribe – have been discerned not merely existing in themselves but also acting for themselves. There is a measure of ideological fiction of course, in all such presentations: on the most local of all possible social stages, within the individual domestic unit, there can be, and after all usually are, deep conflicts of real interest. But on the whole, it is not the fictive flavour of localist representation in Africa which has proved its major political defect. (Even the most class-divided community of residence does in fact possess a substantial range of common interests. Even the most sociologically determinate and culturally homogeneous of classes has a wide variety of divergent interests.) What principally detracts from the merits of effective localist representation in Africa is its palpable threat to the maintenance of national interests. Just as rebellion in the southern African monarchies (in Gluckman's functionalist analysis)[45] on balance favoured the preservation of regnal unity while the preservation of local interests by attempted secession imperilled the kingdom, so in modern Africa efficacy of localist representation has always tended to appear incipiently subversive when seen from the centre.

The plethora of languages and the multiplicity of pre-colonial and colonial units of social and political membership has rendered effective localist representation an aggressive solvent of the somewhat gimcrack national unity of African states. (This issue is commonly discussed in Africa under the rubric of 'tribalism', but it is a just complaint that 'tribalism' is a highly plastic term of common political speech and not at all one of precise social analysis.) Since political secession in Africa, as elsewhere in the world today, tends to be bloodily resisted by incumbent governments with ready access to international arms supplies, it is hard to believe, now that European colonial rule is at last over, that in the great majority of cases localist representation by attempted secession is in fact in the real interests of African populations.[46] Once it has well and truly begun, however, and once the repression is in full swing, the resulting choice between acute evils may be hard to assess rationally and even harder to resolve in practice for the better. Even where secession is not explicitly in question, the (often well-founded) suspicion that the national government is being conducted very much more vigorously in the interest of one ethnic grouping or region of the country than in that of others greatly exacerbates political instability, even when it does not in fact lead to the military displacement of the elected or self-appointed rulers. Only within more geographically constricted confines, where localities in themselves can coincide with localities for themselves with rather little ideological fiction, does a real continuity of representative exploration and exertion subsist, as national governments come and go.[47]

The elusiveness and the often distressingly negative contribution made by political representation within modern African polities underlines, by contrast, the overwhelming significance in Africa, as elsewhere in the modern world, of the presence or absence of good government. As a concept good government is holistic and consequentialist rather than specific and procedural. It implies, *ceteris paribus*, and in relation to the policies that it actually pursues, a high level of organizational effectiveness; but it certainly does not imply the choice of a particular ideological model of state organization: a government of laws but not of men, a minimal state, or dictatorship of the proletariat. Good government is best defined ostensively rather than by semantic prescription. It is what Sweden and Singapore enjoy, and what Zaire and Ethiopia distressingly lack. In principle, heavily repressive regimes may on occasion exemplify good government. But they can do so only where there is a direct and palpable link between the effective contributions of their rulers to popular welfare and the modes of repression they employ – good government is not to be equated, for example, with ingratiating or virtuous government. Since any repressive regime in any public forum, national or international, is likely to justify its coercive activities by their putative contribution to popular welfare, the concept of good government is necessarily anti-ideological in intention. Its analytical purpose is precisely to distinguish the professed or actual self-understanding of ruling groups from their real causal contribution to the prosperity and misery of their subjects. The presence or absence of effectively guaranteed civil and political liberties does not in itself ensure the prevalence of good or bad government. But any set of repressive practices, as Jeremy Bentham salutarily noted, is in itself a direct contribution to human suffering. In Africa as elsewhere in the world today, by far the most important contribution of government to popular welfare in time of peace is furnished by the conduct of economic policy. The conduct of economic policy is evidently a matter of constrained choice, while the ideological resonance of the choices involved is necessarily intense. Viewed retrospectively and causally, governmental economic policy since independence in sub-Saharan Africa (at least north of the Union) has consisted for the most part in a historically readily explicable sequence of errors of judgement.[48] The most plausible exceptions to this sweeping assessment have been the states which have retained intimate relations with their former colonial masters, the Ivory Coast and Kenya being perhaps the most conspicuous and important instances. In the Ivory Coast the intimacy of these links, administratively and indeed militarily,[49] has been such as to make the regime a direct continuation of the colonial order. Not only has the Ivory Coast continued to serve as a haven for French corporate enterprises (with a massive contingent of French expatriate personnel and a very substantial continuing outflow of personal earnings in international currency) but the economic, monetary and security policies of the country are still designed with active French advice and participation.[50]

Neither the Ivory Coast nor Kenya has been particularly delicate in its treatment of domestic political dissidents and neither can be said to have established a very egalitarian social order. But it is a striking fact that the two African governments which have proved most successful in sustaining competitive local agrarian production for the world market and in raising, however unevenly, the real living standards of their rural subjects should both have adopted the neocolonial road with such determination.[51] In attempting to assess the domestic political viability of the two regimes it is necessary to consider their handling of rural class relations. Even the most neocolonial of states requires a domestic class base of some kind if it is to develop any enduring political viability and solidity. The rural political base of the ruling parties in both Kenya and the Ivory Coast was established firmly in the competitive political conditions of the final decades of colonial rule. While the shape of the domestic class structure has been extensively modified since independence, in part by the exercise of governmental power, there remains an important and on the whole highly explicit political alliance between, on the one hand, national bureaucracy and party leadership and, on the other, the larger African agrarian producers of export commodities in each country (now for the most part very considerably richer than they were at the date of independence). In the light of these considerations, it is an understandably vexed question whom precisely the governments of Kenya or the Ivory Coast represent[52] – which is not to say that it deserves to be any less vexed a question in the case of governments which have been compelled by prior fecklessness to abandon control of their domestic economic policies without residue to the International Monetary Fund, or which have inadvertently abstracted their subjects, at least temporarily, from the world trading system altogether. But however ambiguous they may appear as representative agencies, and however ugly the relations of subordination that they have established and the techniques of coercion that they continue to employ to protect these, it can be said without equivocation that the governments of the Ivory Coast and Kenya have on the whole succeeded since independence in providing their subjects with good government. In contrast with virtually all other African countries but the few fortunate beneficiaries of massive rents on foreign extractive activities, Kenya and the Ivory Coast have provided the majority of their subjects with economic opportunities and rewards which have on balance improved rather than deteriorated over the last quarter of a century.[53] The erratic and depressed course of the world market in the early 1980s may have halted this progress but, along with the sharp rise in oil prices in the previous decade, it has certainly harmed them less directly than it has harmed those African states that have stumbled or been pushed backwards towards autarky.[54]

The relations between retrospective causal explanation and prospective political choice are especially delicate in the case of economic policy.[55] It is in the selection of economic policies that in peacetime the holders of modern state power most crucially exert the impress of human understanding and will on the actual life chances of those they rule.[56] Retrospective causal explanation of the choice and consequences of economic policies requires the careful alignment of two very different sorts of explanatory considerations: the objective constraints of local comparative advantage, local and world market demand structures and the limited efficacy of incumbent governments, with the no doubt in principle equally objective constraints of the potential consequences of the full set of economic policies which might in principle have been undertaken. A fatalist vision of the history of economic policy in African countries up to the present underlines the least appealing of these elements: the tightness of the objective constraints, and the more unpleasant consequences of the particular economic policies actually adopted. A consistent fatalism would entail the prophecy of an African future little, if any, more agreeable than its post-colonial past. But at this point, understandably, fatalism is often supplanted by a substantial measure of voluntarism.[57] Since the viewpoint of the maker of economic policy necessarily balances choice against the perception of objective constraints, it is hard for it to exclude either fatalist or voluntarist elements; but it is also, of course, even harder for it to appraise the actual range of choices available and constraints given with any great accuracy. On the whole it is this last difficulty which, given the limited degree of comparative advantage with which African economies were actually endowed at the time of independence, has proved causally most important for understanding the economic vicissitudes of independent Africa. It is also, fortunately, the aspect in which gains made in understanding past experience can most readily and valuably be brought to bear on the taking of future political choice.[58]

One very obvious and currently fashionable contrast is that between fully open economies, operating with sound money (currencies pegged to the franc or the dollar) and enthusiastically committed to the deepening of domestic capitalist relations, and on the other hand a highly regimented economy (at least in intention), with a large and decaying state sector, a rapidly inflating currency whose official international exchange value is fixed quite arbitrarily, and a more or less determinedly implemented hostility to domestic capitalist interests. Presented with a choice restricted to these terms, in the light of the experiences of post-independence Africa it now takes a genuine socialist ideologue to opt firmly for the latter.[59] As a growth strategy, the levying of heavy fiscal burdens on the deployment of local capital, applied to the hasty construction of a substantial import-substitutive manufacturing sector, appears by now to be less a well-considered manner of winning for small African countries the geopolitical and industrial strength that Stalin once amassed for the Soviet Union, than an effective means of eliminating local comparative advantage. But this level of analysis remains unhelpfully gross. It is certainly important that socialist structures of ownership and economic organization are hard to operate successfully and that they are decisively less efficient than nineteenth-century socialist thinkers hoped.[60] But it is, of course, possible to design and operate both socialist and capitalist economic programmes with very varying degrees of prudence, skill and dedication. It would take a real capitalist ideologue (of which there are some) to be genuinely surprised at Crawford Young's finding that the simple difference in ideological colouration between African regimes and between the economic policies that they have chosen to pursue[61] does not furnish a sufficient basis for predicting the extent of their relative economic success and failure. Both capitalist and socialist development can benefit enormously from the organizational efficiency and the simple probity of the state apparatus. Outside Europe and North America the most successful capitalist development in the period since 1945 has occurred in countries with powerful state structures very actively committed to planning and organizing many aspects of the development of their economies.[62] The moral decomposition and almost neurological degeneration of the state structures in some of the wealthiest and most important African territories – Zaire, at some points Nigeria – has not only been ugly in itself, it has also precluded any soundly based local capitalist development of the economies concerned. By contrast, those would-be socialist states in Africa in which the state structures have maintained some organizational effectiveness and a reasonable level of public probity have done dramatically less damage than other regimes which have sought to compensate for their increasingly blatant organizational impotence by the spiralling application of terror.[63] This distinction is of considerable importance for the potential future of socialist regimes in Africa. The absence of institutionalized accountability of rulers to ruled in all existing socialist states in Africa, which is unlikely to be remedied in the imaginable future, has two principal implications for the welfare of the ruled in these territories. The first is that the simple effectiveness with which they are ruled (quite aside from its cruelty or humaneness) depends very largely on the capacity of their rulers to discipline themselves. Pessimism about the capacity of holders of political power to discipline themselves is the central motif of liberal political theory,[64] even if it is not a hazard for which liberal thinkers have yet discovered very precise or reliable remedies. The second implication is even more discomfiting. No regimes in the modern world can be trusted to govern very humanely where their sway is at all actively contested: compare Ethiopia and Afghanistan with Indonesia and the Philippines. Hence, among other things, the extreme ambiguity of the prospective contribution of South Africa's domestic and international politics to the potential political trajectories of its African neighbours. Given the vastly greater prowess of modern state powers at brutal repression than at economic construction, one contribution to Africa's political future which could not sanely and decently be welcomed at present would be a plethora of local insurgencies.

Effective state powers in African territories are unlikely to charm well-informed liberal observers by the manner in which they govern. But, other things being equal, they may at least succeed in furnishing reasonably good government, and in doing so they will be able to spare their subjects the miseries of anarchy and civil war from which the peoples of Africa have suffered so desperately in recent years. In purely domestic terms the other principal contribution an effective state power is in a position to make is in the skilful choice of economic policies. (Both socialist and liberal political theories grossly understate the causal importance of skill in political life. Socialist political theory is especially lamentable in its almost complete failure to acknowledge the exceptionally exigent demands for economic and political skill in the effective design and management of a socialist economy.) Because a socialist economy requires a very high level of causal understanding and a very deft practical control on the part of its political masters (and also because of the intractable inefficiencies of socialist agriculture), it is in many ways ill-suited to enhancing the prosperity of poor and weakly integrated countries. The principal advantage of markets, by contrast, is the extent to which they economize on the need to centralize accurate information. Since the most important actors on modern markets are themselves very large organizations it is, of course, mistaken to think of market and command principles as systematically opposed to one another. But these organizations (especially multinational corporations), where they do operate effectively, are designed in and sustained from comparatively wealthy, highly literate and well-organized societies. To replicate their organizational models in poor, predominantly illiterate and exceedingly disorganized societies gives no better guarantee of securing equivalent levels of efficacy than aping the design of foreign state powers has proved to do.[65]

It is an enormously intricate and specific exercise either to identify the historical significance and explain the historical consequences of past choices in economic policy or to prescribe well-considered policy choices for the future. What can usefully be said in general about such choices, either in explanation of the past or in prescription for the future, is in comparison brutally simple. There is no royal road, proudly autarkic or shamelessly dependent, to a more prosperous Africa. There are a very large number of policy proposals for economic development which have been tried out in one or other African country since the early 1950s which sounded good ideas at the time – at least to those who chose to implement them – and which have proved since to be dismally ill-conceived.[66] Socialist development strategies in Africa, as elsewhere, need to economize sharply on the organizational demands they place on governmental agencies; and they also need to take careful account of the reasons which ordinary economic agents possess for choosing (or refusing) to cooperate vigorously in implementing their projects. Because domestic capitalist interests, especially in agriculture, can be trusted to operate vigorously without government direction or inducement,[67] and because, therefore, they place less severe demands on the effectiveness or probity of government institutions, there is very little to be said against any domestic capitalist development which does not simply depend on the allocation of monopoly privileges by the state.

There is no intellectually cogent formula for synthesizing a dependably well-conceived choice of economic policies with effective political accountability in any form of state and society in the modern world.[68] Political accountability can in principle be quite effectively institutionalized. But no modern population will in fact choose to defend, sustain and recreate it where the accountability itself is perceived to militate against economic prosperity. The synthesis of political accountability with economic prosperity is a contingent and permanently reversible historical achievement. It is not an institutionally guaranteed causal property of any form of regime. African prospects for economic prosperity will continue to depend (as they have come increasingly to do for at least a century and a half) on the credit institutions and trade flows of the world economy. There is essentially nothing that African governments – let alone African peoples – can do to influence this basic framework to their advantage. The gloomy economic and political history of post-colonial Africa is not in retrospect at all surprising and it is easy enough to explain its broad course. But even a despondent (and not necessarily very forgiving) historical understanding does not dictate a fatalism about the future. A very large proportion of the worst that has happened to Africa has happened as a result of foolish or vicious political choice.[69] Many of these crimes and follies are very likely to be repeated in the future. But not a single one of them *has* to be repeated. Africans, like the rest of us, are free agents judging on the basis of imperfect understanding and choosing under constraints. They are as well placed as any other segment of the human race to learn politically from their own history. By now, a good quarter of a century after independence in many countries, there is a good deal for them to learn.

10

Unger's *Politics* and the Appraisal of Political Possibility

What really is politically possible? How different, over any given period of time, could our collective social and political life be caused to become? Just how is it epistemically appropriate and humanly decent to conceive political possibility?

There are few, if any, questions about the meaning of human existence in which the link between personal temperament and cognitive style are as direct and intimate as they are in the case of our conceptions of what really is politically and socially possible. To equate our more edifying desires with the possible consequences of our political actions is merely an agreeable exercise in self-deception. To identify the existing contours of our social arrangements with current embodiments of 'the ancient laws of society'[1] or structural preconditions for social and political existence here and now is an index of the most ignominious superstition. But the happy Aristotelian mean between these two styles of cognitive indignity is as hard to characterize as it is to locate. The most striking feature of Roberto Unger's new trilogy[2] is the confidence with which it presses an answer to all of these questions. The answer itself is in many respects arrestingly novel, though it draws with great cunning and analytical energy upon many strands of modern thinking and historical scholarship.

Its core is impressively integral, a direct expression of Unger's own highly idiosyncratic fusion of individual disposition and cognitive style: unmistakably *l'homme même*. It rests on a taut but oddly stable balance between an intense scepticism and an at least equally intense faith. The scepticism dictates the judgement that we simply cannot ever and under any circumstances know what really is politically possible or know how different our collective social and political life could or can be caused to

ugh!

become. But the faith, what Unger often refers to as 'the radical project', insists that this limit on our cognitive powers is an occasion for exultation rather than a ground for mourning: and never, under any conceivable conditions, an excuse for lassitude, torpor or resignation. To revel in the indeterminacy of the future, for Unger, is the message of modern world history; a history, over and above all its horrors, of human empowerment, invention and self-recreation, individual and collective, a history of the growth of what he calls 'negative capability'. 'Negative capability' is the modernist index of human progress, a startling existential totalization of Karl Popper's falsifiability criterion for scientific inquiry.[3]

Taken on its own the natural impetus of either element in this combination is one which Unger finds deeply distasteful. The sophisticated scepticism of the most advanced modern understandings of the character and development of human cognition yields at the level of practical reason a nasty choice between a radical depoliticization of the imagination[4] or a sinister obsession with the manipulative opportunities potentially afforded by fusing esoteric knowledge with condensed social and political power. In this last guise the emancipation of men and women becomes in essence the task of the social and political cognoscenti.[5] The latter in consequence find themselves committed to claiming a kind of social knowledge which is necessarily unavailable and a degree of manipulative control, presumptively licensed by this 'knowledge', that sets fierce and degrading limits to the freedom of action of the majority of their fellow human beings. These last dangers have been well explored by a wide variety of modern thinkers and Unger himself does not really have any especially decisive suggestions on how they can in practice be avoided.[6]

What he does, however, offer is a compelling picture of the impossibility, short of thermonuclear war, of sundering the potential for drastic social and political reconstruction from the exercise of modern state power everywhere on earth. This is of great importance and interest because it conflicts so sharply with educated political sensibility in the great majority of contemporary states – in the Russia of Mr Gorbachev, the India of Mr Gandhi, and the Japan of Mr Nakasone, as much as in the United States of Mr Reagan or the Italy of Mr Craxi. It is not that Unger in any sense denies the massively routine character of most modern politics at any particular time. But unlike the effectively habituated observers of modern politics – journalists, politicians, economists, political scientists, citizens – he deploys a strategy of understanding which resists with the greatest obduracy any equation of intelligibility with fatality.

This strategy of understanding has a theoretical basis which is set out in the preliminary volume, *Social Theory: Its Situation and its Task*. It is deployed at length on behalf of Unger's own preferred contemporary articulation, political, social and economic, of the radical project in the centrepiece of his present trio of works: *False Necessity*. But it is easiest to see both the source of Unger's own political confidence and the fragility of some aspects of his proposals in the third volume, *Plasticity into Power*, which applies this strategy of understanding to the quest for wealth and power in a wide variety of pre-modern societies. The requirement of plasticity – the capacity to alter social forms fluidly and inventively to face fresh challenges and surmount ancient barriers – is itself simply an especially salient fact of power within modern world history (as it has been more or less importunately throughout the humanly recorded history of our species). To tie it in practice to the steady elimination of personal dependence from large-scale human interrelations (let alone to an elimination of the depersonalization which Unger sees as accompanying this) is an endless and formidable political task. It is the essence of the conservative political wisdom of the western world that this undertaking is one which can already be known to have failed, a task which was always knowably impossible in principle.

Unger rejects this jaded but contemptuous conviction with some virulence, both for the spiritual vices he sees it as disclosing and for the intellectual superstitions it inadvertently exemplifies. But he cannot offer to replace it with a more invigorating and ingenuous conviction which bears the same claim to conclusive epistemic authority. The very scepticism that is indispensable for discrediting the epistemic pretensions of contemporary conservatism precludes the volunteering of counter-convictions that purport to enjoy a comparable authority. To see the imperative of plasticity so unblinkingly as a fact of power is certainly to call into question the political realism of governmental and administrative circles in the modern West with their increasingly enfeebled and Lilliputian sense of alternative possibility. (This is perhaps even more apparent today in the international monetary, trade and strategic relations between nations and power blocs,[7] which Unger on the whole ignores, than it is in the domestic reform cycles of the capitalist democracies and communist regimes which he considers with some care in *False Necessity*.)

But the precariousness of existing routines, while it may be bad news for their more persistent beneficiaries, is not necessarily good news for most other human beings. This is especially apparent in a period in which weapons of terminal destruction are not merely within the scope of human imagination but permanently and all too plastically poised to carry out their tasks.[8] Unger insists evocatively, throughout *Plasticity into Power* and more intermittently throughout *False Necessity*, that the imperative of plasticity has been historically imposed by the relentless pressures of military competition, the quest to augment men's powers of destruction and coercion, as much as by their efforts to create and produce less equivocal goods. But the hope of giving the imperative of plasticity 'the focus and authority it lacks'[9] by democratizing the quest for wealth and power and by breaking down a hierarchical division of labour with its sharp distinctions between task-setting and task-implementing roles looks especially forlorn in the face of thermonuclear weapons. It is far from apparent that what we really need today is any further supplementation of our destructive capabilities; nor is it very plausible that, at least in that field, the notably hierarchical and overbearing organizational apparatuses of the two greatest powers in the world will not serve all too adequately to increase these powers at a dramatic pace. Given the extreme difficulty of controlling nuclear weapons in deployment and the stunningly evident need to do so, this appears to be at least one context in which the imperative of plasticity has at last met its match. Indeed, since it is the prospect of uncontrollable individual improvisation in crisis conditions on the outer fringes of the two great structures of thermonuclear menace which is most likely to precipitate irreversible engagement,[10] there is clearly now a strong case for seeing the central imperative of human life today as the hasty reconstruction of a more dependably hierarchical set of rigidities.[11]

In these ways *Plasticity into Power* indicates some of the darker shadows cast by Unger's vision and brings out, in the perfunctoriness of its ending (pp. 211–12) the contingencies of personal temperament that hold this vision together. In his own presentation, with its elaborate *ricorsi* of leading themes and its mildly elusive overall structure, the reader is left with a choice between a variety of modern superstitions of the left or right and one or other of two theoretical options – super-theory and ultra-theory – each unmistakably of the left which are commended by Unger himself. But the construction of this matrix of choice relies rather heavily on fusing negative epistemological doctrines, pragmatist emphasis on the imperative of social plasticity and the self-estimate of the radical project, as Unger construes this. This fusion, if it is necessary rather than factitious, may lend the imperative of plasticity 'the focus and authority that it lacks' (p. 212). But to anyone who disputes Unger's reading of the radical project or finds any version of the radical project fundamentally uncompelling, it naturally encourages the opposing judgement that the imperative of plasticity, long-term fact of power though it be, in fact possesses no such focus or authority.

The most decisive and bracing feature of Unger's work is its frontal assault on the imaginative torpor of modern social and political understanding. Here he has seen with great acuity something about human existence at an individual, a collective and even a global level which only the most brazenly flippant of modern thinkers have contrived to register – and which the latter's lack of analytical curiosity or energy has largely prevented them from comprehending. It is a point which certainly consorts more comfortably with radical and modernist apprehensions of the human predicament than it does with the sedate enjoyment of assured advantage.[12] But just because it is analytically compelling the most conservative of thinkers or political leaders has every reason to nerve themselves to face it. *Plasticity into Power* gives a vivid demonstration of the force of this lesson and Unger's own evident fascination with the perspective of power throughout his writings lends it still greater emphasis. There could be no more appropriate audience for its stringent implications than the exponents of that broadly conceived politics of social democracy which Unger very justly casts as the current embodiment of conservative political decency in the modern West.

What Unger does is to take the alienated catenal imagery of the setting of modern human existence – the iron cage, the carceral imagination – and gleefully supplant it by the picture of a human habitat endlessly seething with possibility. The site of this susurration of possibility, guaranteeing its omnipresence from the most intimate of individual circumstances to the most global, is simply the human imagination. This is not a metaphysical thesis. It is perfectly compatible with a monistic determinism, provided that the detailing of the latter is a viewpoint necessarily cognitively inaccessible to real human beings. But it certainly is very sharply at odds with the most widely esteemed modern techniques of social, political or economic understanding and with the dominant models of human rationality.[13] It does not, of course, disturb the latter's internal workings nor deprive the former of all analytical force. But what it does do is to cut each and all of them decisively away from any determinate foundation in the flux of human experience and to make their application to this last, in consequence, a matter of improvisatory deftness and good fortune.

A world seething with possibility to a degree that human agents can necessarily never contrive accurately to assess (and in relation to which the very idea of such an accurate assessment is profoundly unclear) is plainly not a conclusive warrant for any particular set of actions. (It is one of Unger's principal theses that there never have been, are not, and never could come to be any such warrants.) But what it is is a stimulus to a style of social vision very different from that which prevails in the positivist social sciences that Unger excoriates (but from which he is perfectly capable of learning whatever they happen to have to teach).

One of the best ways of seeing the force of this conception of social causality (or causal theory of history) is to focus on Unger's understanding of the character and role of institutions. The greatest political merit of his work is its insistence on the centrality of institutional understanding to any honourable and effective radical politics. Here he echoes a very old theme in western political theory,[14] but one which radical political and social thought in the present century has treated in an overwhelmingly frivolous or disingenuous manner, where it has not elected simply to evade it completely.[15] (One possible construction of his programmatic volume *False Necessity* is to see it as a revitalization of Utopian Socialism, inserted firmly into what Unger himself hopes and believes to be a realistic understanding of world history, and thereby rescuing the suppressed promise of petty commodity production: Proudhon Redivivus.[16] Unger takes institutions (economic, governmental, legal, military) very seriously indeed. In a sense, indeed, he takes them more seriously than most positivist social scientists are apt to do, seeing them as not merely subject at any given time to an operating logic and a range of internal constraints but as also in large measure moulders of the personnel who make them up and the clients or victims on whom they principally act. But although he recognizes that institutional niches (or on a larger scale what he calls 'formative contexts') do much to constitute human agents as well as to determine the consequences of many of their actions and to constrain the scope of the outcomes that they can in principle bring about, it is the ineliminable capacity to reverse or transcend these limits that most concerns him. (Compare the more despondent tone of Barrington Moore's musings[17] on the human capacity to become adjusted to the abominable.) The locus of this capacity to negate, once more, is the individual human imagination: the ability to stand back from the importunities of a set of routines or practices, recast this more or less dramatically in one's mind, and try again.

What makes a context formative for Unger is not its unique and historically predestined eligibility but its relative inelasticity at any particular point in time and, above all, its deep impress upon the social imaginations of its denizens. We are never just our habitats; but we are always in large measure their creatures. Formative contexts come into existence in the restless ecology of the struggle for power and wealth. They are shaped by invention and mimesis and by the arbitrary contingencies of historical sequence.[18] But the same forces that shape them can always serve to break them and reshape their sometimes very different successors. Unger's vision of the history of institutions, like the conception of the history of science developed by followers of Thomas Kuhn, stresses both the capacity of human practices to reproduce themselves through time and to protect themselves against external challenge and the sharp discontinuities, inseparable from the exercise of this capacity, between one effectively self-reproducing practice and its successors. Unger's own political programme in *False Necessity* is a programme for weakening the self-reproducing capabilities of institutional contexts and, in its eventual implications, for diminishing the discontinuities between their prior and subsequent forms.

To make this conception compelling he complements his account of the nature of human institutions with an attack on the possibility of determinate causal knowledge of their properties. This attack is best set out in *Social Theory*. It combines a relatively determinate negative induction from the history of human cognition, much stressed by recent epistemologists and philosophers of science[19] with the elusively radical scepticism which some have drawn from the later writings of Wittgenstein, from Quine's critique of the analytic/synthetic distinction or from Heidegger.[20] If all human knowing is simply the expression of a form of life, epistemologically grounded pretensions to conclusive social insight are as intellectually threadbare as they are politically impertinent and offensive.[21] But this negative doctrine secretes no definite positive implications for political judgement,[22] however decisive its criticisms of the claims of others to ground their political judgements in epistemic authority. Indeed by itself it provides only the flimsiest of support even for Unger's vision.

The account of the character of human institutions, by contrast, provides rather more robust aid. It begins from the 'obvious truism' well expressed by Alasdair MacIntyre as long ago as 1971[23] 'that no institution or practice is what it is, or does what it does, independently of what anyone whatsoever thinks or feels about it. For institutions and practices are always, even if to differing degrees, constituted by what certain people think and feel about them'; and it presses this truism to its limits. It does not volunteer to tell us – given Unger's sceptical premises – where exactly these limits lie. Indeed it insists that there is no way of *knowing* where they do lie. But what it does do, still at a truistic level, is to insist that the precise causal character of any institution at any time rests upon what every individual causally associated with it thinks and feels about it. (It should be noted that this implicitly rejects part of MacIntyre's judgement.) Here epistemic analysis directly prompts a sense of social vertigo. The practical dependability and facticity of the social world lurches startlingly and the role of surprise is nicely reincorporated into a vision of human history.[24] How human beings see their social setting is never foreclosed at any level cognitively open to the species to which they belong. The immediate and volatile relations between belief and desire furnish an endless resource for astonishing recombinations. Any human institution at any time can tip and buckle under the impact of these forces. (It is not wholly clear whether Unger believes that this is literally true or whether he merely believes that, for all we can ever know, it always may be: a less exciting possibility and one which would lend less sustenance to the radical project in conditions of adversity.) Human beings, thus, really do make their own history; and they make it most crucially by their precarious construction and refurbishing of their own personalities[25] and by their assessments of the options presented to them by the settings in which they live. Unger's repeated and exhilarated insistence that history is always 'up for grabs' and that all social life is always and necessarily politics is the response of one temperament to this understanding. As against Barrington Moore's resigned pessimism it luxuriates in men's and women's magnificent capacity to find themselves suddenly unable to remain accustomed a moment longer to the odious conditions of their lives. But in truth there is little analytical conflict between the two perceptions. Both see the human imagination, intractably, as the site on which human history is in the last instance determined. Neither arrives at this view through callow inattention to the heavy weight of power or the raw urgency of material need.

It is clear that for Unger the sense of closure and finitude in a given historical setting is in itself something of an affront to human potentiality. But the temperamental basis of this distaste is less his edgy and restless sense of the absurdity of reifying the hopelessly provisional than it is his classically radical revulsion from the subjugation and abuse of huge cohorts of human beings by far smaller numbers of their fellows. It is the residual prominence of such relations of subordination and exploitation, sunk deep into the property order and institutionalized division of labour of the most engaging of today's social democratic communities, that goads him persistently into programmatic expression of his counter-imagination. The telos of a social habitat at last made fit for human inventiveness and antinomianism – the radical project – lends focus and authority to the blank apprehension of social plasticity through the immense gap between the desirable and the actual that it exposes. At times he writes as though he were confident that this gap will narrow ineluctably as time goes by. But at others he recognizes, frankly enough, that the accumulated weight of historical experience gives no firmer warrant for presuming an optimistic eschatology for modern social life than it does for presuming a pessimistic one.

Many critics of Unger's views are likely to wish to concentrate their fire on the character of this telos – his idiosyncratic reading of the Form of the human good. Even those who see a human society as most fundamentally a relation between the imaginations of its members, as a modern communitarian like Charles Taylor is apt to do,[26] are likely to find the ferocity of his insistence on individual imaginative autonomy too extreme to be altogether humanly sane. Those with less euphoric temperaments are also likely to find his sheer zest for novelty and experiment deeply unconvincing as an account of most human beings' strongest and most persistent motives.[27] And others still are likely to see in his recasting of human society as an arena of endless participatory deliberation and choice more a threat of endlessly futile bickering and the squandering of time and energy than a promise of the linking of individuals to their social milieu in a vital flow of interest and enjoyment.[28]

Certainly Thomas Hobbes's estimate of the human rewards of political engagement still presents a formidable challenge to Unger's assessment of the pleasures of a society and a polity made safe for the more loquacious amongst the petty bourgeoisie:

> some will say, That a *Popular State* is much to be preferr'd before a *Monarchicall*; because that, where all men have a hand in publique businesses, there all have an opportunity to shew their wisedome, knowledge, and eloquence, in deliberating matters of the greatest difficulty and moment; which by reason of that desire of praise which is bred in humane nature, is to them who excell in such like faculties, and seeme to themselves to exceed others, the most delightfull of all things. But in a Monarchy, this same way to obtain praise, and honour, is shut up to the greatest part of Subjects; and what is a grievance, if this be none? Ile tell you: To see his opinion whom we scorne, preferr'd before ours; to have our wisedome undervalued before our own faces; by an uncertain tryall of a little vaine glory, to undergoe most certain enmities (for this cannot be avoided, whether we have the better, or the worse); to hate, and to be hated, by reason of the disagreement of opinions; to lay open our secret Counsells, and advises to all, to no purpose, and without any benefit; to neglect the affaires of our own Family: These, I say, are grievances. But to be absent from a triall of wits, although those trialls are pleasant to the Eloquent, is not therefore a grievance to them, unlesse we will say, that it is a grievance to valiant men to be restrained from fighting, because they delight in it.[29]

The public pieties of political life have gone Unger's way rather than Hobbes's over the two and a half centuries since 1642. But it is eminently questionable how far the sentiments of the majority of human beings have accompanied them. The psychological realism or implausibility of Unger's favoured telos and of the conception of human nature on which this rests are obviously important in themselves. But they are also important, as Unger frequently reiterates, in appraising not merely what is politically and socially possible in principle but also what is politically and socially at all likely in practice. One of Unger's rhetorically most compelling lines of attack is the sneer that those who lack a programmatic vision comparable in scope and grandeur to his own are forced back into assessing the realism or absurdity of political proposals solely by the degree to which these deviate from existing arrangements, thus presuming the impossibility of significant change. The resulting torpor in social and political imagination is not merely in Unger's eyes spiritually unbecoming in itself. It is also, by induction from the history of large-scale social transformation, especially over the last two centuries, quite evidently intellectually ludicrous.

For those who cannot fully share his vision of the Form of the human good, it is therefore a key question about Unger's work how far his enriched sense of social and political possibility depends on this vision: how readily and usefully the components of his analysis can be re-combined to serve other perceptions of what most human beings really do want. To judge this, it may help to go back to his radicalization of MacIntyre's truism about human social institutions: that all human institutions are as they are and act as they act in part because some of their participants think and feel as they do. Seen both analytically and practically even MacIntyre's point establishes a minimum of potential instability in the character of all human institutions: a limit point to their capacity for compulsive self-reproduction. At its narrowest, False Necessity is Unger's name for this window of vulnerability in the stolidest and best protected of human arrangements. The necessity is 'false' because it is illusory, secured in many instances through false beliefs which the institution fosters among its denizens and bovinely reaffirmed in the erroneous estimates of its less sensitive external observers. To see the representation of social reality as a sort of codification of the habitual expectations of the occupants of a social territory or of the range of equally habitual expectations nurtured by its more dedicated observers from the outside is to see at least one way in which the possible can be shrunk to the narrow confines of the actual. But it is also to see this constriction as a product of imaginative indolence or capitulation.

What happens to the conceptualization of social possibility if these imaginative shackles are shaken off? What, if anything, more crucially, happens to the conceptualization of social probability? As we have already seen, it is easier to identify Unger's answer to the first of these questions than it is to judge quite how he would prefer to address the second. (It is a matter of some importance that, despite the rich array of eminently causal reflection on the properties of actual and possible institutions – legal, economic and political – set out in *False Necessity* he nowhere offers a very firm account of how to conceive quite what it is for a human state of affairs to be very probable or improbable.) To escape from false necessity, for Unger, is to see the way open once more to the realization of the radical project – not by historical predestination but through the absence of any knowable and conclusive impediment. A vast horizon opens up, far far beyond the thwarted and humiliating intimacies of the politics of the present day. But how should we judge how best to move towards this horizon? What, outside the comparatively domesticated terrain of North American legal education,[30] might particular human beings have good reason to do if they found Unger's vision of the causal character of existing social life compelling that they would not have good reason to do already?

There are at least three ways of envisaging political agency as essentially futile or forlorn on a given type of occasion; and Unger is plainly anxious to shake the imaginative hold of each of them. The first, expounded with baroque exuberance by adepts of game theory and the economic analysis of public goods, focuses on the consequential improbability of the actions of particular individuals proving decisive for securing a given political outcome or on the antinomies between individual rationality and collective advantage. In their classic forms of the free-rider problem and the prisoner's dilemma these lines of thought have exerted a deeply traumatic effect on the exercise of civic imagination, eroding the plausibility or subverting the putative human point of civic engagement.[31] Unger has a fairly brutal touch with modern devotees of civic republicanism,[32] a historical tradition which he correctly identifies with commitment to a savage degree of social discipline and a quite unacceptable degree of flippancy towards the claims of modern liberty – the liberty to act as one pleases.[33] While he is surprisingly (or perhaps unsurprisingly?) cavalier about the potential implications for the radical project of the dilemmas of collective choice, virtually the whole weight of his conception of human nature is brought to bear on the dispiriting cultural detritus of the free-rider problem and the depleted imagery of human reward which this fosters. In contrast with the powerful tendency in modern political thinking to see the implications of free-riding as essentially a sequence of problems in institutional design – and despite his own keen and imaginative interest in precisely such problems – it is plain that Unger regards them (much like the civic republicans whose social goals he repudiates) as above all an index of spiritual failure.

Nor, from his own point of view, is he at all ill-advised so to regard them. For this first image of political futility, the image that has always pressed most heavily on the great majority of human beings, cannot plausibly be shaken by any of the more analytic procedures that he develops. For the purely individual sense of political futility and impotence is for the most part not an illusion at all: not a credulous misidentification of necessity where no such necessity is to be found, but an eminently reasonable assessment of the limits of individual causal powers.[34] To shake the sense of individual political futility, it has to be vision or nothing. Here Unger is compelled to call upon his own view of the solidarizing potential of the radical project: its capacity, once again, to 'lend focus and authority' to the analytically achieved appreciation of social plasticity. (He does, of course, like Hobbes, fully recognize its potential also, along with any other scheme of orientating beliefs that extends beyond the rational imperatives for self-preservation for spawning an endless sequence of bitter quarrels. But, in contrast with Hobbes, this is a prospect in which he is inclined to revel. And equally unlike Hobbes, the potential of the radical project for fusing and inspiring a collective agency that is often self-endangering or even self-sacrificial for each particular individual is one with which he cannot afford to dispense.)[35] For individuals to see their own agency not as a costly and hazardous contribution that is unlikely to secure a directly and uniquely imputable gain for anyone at all, but rather as an element in a collective performance in which it is intrinsically rewarding to participate is for them to repudiate the terms of the free-rider problem on their own behalf.

This is a very different line of attack from Unger's assault on deep structure social theory and the unstable oscillations between fatalist passivity and feckless opportunism which he sees the latter as prompting. His diagnosis of the corrupting and bemusing political consequences of this style of theory – and most particularly of marxism[36] – is protracted, searching and lethally effective. (He has a wonderful ear for leftist cant. But it is in fact hard to imagine an exponent of any strand of modern political faith who could read his work through without occasional twinges of acute discomfort.) But whereas his exploration of the political weaknesses of deep structure social theory is an immediate aid to the formation of political judgement, it is quite difficult to distinguish the agitational from the analytical elements in his exploration of the former. It is also correspondingly difficult, even for the best intentioned, to employ the former directly in the refinement and disciplining of political judgement. This is not simply a matter of inadvertence on Unger's part. It follows from his intense and arrestingly personal ambivalence about the very idea of political judgement itself. Seeing the claim to political realism, in its characteristic modern forms, as an epistemically impertinent pretension to knowing what necessarily cannot be known (a *true* necessity) or as a limp capitulation to the actual, he is intensely suspicious of the very attempt to subject political judgement to systematic analysis. The qualities that he approves in political judgement are in one sense, naturally, on display throughout *Politics*. But they are most accessible in the more condensed version of his sketch of the virtues appropriate to a genuinely valuable cadre in one of the political movements that in his view carry the banner of the emancipatory struggle (pp. 437–41), even though in its ultimate stages this struggle aims at 'effacing the starkness of the contrast between who is and who is not a cadre' (p. 441). 'The realistic, second-best solution to the problem of the cadres' (p. 440), the non-Platonic solution, is the addition of a relatively small number of those who eschew the polar vices of pious conservatism and sectarian bigotry in favour of the benign mean embodied in Unger's own opinions,[37] thus leavening the substantial lump of the remainder of their less discerning fellows. This plainly is to be seen as a true realism, and by no means to be conflated with the 'realism' of the paralytic conservatives whom Unger scorns. It is plain, too, that he regards the elaborate institutional forms proposed for the transformative movement, within their own hypothetical terms, as eminently realistic: and that by 'realistic' he means just the same as the conservative observers whom he views with such contempt. What they disagree about is not what in general it is to be realistic but which particular social expectations satisfy this criterion. It is in their causal beliefs, not in their analytical concepts, that they are genuinely at odds.

Since the late seventeenth century most western social and political thinkers of any great force have been apt to rest their causal beliefs about societies, economies and polities, openly or tacitly, upon some conception of probability.[38] Unger's stress on the desirability of the 'ceaseless exercise of an almost frenzied inventiveness'[39] and on the prospective triumph of the 'principle of pitiless recombination', while presumably in some sense inductively grounded itself, sets him very much at odds with this by now hallowed imaginative framework. But it does not really furnish him with an alternative analytic matrix of his own which could possibly serve to supplant it. A diffuse expectation of forthcoming surprises, however urgent and eager, is scarcely a framework for analysing anything. The link between his vividly imagined and carefully considered programme of emancipation and his more analytic perspective on the human past is correspondingly arbitrary: an exercise of will and a reflection of temperament, not a dictate of the understanding.

Consider the relation between an individual human agent as chooser of her or his own actions and the same person as judge of the potential consequences of the range of possible actions they perceive as being open to them. As choosers of their own actions, human beings perceive, reflect and judge as best they can. Within the perspective of practical reason, and from their own point of view, there is very little to be said for depre-cating their capacity for invention and self-discipline in advance of the attempt to exert either. There are none so inefficacious as those who do not try. From the point of view of theoretical reason, however, the epistemic grounds for pessimism even in relation to oneself may well be dismayingly robust; and these same grounds may carry through, with all too crushing cogency, to any consideration within the framework of prac-tical reason of the prospective conduct of one's fellows. For what reason-able alternative is there for any human agent to representing the space on which she or he can and must seek to act, if they are to act at all, as a set of varyingly possible consequences, surrounded by a blank cliff of sheer impossibility? Few things matter more to any human agent over time than the structure of risks and opportunities furnished by the prospective conduct of others. Except with the extremes of downside risk what is likely to happen is almost always more important to them than what just conceivably might: still more so than Unger's favoured con-sideration – what just (*inconceivably*) might. To dissipate the sense of futility that hovers over the vast bulk of individual political agency, from the most routine and conformist to the most intractably subversive, it is above all the sentiments of those concerned and not their causal beliefs that have to be altered.

Here Unger's attack on two further perceptual sources of the feeling that political agency for most humans most of the time is irretrievably futile comes briskly into play. A fatalist and monistic vision of the histori-cal process deconstructs the very idea of rational agency, offering to individuals (and indeed to classes, states or national communities) a per-spective on their own strivings which renders the latter comically self-deceptive. Even a less extreme and analytically determinate structural explanation of large-scale historical change requires the adoption of a sociology of fate in lieu of one of choice and prescinds firmly from the standpoint of human historical agency.[40] Unger's rejection of this perspective, both in its metaphysically more full-blown and in its analy-tically more modest and controlled version, follows from his emphasis on the intrinsic unpredictability of imagination and on the severely provisional character of all human cognitive achievement. Even if the most metaphysically extreme version of determinism were in fact valid, it would be impossible for human beings ever to ascertain that this was the case and equally impossible for them to construe any definite impli-cations for their own agency that followed from its being so. (Whatever they chose to do would, *ex hypothesi*, have to follow from its being so.)

In a sense Unger adopts the ultra-idealist reading of the fundamental
determinants of historical change suggested by his mid-seventeenth-
century English predecessor as radical legal critic, John Warr: 'But yet the
minds of men are the great wheels of things: thence come changes and
alterations in the world: teeming freedom exerts and puts forth itself.'[41]
But he lends this judgement depth and sociological credibility by offsetting it with his conception of the formative contexts of human agency
and the heavy imaginative weight of habit and cumulative dismay in
crushing those powers of negative capability that he sees as the birthright
of every full human being.

In a similar manner his conception of twentieth-century world
historical struggle adds to a recognition of the causal weight of mimesis,
invention and sheer nerve in determining the course of twentieth-century
revolutions,[42] a particularly illuminating insistence on both the necessarily improvisatory character of most revolutionary political struggle and
on the endless range of institutional discretion open to those attempting
to reconstruct a social world. He is a powerful political critic of the
twentieth-century revolutionary tradition, who understands very well
why this has developed as it has, without displaying the slightest patience
with its tendency to cling on desperately to the most adventitious and
blatantly discreditable of its improvisations. Denying, perhaps a trifle
hazardously, that any set of human circumstances is knowably impossible, he is especially hostile to pretensions that any given set of shabby
accommodations to the temporarily convenient should be dignified with
a title to historical necessity. He is an equally sharp critic of twentieth-
century reformist traditions; but it is striking in this instance how little his
reading of their largely involuntary self-limitation is really at odds with
those of their more pedestrian interpreters.[43]

To reject a closed set of possible worlds,[44] however much it might or
should open up a person's sense of historical possibility, is unlikely – and
for fairly obvious reasons – to be of much direct help in sharpening his or
her political judgement. Addressed to most human beings one at a time,
nothing in Unger's interpretation of *Politics* does anything to shake the
rationality for most inhabitants of the contemporary world of presuming
that political engagement for all but the most obsessive and narrowly
motivated is likely in practice to prove to be hazardous, massively un-
rewarding, or indeed both. What grounds Unger's confidence in human
self-emancipation is in effect a Platonic philosophical psychology in
association with a deeply un-Platonic conception of value for human
beings. (However 'negative capability' is to be understood, it scarcely
possesses the stabilizing and orientating potential of Plato's Form of the
Good.) The judgement that vision shapes desire, and shifts in vision

reshape it just as effectively, is still a powerful challenge to the debilitating impact of Hume's naturalist insistence that what it is reasonable for human beings to do depends fundamentally on their inclinations.[45] It remains not merely the oldest but the most robust foundation for genuinely Utopian social thinking, a genre which Unger's present work dramatically revives. But the direct address to vision as such alters what human agents have good reason to do to the extent, and only to the extent, that it changes how they happen to see. For this reason the only audience for Unger's work that is likely to be able to take it quite as it is intended is in fact the array of ideal cadres – a category, to a perilous degree, predefined in terms of the theory in the first place. Because they share his sense of what really matters for human beings and what truly is desirable they can develop the passionate pragmatism of his exploration of the vulnerability of existing social and political forms in harmony with the goals that he holds dear and not in the service of more disparate and distressingly contingent purposes of their own. But for most others, exposure to Unger's vision, while intellectually striking (and agreeably enlivening in itself) is likely to leave the world of politics very much as they previously supposed it to be. For even the more sympathetic of such readers, accordingly, it is likely to be particular felicities of his institutional explorations that best outlast the diffuse euphoria induced by first encountering his text as a whole.

The role of modernist Legislator for which he discreetly offers himself as inherently more self-effacing than its ancient predecessor. It is scarcely surprising that he should feel the need to repudiate the mantle of 'an omniscient and benevolent Lycurgus' towering over the world of ordinary agents which his historical action has brought into being.[46] But by virtue of its very commitment to institutionalized self-extinction, the role depends both for its historical efficacy and its human authority on the inspirational impact of the vision it conveys. It is therefore a rather delicate and searching test of the soundness of his programmatic 'supertheory' as a whole, just what its effect on the vision of others does prove to be: how plentiful and how ideal the ideal cadres actually turn out.

What is quite certain is that they will continue to have not merely a plethora of fanatical or backsliding colleagues but also a wide array of political opponents. Some of these, naturally, will simply be beneficiaries of privilege, set on defending this for its own dear sake. But others will set themselves against his programme because they cannot share his vision of the Form (or formlessness) of the human good and because they do not trust his political judgement. In politics, in the last instance, it is very hard to get away from the issue of trust.[47] The view, for example, that a belligerently dissident opportunism really is a benign contribution to human life everywhere and always takes a lot of stomaching. The zest for interminable self-reconstitution appears as febrile at a personal level as it does unpromising as a collective political project. Unger himself is rather obviously more excited by the hope of doing good through political agency than unnerved by the fear of doing harm through it. This is certainly one dimension today to the political opposition between left and right. But since it is much easier to do harm by political action than it is to do good by it, it would be injudicious for the left – and more especially for the foes of subjugation and hierarchy as such – to construe it as the sole or even the most decisive line of division between the two. For Unger, like Georges Sorel, the politics of human emotion is in the end every bit as important as (perhaps even, more important than) the politics of consequence. The circumstances human beings do directly encounter certainly are given to them by history. But Unger is as hostile as Sorel was to the sense that they must be taken as given; and his sophisticated attack on the muddled fatalism of modern social theory (which often echoes Sorel's accents) is offered as a negative spiritual exercise in self-strengthening. Those whose selves are likeliest to draw strength from it are radical intellectuals, plainly in the West but also possibly in the Third World: a group very apt at present to find their identities in urgent need of reinforcement. The union between radical intellectuals and oppressed masses has been the most turbulent and consequential liaison in modern politics. It is not an easy romance to chronicle justly. But it seems unlikely that it will on balance be described more honestly or understood more clearly simply by restoring the self-confidence of radical intellectuals.

We may be unable in principle ever to know just what has to be taken as given in human affairs. But it is a criterion of sanity for every human being to recognize that very much must always be taken as given. Even to formulate coherent intentions requires a human world the properties of which must be very highly interpreted. To formulate political intentions of any ambition and determinacy requires a correspondingly sharper degree of causal assessment. The urgency, and on occasion the flair, of Unger's institutional imaginings indicates the limits of the hostility of even the most modernist of Legislators to a strictly political division of labour. But it does not wholly still the suspicion that there is more in this rethinking of the radical project for radical intellectuals than there is for their indispensable partners, the *malheureux*, who no doubt potentially remain *les puissances de la terre*, but who are for the most part less heavily preoccupied with self-reconstitution.

With magnificently reckless self-exposure Unger concludes his central volume[48] by affirming as the goal of his programme for radical democracy 'a better chance to be both great and sweet'. The wish to be both great and sweet is a recognizably modern yearning: the wish to be sweet being, for example, comparatively undeveloped among the Roman governing classes. A social world made fit for radical intellectuals is a natural goal for a radical programme. But it is perhaps less reassuring as a rubric for political action. In particular, it gives too little weight to the dangers to others of political miscalculation by the best intentioned of leaders or to the thoroughly demotic realism with which most human beings still view the hazards and frustrations of ambitious and vague projects for political and social reconstruction. Only a more pedestrianly consequentialist approach stands much chance of distinguishing between wise and foolish instances of such projects; and only the conviction that there are solid and dependable reasons for undertaking them can render them (through all the political turbulence, ambiguity and anxiety which Unger rightly insists will always accompany them) exercises in rational cooperation for great masses of human beings rather than exhilarating adventures for the talented, daring and determined few. Human fragility does not make social oppression any more forgivable than its radical critics supposed it to be. (It is precisely human fragility that makes it such a clear evil.) But what it does do is to make the burden of judging accurately the central responsibility of anyone who aspires to guide political practice. Human life is too short, too tiresome, too sad and too beset by danger for Unger's sense of the heroic to furnish a compelling basis for political judgement for mankind at large. Gracchus Babeuf, precarious bridge between the thought world of classical republicanism and the harsh manipulative adventures of the professional revolutionary tradition, put the case admirably:

> The republican is not a man in eternity, he is a man in time. His paradise is on this earth; he deserves to enjoy there liberty and happiness, and to enjoy it for as long as he has being, without postponement, or at least with as little as possible. All the time he spends outside this condition is lost to him, he will never recover it again.[49]

What to do in politics always depends on what can (and will) be caused to come about. Unger is quite right to insist that we can seldom or never *know* this. But what follows from such epistemic opacity is merely that we must learn to judge it better in practice: an endless task. For this purpose, and over time, Unger's scepticism and his preoccupation with institutional form are likely to prove more instructive than the ardour of his faith.

11

Elusive Community:
The Political Theory of
Charles Taylor

In the introduction to the two volumes of his collected *Philosophical Papers* Charles Taylor describes himself, rather engagingly, as a monomaniac.[1] Only someone with a range of interests and of knowledge as broad as his own would be likely to sense a need to insist on their underlying unity in contrast with their 'appearance of variety'.[2] Both emphases, however, certainly have their force. To say, as he does, that the set of papers collected addresses a rather tightly related agenda[3] is to say a good deal more than simply that they all reflect the preoccupations of a single energetically self-interpreting person. But to acknowledge the variety of their subject matter is merely to recognize the obvious.

The heterogeneity has been apparent enough from the earliest phase of Taylor's published work. It has given him over the years at least four rather sharply segregated reputations, quite aside from his standing as a participant in Canadian national politics. The first of the four is a reputation as a philosophical critic of modern empirical psychology, animal as much as human, as a would-be natural science, commencing with his trenchant assessment of the behaviourist movement of the 1950s and early 1960s in *The Explanation of Behaviour*,[4] and continuing through a lengthy guerrilla struggle against a miscellany of less drastically pejorative representations of strictly human capacities down to contemporary cognitive psychology. (It is these themes with which volume I of the collected *Papers, Human Agency and Language*, is principally concerned.) The second reputation, stemming principally from a single article 'Neutrality in political science', first published in 1967,[5] was as a philosophical critic of North American political scientists' then stalwart pretensions to have eliminated value from their understanding of the character of politics. This was a particularly cunning line of attack since Taylor chose to insist on the degree to which their writings were suffused with evaluative commitments not in order to rebuke them for their epistemic impurity but to felicitate them upon their sanity. The third reputation, again stemming principally from a single article in the *Review of Metaphysics* in 1971,[6] was as a defender of a hermeneutic as opposed to a scientistic model for the sciences of man and of a set of associated conclusions about the directions in which it was or was not desirable for these sciences to develop: a plea for what Taylor himself called (perhaps not altogether fortunately) a 'science of interpretation'[7] as against a science of behaviour. The fourth reputation, based on a distinctly bulkier contribution than these last two, has been as an indefatigable interpreter of the philosophy and social thought of continental Europe, and most particularly of Germany, to the Anglophone world: not just of Hegel in two substantial volumes[8] but also of Herder, Humboldt and Heidegger to name only another three.

None of these four reputations is exactly a reputation as a theorist of politics in his own right, though large segments of the two volumes on Hegel would certainly pass for contributions to contemporary political theory if they were offered as such. But I think it is right to say (and partly no doubt because of his more practical contributions to Canadian politics)[9] that these four relatively obtrusive and definite reputations have been shadowed throughout by a fifth and slightly more surreptitious reputation (partly derived from his impact as a teacher in Montreal and Oxford and as an intellectual friend and companion in a much wider range of settings) as an original and imaginative political thinker in his own right.

In these two volumes something of the grounds for this fifth and more shadowy reputation edges more firmly forward into the light of day. It is principally the upshot of this endeavour – monomania or genuinely heroic attempt to rethink the character of modern politics – on which I should like to concentrate on this occasion. What, as constructive political theory, has come out of this remarkably tenacious, imaginative and original address to the problems of modern political understanding? What aspects of modern politics does it help us to address more effectively? (The criterion of aid to effective practice is one which Taylor himself defends as apt for a political theory.)[10] In the face of what, if any, aspects of modern politics does it rather palpably falter? What are its strengths and limitations?

Taylor's contribution to political understanding, like his contribution to an understanding of the human predicament more generally, rests upon a stubborn (and in my view in some respects often an exceedingly well-justified) commitment to the validity of a set of personal intuitions: or, to put it more bombastically, to a range of truths of his own experience. This is certainly not what systematic beliefs about anything are supposed to rest upon in the post scientific revolution metaphysics of the western world; and it is, of course, quite easy to overestimate the degree to which particular beliefs can afford to rest merely on any such foundation. What the epistemologies spawned by the scientific revolution have in the long run especially stigmatized have been human subjectivity and human value. For Taylor the view that a human understanding of human affairs can be in the last instance disdainful of either subjectivity or value is simply deranged. What it is to be human at all is to experience a self for oneself from the inside, to interpret the character of that self actively for oneself and to seek to mould or remould it in terms of an interpretation of values (what Taylor calls 'distinctions of worth')[11] seen as located outside an individual within a social and natural habitat to which that individual belongs.

In one of the most stimulating modern discussions of the place of subjectivity in a world of fact, Thomas Nagel addressed the question 'What is it like to be a bat?',[12] insisting essentially that however necessarily inaccessible it might be to us there was something for bats which was what it just *was* like to be a bat. What holds Taylor's work as a whole together is a stubborn defensive commitment to his own sense of 'what it is like to be a human being'. Of course we know today that there is a staggering range of answers to the question of what it has been like and is at present like to be a human being; and there is no very dependable modern technique of analysis that establishes clearly whether there has in fact been or must necessarily have been any definite common core to what it has been like to be a human being over even the last few thousand years.[13] Taylor's conviction[14] is simply that, whatever it may have been like in the distant past and far away, at least in the post-Romantic, post scientific revolution, industrial civilization of the West what it has definitely by now become like to be a human being (and has in fact been like for as long as we have any very instructive evidence on the matter) centrally includes subjectivity, self-interpretation and the active location and amendment of the self in relation to a world of external values which he calls strong evaluation. (Of course, as Taylor has described as extensively and as eloquently as any modern thinker, the sense of the significance of this process of self-interpretation and self-modulation has changed dramatically over the last three hundred years in the West. But it is essential to Taylor's strategy of understanding, in contrast for example with that of Alasdair MacIntyre,[15] that the practice of strong evaluation is as readily located in the verses of the *Iliad* as it is in the pages of the twentieth-century novel.)

No account of human agency or of the human predicament more broadly which was trimmed to the epistemological canons of an absolute conception of reality could accommodate these central features of what it is to be a human being, since the features themselves are of an essentially anthropocentric or subject-referring character.[16] An absolute conception of reality is a conception of reality seen in a manner which was no longer contingent on the perceptual or cognitive idiosyncrasies of the human species,[17] a conception of the universe, for example, as seen in the steady gaze of its omniscient Creator.[18] Anthropocentric properties – secondary qualities like colour and so on – are *ex hypothesi* to be excluded from an absolute conception. But precisely what makes them ineligible for inclusion in such a conception also, in Taylor's eyes, renders them indispensable to a human conception of human reality. Like Strawson,[19] Taylor doubts the possibility of our coming to regard each other purely as more or less benign or menacing physical objects whose future trajectory is causally determined by a prior state of the universe. (He does not, as far as I can see, seek to deny that this may be a metaphysically valid verdict on what they in fact are.) But more interestingly he also regards the temptation to regard human beings in this way as a form of protracted imaginative self-hypnosis, going back at least to the seventeenth century and powered increasingly through time by an essentially moral and aesthetic response which is itself a component of the strongly evaluative reformulation of the experienced self on which he lays such emphasis.[20]

Applied at this point the hermeneutic approach, with its mildly condescending charity, volunteers to explain better to us why we think and feel as we do about ourselves and about how these are most clearly and stably to be understood – and by so doing, to weaken the sentiments and suspend some of the burden of the vision itself.[21] This is an ingenious line of thought; but it more suggests a mildly forlorn rearguard action than an arrest and reversal of the powerful imaginative currents of the last three centuries. The principal burden of Taylor's critique of large areas of empirical psychology has been the complaint that they greatly underestimated the intelligence and resourcefulness of the creatures whose behaviour they purported to explain: in the case of *The Explanation of Behaviour*, a complaint pressed as vigorously on behalf of rats as it has been later of human beings. The outcome of this epistemologically punctilious travestying of the practical abilities of the subjects under investigation was, in Taylor's eyes, a tissue of prevarication and confusion: just extremely poor science.[22] And the same in his view, a good deal more contentiously, has held true of much recent cognitive psychology and computer modelling of human mental operations.

In relation to political theory, fortunately, it is less important to judge the cogency of Taylor's criticism of empirical psychology (either as this has been or as it could in future become) than it is to assess just how strong and clear implications his arguments carry for the understanding of politics. Only very foolish students of politics any longer suppose that their own subject matter can in fact be understood with any power and precision without a close consideration of – or at least a wary regard for – human values (1967 is over twenty years ago). But they do, of course, have rather substantial disagreements as to just how human values are to be appraised and taken into account. On the whole the current confrontation between hermeneutic approaches to political understanding and the somewhat adulterated vestiges of the scientistic approach is as much a political conflict in itself as it is a disagreement between two analytical judgements about a common object of analysis.[23] The hermeneutic approach is admirable (especially in the hands of those with some literary gifts) for furnishing a feeling account of how some more or less deplorable political state of affairs was or is. It is distinctly less well adapted for convincing those who feel rather differently that that indeed *is* the way it is. And the fact that in the face of such obtuseness the hermeneutic approach can almost always provide further (and invariably somewhat pejorative) explanations for the existence of this gap in intuitions merely adds, from its opponent's point of view, insult to injury.[24] More importantly, perhaps, the hermeneutic ideal of the fusion of horizons, the linking of distinct perspectives on the world by the mutual adjustment of perceptions and values, is apt to be seen by the embattled liberal sceptic as a threat of enforced evaluative uniformity rather than as a promise of the discovery of evaluative harmony.[25]

Here I think Taylor's choice of terminology is a trifle incautious. To speak in the English language of 'a valid science of man' or simply of 'the science of interpretation'[26] appears to promise (or threaten) a degree of integration (and thus of epistemic regimentation) in the understanding of human affairs which nothing else in Taylor's extremely extensive writings suggests that he either expects or would welcome. Presented with a choice (and this is in fact never the choice with which anyone is presented) between a hermeneutic approach and what I suppose for purposes of brevity may still be called a positivist approach (an approach relatively insouciant about agent self-understandings) I would myself incline on most occasions to the hermeneutic. But I would do so, to be sure, essentially as a heuristic: not as an, in any way, self-validating cognitive procedure. And I would expect to meet the objections to my 'findings', as they came and one by one, as best I could: not by attempting to design some comprehensive piece of pseudo-epistemological appara-tus which could somehow rule them out of court in advance. Whatever else the term 'science' now means in the English language, most English speakers who have thought at all about it in recent decades do at least understand it as referring to rather strongly institutionalized and (for better or worse) effectively self-disciplining human practices. Given this understanding of the word, it does seem most unlikely that we will soon (and fairly unlikely that we will *ever*) have good reason to look forward to the firm institutionalization and self-disciplining of a single science of man or science of interpretation. Humanly speaking, the interpretative commitment is a good deal more enticing as a declaration of intention[27] than it is as a claim to achievement, let alone as a claim to effectively routinized achievement.

Indeed the very confrontation with positivist conceptions of the human sciences on the terrain of method as such seems on balance ill-advised – ill-advised, at any rate, if it takes the form of counterposing one hypothetically sound method to another putatively unsound one. The view that it is essentially method that guarantees claims to valid under-standing was (and no doubt in some sense remains) the ideological core of positivist social science. It is a view that no longer retains a shred of intellectual respectability.[28] The role of uncodifiable judgement and speculative theoretical choice and invention in constituting the sciences of non-human nature simply rules out of court any such conception of procedurally self-guaranteeing knowledge. What the human sciences need is not a method which ensures their success (which they simply cannot have, whether they would welcome it or not), but simply a variety of approaches genuinely apt to the heterogeneity of their subject matter that at least *permits* them to illuminate this sharply and plainly, both to their own practitioners and in somewhat more summary fashion to the populace at large.

I am not at all confident that Taylor in fact disagrees with this judge-ment. But he has certainly convinced some of his readers that he does so; and, if the impression is erroneous, the misunderstanding is of consider-able importance.

It is particularly important in relation to two of Taylor's most ambitious and fruitful themes: the conception of the self-interpreting individual as metaphysically dependent upon rather than independent of society,[29] and of the self-interpretation of that individual as in turn dependent upon the resources of the language of a particular language-community[30] for capturing and revealing a range of human values which can lend to this self-interpretation real depth and dignity of insight.

('Lend' here is better than 'give' since it is central to Taylor's vision that the idea of the individual as potential container (or site) of the full significance of his or her own self-interpretation is utterly incoherent, despite its furnishing the fundamental premise of atomist social and political theories and the theoretical strategy of the radical objectification of the self.) The claim that the individual as speaker 'is in fact enmeshed in two kinds of larger order, which he can never wholly oversee, and can only punctually and marginally refashion'[31] is Taylor's strongest rebuttal of the 'atomist' vision of society[32] and the objectified conception of the individual. (It seems right to distinguish vision from conception in this way since 'atomism' in Taylor's vocabulary is essentially the presumption that nothing real in fact corresponds to 'society' – that 'society' has only an aggregative reference – while his doubts about the objectification of the individual are not doubts about whether any such entity exists but simply doubts about whether what does exist is aptly conceived solely in these terms.) In the end what Taylor hopes to do (as the conclusion to his introduction avows, and as has been at least intermittently apparent throughout his earlier writings) is to vindicate the standing of these two kinds of larger order (or at least of some integrated component of the two) as the true locus of value for human beings: not value over against individual consciousness, but value in and for and through individual consciousness. What he hopes is that it will in the end prove to be within the capacities of practical reason to furnish such a vindication.[33] This is, of course, an old hope, present in very different forms in the great Greek political philosophers, in Aquinas, in Hegel and in my view also, at least for most of his life, in the allegedly 'atomist' Locke (though the latter of course located his larger order in part outside the frame of terrestrial nature).[34] It is also a spectacularly intellectually unfashionable view.[35]

What has made it so unfashionable, evidently enough, is the very objectification of the individual against which Taylor sets himself so obdurately. It is worth asking very briefly what, if anything, might prove sufficient to restore it to intellectual favour. One natural answer might be the countervailing objectification of the larger orders in question: society, economy, language, perhaps even polity. This answer has in fact been pursued very actively in modern structuralist thought in recent decades, as it has in the marxist tradition over a lengthier period. But Taylor in the end rejects this strategy, even in its most glittering and imaginatively seductive recent avatar, the oeuvre of Michel Foucault, because of its unyielding contempt for agency and individuality as such. On the whole he is, I think, right to reject it[36] (though not necessarily right in all the criticisms he levels at Foucault himself).[37] But what he has to put in its place, as the necessary link between the microcosm of the individual and the two larger orders in which that individual is always enmeshed, is the somewhat precarious substance of intersubjectivity and a public domain constituted by the elaborately recursive patterns of mutual recognition of intentions between individual human beings. What is precarious about this substance is both practical and epistemological. Epistemologically it is vulnerable to the objectifying atomist drift of modern thought. Nothing intersubjective will be vindicated as genuinely present in the objectified representation of a particular community unless it is individuals in whom it is present. Its standing cannot be established, on the battleground chosen by modern epistemologies, by the deployment of superior cognitive power. To be induced to desert an objectifying representation for a more subject-responsive representation what is required is not external force (conquest); it is internal enticement (seduction). But by the same token intersubjectivity is also vulnerable to the cultural drift (or perhaps simply to the more nakedly apparent cultural realities) of contemporary societies throughout the world.

Intersubjectivity is either present or it is not. If it is present, the hermeneutic theorist can perhaps illuminate it a little more fetchingly and reinforce it somewhat by doing so (a little like the minister in the face of the current spiritual receptivity of a Protestant congregation). If it is absent, the hermeneutic theorist can identify the absence and perhaps, if she or he is particularly eloquent, elicit a measure of pain, regret or even nostalgia at the absence which they have disclosed. But no hermeneutic theorist can reasonably expect, out of their own histrionic resources alone, to conjure intersubjectivity into life. In the face of a true void of intersubjectivity – a radical gap in intuitions of value – the point is not so much to interpret this as it is to change it. But of course the question remains of how far and how (if at all) it actually can be changed. History, as Marx pointed out, is a very resistant medium.

It is because of his responsiveness to these dilemmas that Taylor is such a fascinating political theorist. In the face of distressing choices he is apt to cling tenaciously to both horns of the dilemma, refusing, for what are often humanly excellent motives, to let either of them go. What induces him to do so, presumably, is in the end his own sensibility: the set of truths furnished by his own experience. Crucially – and most unusually among modern writers – this experience not only engages him deeply and arrestingly in the modern post-Romantic project of self-exploration, both as spiritual odyssey and as analytic dissection; it also engages him just as deeply in a distinctively pre-modern project of locating himself and other human beings within an independent and objective order of natural and social value.

Most modern philosophers see this last project as not merely pre-modern in historical derivation but as rather blatantly epistemically impermissible within any modern system of beliefs – and hence as evidently absurd for any thinking person, let alone any serious intellectual, to credit today. Aside from the lower reaches of religious entrepreneurship (Hare Krishna and so on) and from the institutional relics of the grander pre-modern readings of this order (the Holy Catholic Church), the only setting where any such perspective is likely to appear attractive in the contemporary world is in the more or less coercive practical construction of supposedly socialist (or perhaps in due course truly Islamic) political communities in the face of an unfriendly world. And its attractions in these settings are plausibly more instrumental than they are intrinsic: the attractions of a bullying idiom of public moralizing rather than of an authentic mode of experiencing what the human world is really like.

This is where Taylor's *oeuvre*, in my view, really does falter; and it falters not because it is wrong but because the resources it disposes of are inadequate to the tasks which it implicitly (and occasionally rather explicitly) sets itself. In effect it seems to me in the end excessively grounded in the contingencies of one individual sensibility and insufficiently turned out towards a practical world. It is not so much the epistemic self-certification of Taylor's own consciousness that is at fault here. I think Taylor is quite right to suppose that in the understanding of human value the only resource there is is the exploration of one's own subjectivity and a reflective communication with other subjectivities on the results of this exploration. (The communication will obviously need to go in both directions; and the wider the range of interlocutors the more promising the epistemic prospects of the interchange.) In such communication intersubjectivity is what, if one is fortunate, one may hope to discover. But it is not something whose availability can ever be confidently presumed. The sceptical astringency of modern understandings of the character of human value may be rendered a trifle less painful by reflective exploration. But it is not going to be simply thought away. (It is important that even in ancient Greek philosophy – and long before Descartes and Hume and Kant and Wittgenstein and Quine had deepened epistemological scepticism about our knowledge of the natural world – there were powerful currents of value-scepticism.) Where the weakness of his thinking as a whole as thinking about *politics* really does lie is in the degree of its preoccupation with self-understanding and self-interpretation and in the comparatively thin rendering that it offers of the real setting of modern political life and of the practical problems with which this life struggles so unreassuringly.

This does not prevent him from being a powerful critic of much other

modern political theory. His attack, for example, on the moral uncouthness and the analytical incoherence of the still dominant atomist strand
of political and social understanding, especially in North America,[38] is as
effective a rebuttal of an entire perceptual style as one can find.[39] The
insistence that the elevation of autonomy as master value (indeed sometimes the sole value) in modern liberal theories can only retain any
cogency at all within a human setting which affords a real spectrum of
values among which to choose[40] is an exceedingly important strategic
commentary on the most fashionable wave of recent political theory. And
there are plenty of other examples.

But even his critique of atomism is a little weakened by its lack of
attention to the political motivation of the great intellectual forerunners
of atomist political theory. Even in the case of the political theory of
Hobbes, for example, what motivates that theory is certainly not a lack of
sensitivity to the dynamism of intersubjective strong evaluation. Rather,
it is a political judgement about the difficulties of combining individual
conceit about the merits of one's own judgement (hardly a condition
which the strongly evaluating self-interpreter can be wholly confident of
avoiding) with a plurality of groupings pretending in all ideological
authenticity to be entitled to monopolize political power and credal
authority. Both in *De Cive* and in *Leviathan* Hobbes's political argument,
an argument against the fusion of classical democratic or republican
claims to political choice and post-Reformation sectarian pretensions to
religious monopoly, is not well captured in the conventional account of
the necessary conflicts between individual desires for scarce goods and
the consequent imperative of subordinating these desires to a single
definite locus of coercive authority. Both of these claims, of course,
remain of rather evident importance in the contemporary politics of
those societies where 'commodious living' has come to be seen, without
absurdity, as a historical civic right. But the former, unlike the latter, lies
precisely within that space of the problematic politics of intersubjectivity
to which Taylor has so graphically drawn our attention.[41]

Taylor's sharpest recent liberal critics attack him in essence for invok-
ing or promising a form of community which he is in fact unable to
deliver, and which they strongly suspect that they would find pretty
odious if he did contrive to deliver it.[42] (I think that in this latter suspicion
they underestimate the degree of his commitment to the intimations of
the firmly self-interpreted self, which is as liberal as such commitments
come.) It is quite true that some of Taylor's strongest intuitions are
communitarian, and that they lie, as he makes quite explicit, within the
republican tradition of the priority of public over private: both the entitlement to participate in a public realm and the duty to commit individual

energies and resources to sustaining and defending that realm.[43] He i
certainly a tart critic of the privatization of individual lives within moderi.
capitalist societies, seeing this in practice more as spiritual deformation
than as opportunity for the cultivation of a fuller and richer individuality.
(Indeed he tends at times to suggest a measure of real spiritual discomfort
on the part of many of the citizens of these societies at their own sense of
the centrality of material consumption to their lives[44] – an assessment
which I find pretty unconvincing.) But the combination of his personal
sensitivity and his acceptance of a hermeneutic approach together ensure
that he also sees quite clearly the heterogeneity of evaluative conceptions
and the variety of practices that go to make up the advanced capitalist
societies of today. Indeed he is particularly sensitive to the anomalous
and disharmonious relations that frequently obtain between these
practices, arguing, for example, that they constitute a major threat to the
legitimacy of these societies in the eyes of their own citizens and that
they preclude the acceptance by the latter of a single standard of distributive justice.[45] In particular Taylor argues (perhaps with the experience of
Quebec centrally in mind) that the sense of political community is often
not felt most strongly today at the level of the nation state and that the
distant bureaucratic structures that regulate economic activity today,
whether under notionally private or notionally public control, fail to
register a convincing sense of a community of production.[46] For both
discontents the principal remedy which he suggests, not for the first
time[47] and, of course, along with numerous other recent writers,[48] is the
decentralization of political choice and the extension of control by producers over their own production.[49] There are definitely some attractions
to these proposals. But there is also an abundance of potential snags; and
it cannot be said that at present either looks very much like the wave of
the future ('the real movement of history') anywhere on earth.

Nor do they necessarily represent a very effective remedy either for the
particular problems that Taylor underlines or for the miscellany of other
more or less pressing difficulties that confront the populations of all
advanced capitalist countries. (Many of the same problems in fact also
confront the populations of those socialist states that have succeeded in
becoming industrialized, along, of course, with a heavy endowment of
additional problems which are peculiar to the latter.[50] A sense of
community, as reflected in the consciousness of individual human agents,
is perhaps spiritually desirable because it permits (and in some measure
compels) a saner and more reflective understanding of the setting of individual lives and because it fosters less resentful and more generous dispositions to cooperate across the space on which such lives depend for
their viability. The sense of community is itself a form of perceptual and

motivational edification. But the sense of community, whether or not it is present on a particular occasion, must always itself be the product of a causal process, an outcome of the way in which particular human beings have been caused to see the world. To prescribe a sense of community for those who lack it (a familiar feature of the politics of recently post-revolutionary states) is in effect to will them to be (or to become) different persons. In this sense community cannot exactly be a remedy for present political discontents since its absence is in large part what constitutes these discontents. What has eroded the sense of community in practice is, as Taylor is well aware, the extension of the physical scale on which human life is now organized – from villages to great cities, from local market regions to a global tissue of exchange. Even those modern societies that retain a much stronger sense of community[51] (and a consequently much greater capacity for large-scale cooperative actions) have undergone the same process of communal etiolation and deepening instrumental commitment to relatively short-term material enjoyment in drastically diminished human groupings.[52]

If the absence or thinness of community is one of the central modern political problems (already signalled, albeit a trifle ambiguously, in Benjamin Constant's insistence on the supersession of ancient by modern liberty),[53] then the mere prescription of such community cannot itself be the remedy for this problem. If the problem can be remedied at all, it can be remedied only as and where it is located, within the perceptions, judgements and sentiments of the denizens of the modern world. This was in fact quite clearly seen in the first really powerful attempts to understand the significance of modern commercial civilization, both in Smith's (and Dugald Stewart's) reflections on the political and cultural implications of a drastically deepened division of labour[54] and in Constant's anxieties about the strictly political viability of a regime of modern liberty.[55] The remedy which Smith, Stewart and Constant all invoked was a system of public civic education. But whatever services such a system may have performed in the nineteenth and early twentieth centuries in turning peasants into Frenchmen or polyglot immigrants into Americans, the more recent experiences of such systems in advanced capitalist societies make this remedy on its own something of a counsel of despair. Nor does it gain greatly in immediate appeal, if it is thought of as merely a complement to that other key component of the civic republican recipe for forging political community, the shaping action of a Legislator or a durably institutionalized political leadership. Indeed the political experience of the twentieth century tends to suggest two quite different guises for this proposal, one comically inefficacious and the other, although probably in the end almost equally inefficacious, at least in the meantime quite spectacularly repulsive. In the face of the pluralist and instrumental political and cultural dynamics of contemporary capitalist democracies, the very idea of morally didactic political leadership borders on the farcical, while in the chequered history of twentieth-century authoritarian socialist states its resonance is almost unequivocally sinister.

It is possible to see these in many ways singularly oppressive experiences as disclosing the ineluctable systemic properties of all known ways of organizing a modern society and perhaps even as exhausting all possible ways of organizing one, at least in broad outline. I suspect that, despite his invocation of the merits of decentralization and self-management, Taylor today finds himself a good deal closer to these two beliefs than he would at all care to be. But I do not myself think that there is any sound reason to embrace them in this form. In particular, to do so gives far too little weight to the dynamic economic, social and also political instability of the modern world and to the comparatively torpid intellectual (and imaginative) history of the last three decades. It also fails to register the extent to which this history itself represents a massive political and cultural failure, a simple wilting of human intelligence, imagination and practical skill in the face of the challenges with which the exercise of these human attributes by others in the past has confronted the generations to which all of us belong.

There is no doubt at all that this failure goes exceedingly deep; that it is a failure in reflective understanding of the ecology within which we now exist, a failure in the interpretation and transmission of humanly compelling values (who indeed is going to educate the educators: in homes, in schools, and in the universities?), and a failure even more spectacularly at the level of the exercise of state power to take the measure of the perils of modern global politics. But within the educational and political institutions of capitalist democracies there is at least little ambiguity about who it is that has failed. Democracy, in even its most bureaucratized, alienated and distanced forms, has at least *that* to be said for it.

In the end it can only be we who have failed, failed in what we have asked our political leaders, in what we have been prepared to accept from them, and failed no doubt too in what we have in one setting or another ourselves been prepared to give. In the end there can only be us to blame. Of course the 'we' in question here is a pretty expanded and polymorphous entity and there are many occasions and respects in which it is ridiculous for us to think of ourselves as a single unit – as a community. (I do not, for example, often spontaneously identify myself with Mrs Thatcher, let alone with President Reagan or Mr Gorbachev, to say nothing of M. Le Pen or Colonel Gaddafi.) But there are a number of other exceedingly important respects, eminently pragmatic as well as moral, in which all the human beings now alive on earth simply *are* a community and have in a sense been forced back into that 'great and natural Community'[56] which Locke saw as the casualty of human sin and the fragility of which he saw as the very occasion for the existence of political power at all. There are also other and more elaborately and insistently relevant respects in which all the citizens of any modern democracy belong to a single community. And so, *mutatis mutandis*, across one institutional arena after another of the space in which we now live.

If modern political community is to be elicited at all, if it is to be repaired and reconstructed rather than allowed to subside into ruins, it must be elicited where it practically obtains and elicited through a bringing into consciousness of the fact that it does practically obtain there. This is a challenge to our powers of understanding and of the communication of the results of such understanding: a challenge to professional politicians and entrepreneurs and workers, to teachers in schools and universities, to parents and children, to bankers and union leaders and farmers and policemen and soldiers. It is certainly an appeal to the resources of language, of speech, even of rhetoric. But it is most emphatically not a threnody to the ideal speech situation. Rather, it is a challenge to our capacity to *think* more perceptively together. And it rests in the end on the judgement that, however sensible most of the actions that have gone to make up the present world conjuncture may have looked at the time to the myriads of agents who have performed them, when taken together many aspects of them now look exceedingly stupid and short-sighted: just overwhelmingly unwise.

What keeps a community together through time is a sense of shared fate. Human beings today share fates with very many others in different settings and in different respects just as much as they have ever done in the past. They are very much in danger of sharing a single and definitive collective fate, as they of course in one sense have always individually shared in the end a single fate. But their capacity in practice to grasp, and to organize themselves in the light of, these common fatalities, is today exceedingly unimpressive. I think it is time that they stopped glowering resentfully at the past for having landed them in this predicament and made a rather more adventurous and adult attempt to meet it.

This is why I feel that Charles Taylor's work, extraordinarily rich and fruitful though it is in so many ways and greatly though I admire it and envy the gifts and energies which have made it possible, goes off the air at just the wrong point: at just the point where its greatest contribution might indeed begin to be made.

12

Reconceiving the Content
and Character of
Modern Political Community

The purpose of political theory is to diagnose practical predicaments and to show us how best to confront them.[1] To do this it needs to train us in three relatively distinct skills: firstly in ascertaining how the social, political and economic setting of our lives now is and in understanding why it is as it is; secondly in working through for ourselves how we could coherently and justifiably wish that world to be or become; and thirdly in judging how far, and through what actions, and at what risk, we can realistically hope to move this world as it now stands towards the way we might excusably wish it to be.

Both the first and the third of these skills – judging how the human world now is and judging how it could be brought closer to our present desires – plainly require a large measure of objectivity: a deliberate distancing from the contingencies of our own desires and sentiments. But the second skill is considerably less explicit in its demands for imaginative self-discipline. With it, unlike its two companions, it is hard to be very specific, even at this intimidating level of abstraction, without becoming rather evidently partisan.

Adepts of liberal and socialist political theory are apt to differ sharply from each other on their interpretations of the practical demands of both the first and the third skills. But neither has the least claim to monopolize these skills and neither perhaps in fact enjoys a very convincing claim even to possess them with much security. More interestingly, too, it is far from clear that adepts of either style of theory are in any way committed to disagreeing with their opponents over these two matters. And, more interestingly still, it is still quite unclear that adepts of either theory derive much aid from their theories for meeting these important challenges of practical reason.

Where liberal and socialist theories do indeed clash repeatedly and systematically is in their conceptions of how we could coherently and justifiably wish the human world to be or become. This is certainly not a trivial terrain on which to quarrel. But quarrels which take place essentially within it do not necessarily contribute greatly to political illumination, being more apt to cement a self-righteous enmity than to prompt a socially more detached and balanced view of one's own interests and entitlements within a world made up – *inter alia* – of a multiplicity of the interests, entitlements and purposes of other human beings.

All three of the skills which a political theory aspires to nurture can be thought of from a range of different viewpoints: individual, domestic class, national political community, international class, international bloc, the human species as a whole, perhaps even the set of all sentient creatures. Of these viewpoints only the very last is simply fictive (if that). But all are in a variety of ways conceptually and epistemically problematic. Liberal and socialist quarrels over the character of a desirable human world often turn on the selection of contrasting viewpoints as ultimate standards of value. But both political commitments tend to overestimate the real cognitive or moral authority which could in principle be derived merely from brandishing a chosen standard of value. The different viewpoints themselves also each enjoy a measure of practical evaluative relevance. But none, in a world that lacks a monopoly either of secular or of religious authority, has any plausible claim to conclusive weight. (The best candidate for such a weight – the possibility of human extermination as a result of thermonuclear war – has only recently become of immediate practical relevance;[2] and its relevance has as yet no very effective agency through which to make its presence felt politically.[3] The protracted squabble between liberal and socialist political theories – 'the order of egoism' and 'the order of equality'[4] – has been more instructive about the character of social and political value than over the interpretation of contemporary society or future social possibility. But even on the terrain of social and political value it has been heuristically rich – vivid and revealing about the diversity of goods and harms that it has uncovered – rather than analytically conclusive.

If the content of all three skills is in this way open to question it is important to ask how far political theory can hope to attain any determinacy at all. Most contemporary political philosophers are wont to assume that it can only hope to do so – and must therefore attempt to do so – by systematic conceptual analysis of the sole component of its subject matter that permits precise and controlled analysis: the theory of human value. Most contemporary political philosophy, accordingly, consists largely in the application of ethics to political topics: the bringing of philosophy as an achieved academic practice to bear upon the sorry conceptual disorder of public affairs. In adopting this orientation it harmonizes reassuringly enough with the massive concentration on issues of distributive justice in modern ideological conflict, both domestically and internationally. But this comforting resonance is less a token of the achieved cognitive or normative authority of political philosophy than of its radical domestication, its complete subordination to the dynamics of an existing ideological field. Indeed even a (miraculously and unfallaciously derived) convergence of normative judgement within the theory of value could only have any definite political implications if this extended also to some clear understanding of the appropriate modalities for its historical implementation. Such understandings themselves cannot in principle rest merely on the theory of value and necessarily consist predominantly in highly complex causal beliefs about the interaction between a huge range of human agencies of many different kinds. In the absence of such schemata for application, even the most elaborate specifications of human value can possess only a quite illusory political determinacy.[5]

The verdict that no sound understanding of politics can be founded on an essentially pre-political or extra-political conception of the human good is at least as old as Aristotle's criticism of the political theory of Plato. But it has lost nothing in cogency over the intervening centuries. Since the seventeenth century, and more particularly since the close of the Second World War, it has drawn powerful imaginative reinforcement from the dominant model of valid understanding prevalent in the modern world, the sciences of nature. True understanding, on this model, is the systematic analysis of natural causal systems. In the domain of politics such systems are difficult to identify with any great precision and their causal dynamics are harder still to grasp accurately. Valid understanding of politics, accordingly, focuses increasingly on current political circumstance; and any form of understanding which aspires to extend at all boldly beyond such circumstance comes to appear increasingly licentious and undisciplined. Only within the confines of the academic professions, with their ready and culturally all too well sustained moralism, can this narrow registration of political circumstance (as this now happens to be) consort comfortably and without tension with the confident judgement of the disparity between social fact and human good.

As already indicated, I doubt the ultimate intellectual coherence of these preoccupations.[6] But, more to the point, I also doubt their suitability for defining the viewpoint of political theory. In my view, by contrast, it is essentially the third skill, the causally adequate analysis of the human world in terms of its openness to human betterment (or even human preservation), that has priority in political theory. History, if anything, can tell us how we have come hither; moral philosophy, perhaps, what to make of the fact that this is where we now are. But political theory has no choice but to try to tell us how to act, given that this indeed is where we now are. This assignment does not lack stimulation. Yet it is not altogether good news for political theorists as academic practitioners. History and moral philosophy, perhaps even a modest and reasonably parochial political science, can all be turned into finely tuned academic routines. They are all open to what may often be genuinely benign intellectual routinization. (They are also, of course, open to less benign forms of intellectual routinization. But in these instances it is not routine as such which gives the grounds for objection. The conception of potentially benign intellectual routinization is the core of modern understandings of natural science as a human practice.) But judging what to do in the face of a disorderly world is not plausibly open to benign routinization of any kind. And a genuinely deep understanding of its requirements, at any rate in the world in which we ourselves happen to live, certainly at present precludes the least susceptibility to comfortable intellectual routines.

It is history directly encountered which sets the problems of well-considered action. But, contra-Hegel and therefore contra-Marx, we have no good reason any longer to presume that History has necessarily been charitable enough to furnish us with answers to these problems. The urgency and enormity of these problems obviously varies drastically from time to time and place to place. But at no time and in no place is there ever any ultimate guarantee that they will prove to be benign, simple and reassuring. The world of politics has its halcyon days, and even its more smiling epochs. But it is by its very nature a world of danger and potential extremity. It does not condemn political theorists to low levels of moral ambition – let alone to dulled moral sensibilities. But what it does do is to compel them, on pain of terminal bad faith, to locate the levels of moral ambition which they do espouse within their best causal understanding of the human world as this is, and to preclude them in consequence from subordinating their understanding of how it really is to the importunities of their own projective desires. (Hence the severely limited intellectual felicity of a political theory confined to articulating the general theory of the right or the good.)

The world in which we now live is a world of very obvious danger and potential extremity, the first epoch in human history in which it was readily open to millions of human beings to see the earth over time as a natural habitat perilous for the entire species to which they belong and, above all, the first epoch in which men and women could soberly confront the possibility of a natural end to their own species brought about through human action itself. These dangers, to be sure, for most of us bewilder more than they enlighten. The passion of fear on which Thomas Hobbes hoped to build so much is here woven too deeply into the occasions for experiencing it to lend us any very enlightening guidance on how to lower it to more tolerable levels. The classical preoccupations of political theory with legitimate rule, a domestic social good, and the casuistry of just or unjust warfare are not comprehensively irrelevant to this menace. But they fall rather obviously short of showing us how to confront it.

The two great English political theorists of the seventeenth century, Hobbes and Locke, both agreed that in an unsuperstitious idiom of human value, hedonic, utilitarian and overwhelmingly preoccupied with terrestrial consequence, the sole possible basis for establishing a stable shape and a clear structure of priorities for human practical reason lay in the identification of a human *summum malum*.[7] But neither of the two candidates which they selected for this role – individual bodily death for Hobbes or Locke's somewhat depleted conception of eternal damnation[8] – has served very effectively in this guise over the centuries that were to come. Today, however, the potential extermination of the species itself does at last offer a compelling candidate for a *summum malum*, an outcome which no sane and minimally coherent human agent could voluntarily promote. No one could be optimistic enough to expect its mere identification to clarify and simplify political rationality as dramatically as Hobbes proposed. But what it can and should do is to establish one single dominant value as the ultimate standard of political evaluation. Hence the centrality of prudence to any minimally alert modern conception of political value: the sad index that human beings have at last come politically of age and found themselves left face to face with their own intimidating powers of agency.

Prudence, for us, is not an adult psychic and cognitive privilege of the individual life cycle but an elusive collective project in which we still have almost everything to learn. At least in the domain of nuclear armaments, however, it can hardly any longer be denied that it is ours to learn as best we can. But the domain of nuclear weaponry and nuclear strategy is an almost intolerably difficult domain in which to learn anything rapidly and with much clarity. Its sheer factual complexity alone cows amateur judgement. Its hectic dilemmas leave little space between a contrived and heavily selective ingenuousness and the fearsomely institutionalized and myopic conceptions of prudence nurtured in the military and security apparatuses of the great world powers. To single out the capacity for inadvertent human extermination as the fulcrum of modern political theory must in the short run be more a recipe for despair than a ground for expecting this soon to assume a more shapely and instructive guise. In political theory, however, the short run is emphatically not all; and even the cultivation of a comfortable academic fluency need not constitute the exclusive goal of intellectual ambition.

There is much to be said for democratizing a preoccupation with the possibility of human extermination. But democratizing this preoccupation could hardly itself, in the human world in which we live (or perhaps in any possible human world in which this possibility continued to exist), democratize the responsibility for confronting this danger and handling it on our collective behalf.[9] And because it so manifestly could not, the natural human response to this threat is one of massive but angry irresponsibility – a thrilled passivity in the face of the apocalypse or an irked and touchy repudiation of either the capacity or the duty to do anything whatever about it. Most of those who do seriously consider the topic at all conclude in practice, whether they favour the retention of nuclear arms by their own state or march and demonstrate to secure its repudiation of them, that this is an area in which (as Cardinal Richelieu sought to persuade the aristocracy of early seventeenth-century France[10]) they have no choice but to let their prudence in the end be done for them. Here, as so often in political theory, only a very clear head indeed can hope to keep wholly distinct issues of well-considered social good and issues of the social and political division of labour.

The case for placing the value of prudence at the centre of modern political theory can therefore be considered more readily on a less alarming terrain: that of economic organization. If history directly encountered menaces us with the possibility (slight, substantial, or all too insistent) of the imminent extermination of mankind, it has also for several centuries confronted growing numbers of human beings with their dependence on an economic habitat that extends over the greater part of the globe. Thinking about human welfare and human entitlement since at least the days of Locke and Adam Smith has meant considering the causal complexity of an enormously complex international system of production and exchange. Over the average lifetime of a citizen of a modern industrial country almost every such citizen's prospects for enjoyment, self-development and the avoidance of physical suffering depend heavily on the terms on which and the mechanisms through which the domestic economy of their country is linked to this wider system. They depend, too, of course, at each particular point in time on the domestic politics of class struggle and its distinctive outcome.[11] But the latter dependence is one of which only a genuine political imbecile could now be comprehensively unaware, while the former, which in many respects may shape the circumstances of individual lives through time far more profoundly, has an altogether more shadowy and fitful presence in the domestic political imagination. In this field the value of prudence can hardly claim the same peremptory primacy over other values that it deserves in the face of potential annihilation. Nations can be (perhaps often are) more deeply and sincerely devoted to their cherished cultures of class antagonism, subservience or vanity than they are to the instrumental quest for a widening range of individual choices. And the view that either market or state allocation must at any point in time provide a neutral and undistorting medium for personal welfare and self-development is at best a trifle credulous. But, on balance and over time, enmity is scarcely more energizing than personal hope; and nations which find themselves imaginatively imprisoned in historical cultures of class odium and class complacency are more likely to be held there by the game-theoretic difficulties of engineering dependable improvements in anyone's welfare than they are by the sheer compulsiveness of hatred or smugness itself. The feeble impress of prudence in rationalizing modern domestic politics is, in this judgement, less a measure of the degree to which it is genuinely contested as a guiding value than a consequence of the sheer cognitive difficulty, in applying it, of lending it a convincing interpretation. (We would all of us prefer to be prudent, if only we quite saw how.) This is obviously just as much of a difficulty within practical politics as it is in abstract analysis.

On the terrain of modern politics there is evidently much to be prudent about, even if judging just what actions prudence really requires remains a dismayingly difficult feat. The great merit of prudence as a potential fulcrum for modern political theory is that it is at least fully open to the major challenges of modern politics and that it is capable of registering urgency and priority. A subsidiary virtue, political as much as moral in the spuriously democratized modern idiom of political legitimacy, is that it does take individual human beings one by one and that it addresses them in the first instance just as they actually happen to be.[12] Without being in the least sentimental about the existing cultures of particular societies, or classes, or the existing cognitive endowments of individual human adults, it does at least offer us an egalitarian and democratic idiom in which to address one another. There are many worse places from which to begin, to say nothing of less becoming tones of voice. (No real democracy is ever an exemplar of political justice. But even depleted forms of democracy are at least an expression of minimal political fellowship.)

What then is modern prudence? And what, most emphatically, is not? There is a strong tendency in modern thinking to wish to define prudence by its form rather than by its content. Prudence, modern thinkers are inclined to suppose, reduces to instrumental rationality; and instrumental rationality in turn is defined firstly in terms of given desires and given causal beliefs: as a relation between ends and causally adequate means for attaining these ends, with the causal beliefs about effective means perhaps then corrected for errors in their estimation. This is not, however, at all an adequate way of conceiving what I have in mind in employing the term 'prudence'. For me it is important to define it not positively and a priori by form but negatively and ostensively by content – and to insist, by the same token, on the open heuristic character of practical deliberation.

What is imprudent in modern political thinking is not any general aversion to precision or disinclination for closely considered instrumental calculation: very much the contrary. Rather it is our myopic sense of what needs to be considered, its insensitivity to the dynamics of relations between human individuals, groups and collectivities, its thin and impoverished grasp of the relevant causal setting within which human life now takes place. And, partly as cause and partly as consequence, the extreme difficulty which it experiences in thinking realistically about the nature and force of human values and their embodiment in the cultural and institutional substance of modern political communities.

What prudence, as I mean it, tells human beings does not take the form of clear, brief and authoritative instruction on how to act (although it might on occasion muster pretty brief, clear and authoritative suggestions on what it cannot possibly make sense to continue to do). Rather, it shows human beings why they need to see the settings of their lives in certain ways – and what sorts of practical implications follow from seeing these settings thus – and not as they at present happen to do.

One especially evocative and contentious issue in assessing the setting of the life of modern human beings is the relation between individual and community. The essence of a political community lies in a range of peculiarly insistent and morally peremptory demands on its members which are, at the same time, deeply linked to these members' own identities. This relation, it seems clear, has become deeply problematic in all modern political communities. It is now, indeed, seriously questionable how far there *are* any such things as modern political communities, as existing cognitive and affective facts rather than objects of fraud and intimidation. But it should not be supposed that this is a very novel doubt.

Thinkers as historically distant from one another as Plato and Habermas[13] have insisted that true community is incompatible with the systematic suppression of real interests. The rational priority of private preoccupations and a leisure that permits genuine contemplation over public commitments with their voracious demands on human energy has been affirmed and contested ever since systematic reflection about political life in the West first began. Ancient philosophy and Christianity state at least as powerful a case for the priority of private over public concerns as the most untrammeled or sceptical forms of modern individualism. Rameau's nephew would have held few terrors for Callicles.[14]

It is certainly not convincing to see the contrast between pre-modern and modern forms of sociality (a bleary enough categorization in itself) as resting on a putative transformation, for better or worse, of the spiritual quality of human motivation: a more insistent modern obsession with the demands of self, a less effective impress upon modern imaginations of socially inculcated structures of repression.[15] But what certainly *is* characteristic of modern sociality is a deeper suspicion than prevailed in most previous societies that the claims of communality are instruments of arbitrary power and a far richer registration of the entitlement of adult individuals to judge and value for themselves. Both of these aspects of modern consciousness have their historical precedents. But there is little doubt that their joint presence does lend modern politics at least a different tone and perhaps in some respects even a measure of distinctive content. (More external features of the modern world also of course lend to its politics plenty of further and at least equally distinctive content.)

If we take this tone essentially as given, how should we see the character of unforced and genuine political community today? Is this now simply a contradiction in terms? Is it a challenge to some comprehensive charismatic transformation of human nature – to Mao, or Pol Pot, or the Ayatollah Khomeini? What a modern political community is, I take it, is an assemblage of persons constituted as a community by the interaction between amateur, professional and official social theories[16] in the face of a varyingly shared and elusively demarcated predicament. To grasp its character it is necessary to attend not only to the distinctiveness of modern commonality but also to the distinctiveness of modern predicaments: necessary to think about these two not on their own but in relation to one another. *All* political communities, to be sure, are political artifices, dependent on cooperative and competitive skills, expressed through a more or less overt and rigid political division of labour in the face of real perils and opportunities. Modern political communities, rather palpably, find extreme difficulty in seeing themselves in just these terms and hence have historically been over the last two centuries (and emphatically remain) exceedingly bad at judging just what real perils and opportunities they do face. The distinctiveness of the predicament in which modern political communities are situated requires a far fuller treatment.[17] But here I shall principally emphasize the importance of the cohabitation of amateur, professional and official social theories within these communities.

Why should modern political communities be constituted, in this way, by the interaction of amateur, professional and official social theories. All historical states, of course, have contained both official and amateur social theories. But most historical states showed pretty muted interest in the amateur social theories of their subjects, as long as these remained reasonably discreet. Only in a small number of instances – such as the enforced community of participatory belief and practice characteristic of western European Christendom at home and abroad, and the role of the Holy Office in policing this participation [18] did amateur social theory as such become a vivid focus of governmental attention. (It is worth pondering the historical deconstruction of this enforced participation through the militant extension of the principle of toleration, which John Rawls explicitly sees as a precursor to his revised (or authorized) interpretation of the principles of justice as political rather than metaphysical.)[19]

Modern political communities for the most part purport to take amateur social theories rather seriously, because of their populist idiom of legitimacy (an idiom which has complex roots in Christianity and in the participatory requirements of an economy based on free wage labour, and which has now been extended, at least verbally, across the greater part of the world).[20] But what is diagnostically more revealing about modern political communities is not that they purport to take more seriously than their predecessors the amateur social theories which all human societies have always nurtured. Rather, it is that they also contain a new sort of social theory – professional social theory – which is institutionally distinct from the structure of government or public administration and supposedly organized around the project of systematic and open-ended causal enquiry for its own sake. If one asks *why* modern political communities (Mali, Ethiopia, the United Arab Emirates, Singapore) should all be partially constituted by this relatively novel presence – or even just why it is so omnipresent – the answer, once more, plainly lies in the prevalence of a highly developed division of labour, articulated through a global system of exchange. Of course the modern social sciences (and particularly modern economics) all have rich and complicated internal intellectual histories. But these intellectual histories are apt to be focused teleologically on the present (showing how the wonders of modern professional social theory have come to be) or else to be dissolved into a sort of pointilliste historicism in which their movement through time and space is not in itself considered as a potential bearer of significance at all.

But a major element in the political significance of modern professional social theory in fact lies just in this very movement through time and space, this steady infiltration of the terrain of modern political life by a new style of social understanding. This infiltration is itself a consequence of the increasingly obvious need to represent domestic and international social, economic and political orders as highly complex causal structures in order to cope with them in a relatively coherent way.

Neither the professional, the amateur, nor the official social theories that go into the constitution of modern political communities are at present very deft; and they are perhaps especially unimpressive (and, if one investigates the requisite history of ideas with sufficient care can perhaps even be seen to have been built historically so that they were *bound* to be particularly unimpressive) in their capacity to take sensitive and prudent account of one another. All of them, as at present shaped, urgently need to reflect upon and respond to the problems raised by this coexistence: on their co-constitutive role in forming any modern political community, in making it what it is.

Amateur, professional and official social theories, as we encounter them today, all possess their own debilities. But it is sensible for professional social theorists (political scientists, economists and so on) to address these deficiencies in the first place as these appear within their own products (even if it would not be at all sensible for them to confine their attention to doing this).

How, then, are these weaknesses to be remedied? Charles Taylor has argued illuminatingly that the most important deformations of modern professional social theory derive either from its adoption of an inappropriate epistemological model for valid understanding or from a defectively atomistic social ontology.[21] They have also derived, it should be added, from a more or less dogmatic range of presumptions about the conditions for modern economic flourishing. The inappropriate epistemological model (especially blatant in the more rigidly behaviourist zones of the human sciences) is important not merely because it in fact guarantees the generation of conclusions which are, both as stated and as naturally interpreted, actually *false*, but also because of its intimate relation to the least edifying feature of the professionalization of social understanding: the claim to an essentially spurious cognitive authority. (It is not, of course, the case that social scientists routinely do not know what they are talking about – any more than it is that politicians or civil servants or bankers or industrial workers routinely do not know what *they* are talking about. It is just that the professional afflatus of social scientists overwhelmingly encourages them to claim to know something about knowing about society which no one else knows so well – and to know it by virtue of a special set of procedures.)

The defectively atomist social ontology has an especially unfortunate impact on the understanding of the nature of human values. It does so in two distinct and not obviously rationally compatible ways: firstly by specifying the contingent current evaluative awareness and attitudes of a given population (at least towards themselves) as an evaluative standard beyond which there can be no non-superstitious form of appeal (a morally lunatic view, if ever there was one); and secondly by presenting the evaluative standard which Constant christened 'modern liberty' – the liberty to enjoy whatever one happens to find enjoyable[22] – as a right to which every individual person is evidently entitled, in and of themselves and irrespective of their attitudes, beliefs and social contribution, and not as a personal and historical privilege dependent on the good fortune of membership in a particular sort of political community and on the practical skill with which this community is kept in a condition to provide some measure of modern liberty. If one considers the plight of the hapless majority of the populations of Ethiopia, or Indonesia, or Uganda, or even the Philippines, to think of modern liberty as a right of their individual citizens which just happens sadly to be unavailable is a brutal folly. Modern liberty depends upon the organized productive powers of modern populations. These do not by themselves guarantee its provision to the majority of any population. But their absence precludes its provision. If modern liberty is an individual right in any sense at all, it is most emphatically not a *natural* right or a right of human beings as such.[23] The terrain on which modern liberty as a substantive privilege is available at all to the majority of a modern population is a system of international trade in which, as Constant himself pointed out, trade is a rather strict functional analogue of warfare on the terrain of ancient liberty.[24]

But the most crippling weakness of professional social theory lies in its incapacity to conceive itself as merely a single contributor to a complex process of mutual deliberation on the question of what we as citizens of particular communities have good reason, on one occasion after another, to *do*. This is not to say that the findings of professional social science as at present proffered, have nothing to contribute to such deliberation. It is just to insist that, despite the Augean labours of Professor Habermas, they do not conceive themselves merely as modest individual participants in collective deliberation of this kind. This is not what a modern professional socialization in social science *does* to a person: and the better it works as a socialization, the less is that the impact which it actually has.

(We all know this all too well, though we may prefer it not to be expressed in quite this manner.)

There is no doubt at all that professional social theorists already dispose between them of much understanding that collective deliberation urgently needs to take into account: that they are already major depositories in detail of the lessons of modern prudence. There is also every reason to suppose that they could amass decidedly more, if contributing to such conversations in an appropriate tone of voice was more centrally their goal. Unless, for example, we understand better than we yet do *why* states today act as they act, we can hardly deliberate very fruitfully on how they could have (or could be given) good reason to act in a more risk-reducing and need-responsive manner. (Contrast, for example, the burgeoning epicycles of marxist analysis of the performance of capitalist states with the limp ingenuousness with which the same theorists consider – where they deign to consider at all – how socialist successors could hope to build institutions that can be trusted to behave benignly and effectively.) Unless we can learn to pick out more discriminatingly which organizing doctrines of political agency loose in the world today are irretrievably superstitious, no group of persons, whether they be amateur, professional or official social theorists by vocation or avocation, can have a well-founded confidence that they are acting in a politically well-considered manner.[25] Sensitization to political or economic superstition is a very proper task for professional social theorists, even though the practical purgation of such superstition would have to be a collective project involving all three types of social actor. The urgency of such purgation is particularly acute for countries locked into these superstitions in a rigid and doctrinaire form: Albania, Chile. But in a less hectic fashion the shadow of quite evidently rationally indefensible social, political or economic belief falls patchily across the day to day political life of every community on earth. Diagnosing how things stand in a particular setting from this viewpoint is a task which professional social theorists may on occasion be genuinely equipped to carry out very much *de haut en bas*. But when it comes to proposing remedies for the ills detected, their standing requires them to proceed in an altogether more egalitarian manner.

Yet it is important also to realize that amateur social theory as this exists in the modern world is every bit as much in need of remedy as professional social theory.[26] Why is amateur social theory so inadequate today? Part of the answer is obviously, on any analysis, purely cognitive; but part also is plainly normative. The cognitive deficiencies arise especially from the spatial extension and dizzy deepening and differentiation of the relevant domains of causality which now confront amateur social theorists. Compare, for example, the problems of assessing the public interest for the Athenian *polis*. The gap between the assessment of Athenian interests by professional politicians and their assessment by ordinary members of the demos in the Assembly or in private conversation no doubt was, as Moses Finley emphasized,[27] extremely wide. But in terms at least of intelligibility there can be little question that it was a bridgeable gap – that the Athenian demos could for the most part, despite Plato, understand, if it bothered to attempt to do so, the main outlines of what it was being asked to choose about. Consider today, by contrast, the nature of decisions on energy policy, the regulation of international trade, or the design and deployment of weapon systems. In these instances it is increasingly difficult to believe that anyone at all, let alone a random member of a particular electorate, is actually equipped to understand what is being decided about.

There is certainly some consciousness of dependence on a corporate capitalist economy among the populations of advanced capitalist societies. (Human beings are not *that* unobservant.) There is also now, incipiently, some awareness of dependence on an international capitalist economy: greatest perhaps in social democratic corporatist polities heavily reliant on international trade, like Sweden and Austria.[28] But there is also among the same populations a very narrow and in many instances potentially self-frustrating understanding of the implications of this dependence. It is futile to hope to remedy the cognitive aspects of this deficiency without at the same time addressing its more intractably normative aspects.

The widening of the stage on which human life is now lived, socially, politically and economically, has certainly not by itself engineered an accompanying rise in collective moral capabilities: the capacity through mutual awareness and concern and enhanced analytic understanding to act together to generate better outcomes. (This disparity may well in the long run prove the true Achilles heel of marxism as an idiom of political understanding, investing it with an ineliminable and gratuitous optimism long after its miscellany of more specific economic and political superstitions have been laid painfully to rest. The view that History solves its own problems is a stupendously optimistic one.)

Three particular cultural and moral distortions in the political consciousness of advanced capitalist societies either arise directly from or contribute extensively to this widening gap between the collaborative skills of human populations and the complexities of the predicaments with which these are now confronted.

The prevalent political focus on instrumental interest brokerage (impeccably realistic in its own terms and incontestably connected with processes which are at work in the world) yields an accumulated outcome of frenziedly myopic greed, ecological fecklessness, confused and obstinate stasis in the relations between wealthy and poor countries, growing rigidity or aberration in the reproduction of both advanced capitalist or advanced socialist economies and of international trading regimes. The constriction (especially in the United States) of a sense of authentic belonging to narrow communities of immediate residence, as opposed to broad communities of interactive dependence, and the restriction (which may not be as novel as we like to think) of strong commitment to a national polity to occasions for chauvinist hostility towards the polities of others leaves little with which to offset imaginatively the vision of competitive interest-brokerage, and makes it hard for the citizens of a modern polity to think intelligently and politically together about the implications of the relations between their several interests.

Even the moral afflatus which Charles Taylor discerns in the values of expressive individualism[29] tends to reinforce the cultural impact of this fusion of internal manipulation and regressive and externally directed malice.

Taylor is right to insist that a hermeneutic approach is indispensable for understanding these normative distortions: that one must try to grasp (in the first instance, sympathetically) why the political, economic and social world which they inhabit and the lives that they live should appear to the denizens of advanced capitalist societies in these terms. This is not necessarily a heroic feat of the imagination for those who happen to reside in such societies themselves. In each instance the perceptual and affective orientations rest on exaggerated or caricatured representations of eminently real factors. Much of the politics of all human societies just does consist of instrumental interest brokerage (however the interests in question happen to be culturally defined). That is always a good deal of what is going on. The chauvinism that attends military action by a national state today (especially one that can plausibly represent itself as a victim of foreign aggression) may be ugly in itself and may vigorously distort understanding of the circumstances which prompted the taking of military action. But there simply is no more evocative representation of what a state is than a community mutually committed to each others' protection despite acute personal risk and in the face of real danger. It may seem an arbitrary irruption into the distributive quarrels of a regime of modern liberty; and it certainly does often have unwelcome and politically regressive consequences. But it also, necessarily, brings out unpleasant realities which are likely to lie behind collective human life until the end of human time.

Expressive individualism, then, may offer a disagreeably narcissistic and a politically obtuse conception of what it is for human beings to live well. But it also offers, as one can perhaps see in the more exploratory works of Constant himself, not just the most moralistic but also the morally most urgent construction of the human *point* of a regime of modern liberty.[30] If modern liberty is simply the liberty to enjoy whatever individuals happen to find most enjoyable, it is only likely to elicit much external respect if the pursuit of happiness is seen as a mode of strenuous self-exploration and not merely as a more or less gluttonous exercise in personal consumption for its own sake. What is politically destructive about expressive individualism is the solipsistic denial of its human context with which it is so readily combined: the tendency to treat it not as a single value among other values but as a *unique* value, the source of rights and freestanding on its own. It is barely imaginatively possible to entertain such a view without adopting a ludicrously narrow causal focus, and even harder to retain it once the causal focus has been broadened out to take in the complex communal preconditions for the collective valuing of individual enjoyment and self-exploration. Indeed, once the focus has been broadened out in this way, it is hard to avoid recognizing that modern liberty in any minimally morally coherent form practically requires the maintenance of a milieu and a world (and everything in between) propitious for modern liberty[31] – and that this maintenance can only be a complex cooperative project calling on the skill and imagination of all its adult beneficiaries, and even then depending rather amply on the generosity of Fortuna.

The remedy for the debilities of amateur social theory, then, can only be the drawing of entire adult populations more effectively into public dialogue on how such cooperation can best be sustained, a dialogue which must itself serve extensively as a medium of civic education. All projects of civic education in which official social theory, deployed through the coercive agencies of the state, forms the medium of education falter on the question of who is to educate the educators. The true heresy of the modern political imagination is the presumption that just *one* of the three contributors to this dialogue, amateur, professional or official social theory, might hold authentic and final authority for a modern society – and modern political process then become firmly didactic under its aegis. (It is a heresy, naturally, that is especially prevalent amongst those who are themselves in a position to determine the content of official social theory.) All three contributors have pressed their claims frequently enough. But in the end the idea of *monopolizing* legitimate authority in a modern political community is a contradiction in terms.

To remedy official social theory is a more uphill task virtually everywhere. In capitalist democracies it is hard to distinguish from the project of reconstituting a more compelling and effective embodiment for political community itself. But this is because the locus of imprudence in the official social theories of advanced capitalism lies less in the formal doctrines of state, or even perhaps in the fundamental forms of the productive order,[32] than in the vast tissue of accumulated causal belief that swathes its state apparatuses (and extends more diffusely out among the amateur social theorists of the demos at large). In those societies where official social theory (of a deeply injudicious kind as at present understood) is impacted upon the very form of the state, its remedy is a still starker challenge (though, of course, one can also see, more encouragingly, almost the entire history of these regimes as a densely but erratically obstructed quest for a consequentially somewhat less imprudent economic and political order than that they first thought of – or initially improvised). Certainly, making a prison and calling it emancipation has proved in the longer run a bad recipe for extending anything which one could defensibly refer to as modern liberty.

Modern political association, as we encounter it and seek to understand it and act within it, exhibits a massive (though, to be sure, a far from uniform) range of deficiencies. These deficiencies can be seen in many different terms: as contingent and unintended outcomes of intended actions which were readily historically intelligible and perhaps often, in an unexacting sense, even *rational*, as failures in socialization (a particularly treacherous zone in both modern liberal and modern socialist thinking), as failures in cultural reproduction or in political imagination. (These differences in vision do not necessarily reflect causal disagreements. They may simply reflect preferences in the allocation of blame.)

What is important, once again, is to refuse in the first instance to privilege one set of these terms against the others. Human beings today live in an extravagantly complicated world. What they need to learn to do is to acknowledge, understand and respond to its complexity. Learning to acknowledge this is in the first instance potentially an exercise in individual self-discipline. But learning to understand it, and above all learning how to respond to it are practical skills which they can only learn *together* (if at all): can only teach themselves and teach each other in active political dialogue with one another.

Both professional and official social theories in the modern world are apt to enter this dialogue in decidedly the wrong tone of voice, as instructors proffering solutions and not as joint explorers, bringing the resources of special experience to bear on a common predicament of which their personal understanding is necessarily severely partial.

If political community is to be revivified and rendered heuristically more sensitive and morally better disciplined, rendered more capable of identifying and reproducing a habitat genuinely propitious for modern liberty, it cannot hope to be so under the aegis of any simple doctrine of objective social good, still less one which is the private possession of the holders of state power or the privileged cynosure of a particular academic profession, like economics. Nor can it hope to be so by deploying a conception of the real character of collective human life from which the idea of social good has been eliminated (except as a contingent feature of the psychic history of individuals or collectivities) in favour of a purely causal vision of mutual manipulation. The social good for a particular collectivity is something which its members must seek to discover together, with whatever mutual tolerance and patience they can muster. It is not something of which they could in principle be authoritatively informed from without. The claim to a privileged, or an extrahistorical and procedurally guaranteed, access to the content of the overall social good on the part of any subset of a human population is politically perni-cious in the world in which we live. (No doubt in fact it became politically pernicious in many settings an exceedingly long time ago.) Where the objective social good is seen today as the private possession of a ruling organ like a party, it is not a whit more acceptable than its historical fore-runners in the construction of modern state power, the absolute monarchies defended by Bodin and Filmer.[33] Like absolute monarchy, the coercively sustained and monopolistic claim to political authority by a separate ruling organ is not a form of civil society at all.[34]

In the relatively prosperous territories of advanced capitalism, however, the immediate impediments to political progress are a good deal less condensed and obtrusive (which is not to say that there is any inordinate difficulty in identifying many of them). But there is one area that does impede such progress in an especially tenacious and dangerous fashion. It is the understanding of the nature and implications of the poli-tical division of labour in every modern society. It has been clear since at least the eighteenth century that the fundamental basis of the societies that take modern liberty as their goal is an ever deepening division of labour, both technically and spatially. Many of the most glaring instances of imprudence in the politics of advanced capitalist societies (to say nothing of on the whole slightly less advanced socialist societies) are actually located in the ways in which the political division of labour is itself conceived. (Consider, for example, the question of safety in the design of energy installations, or the provision of effective territorial defence for human populations, or the monitoring, domestically and internationally, of the trade-offs between pollution and the growth of productivity.)

There are, to be sure, modern doctrines of political right which brush such issues aside, entrusting power and responsibility firmly either to politico-moral specialists (bureaucrats advised by social scientists) or to the fitful and poorly informed caprice of the populace at large (an effective denial that there either is or needs to be any serious division of political labour at all). But it does not take a very subtle political sensibility to grasp that any of these is likely to generate (as each very abundantly has) a singularly corrupt and evasive style of social understanding. Liberal democracy, of course, does not itself endorse any of these models. (For that matter, no self-respecting democracy could do so.) It prescribes that official social theory should be the outcome of a free and open encounter between professional and amateur social theory. But this prescription is very often not offered in good faith; and it is virtually never fully implemented in practice.

There are many areas in which it could be instructive to consider the problematic relation between official, professional and amateur social theory within the political life of a modern capitalist democracy. One particularly important one, which must here serve as exemplary, is the relation between official, professional and amateur political economies.[35] Every denizen of a modern society has some more or less hazy set of beliefs about the economic habitat within which they exist. Every modern government has a corresponding, and immensely more elaborate if not necessarily any more coherent, set of beliefs on the same topic; and most modern societies are also extensively endowed with professional economists, in and out of public service. Reflecting on the problematic relations between these three bodies of belief was in a sense where modern professional economics began. Liberal political theorists have brooded anxiously since at least the later eighteenth century on just how the putative lessons of professional political economy can be brought dependably to bear on the consciousness of those who exercise the power of the state (and thus determine the content of official social theory in the relevant respects). Not long afterwards they turned their attention to the even trickier question of how these putative lessons could be dependably extended to the politically recognized populace at large (or the latter, instead, continue to be restricted in its personnel to those judged capable of appreciating them).[36] As we all know, they are very much brooding still – and on their own terms quite rightly so.

Rulers, again, since at least the early nineteenth century[37] have wondered anxiously how their own interpretations of the implications of these lessons can be transmitted to the political body to which they find themselves effectively responsible. On this score – alas and bizarrely – the socialist tradition (which one might naively suppose to be especially intimately and challengingly confronted with the issue) has until recently had little more to offer than a habit of imbecile evasion.[38] From one angle the political history of advanced capitalism for the last two hundred years has consisted quite largely of a dialogue between these three versions of political economy. (The same would also have been true of the somewhat briefer political history of socialism, if the holders of power in the relevant countries had been sufficiently modest to permit rather more of such dialogue to occur.) Both this history and the intellectual history of economics as a professional cognitive practice turn extensively on disagreements over whether the putative lessons offered at each point by professional economists are to be judged as brutal or feckless dogmas or as predominantly rational beliefs. (Certainly they have proved over this timespan to be dogmas no more brutal or feckless, and beliefs no more questionably rational than those which have adorned the shorter tradition of socialist economic practice. Compare the Irish famine with that engendered by the Great Leap Forward.)

What requires to be underlined is the very evident need at present on the part of all participants in this dialogue (or cacophony, or bemused and resentful brawl) to reach a more self-disciplned, mutually attentive and genuinely inquiring level: a more *adult* level.

What follows from looking at modern politics (and particularly at the modern politics of advanced capitalism) in this light? Not, I think, either despair or a contrived ingenuousness. Despair may be an analytically correct conclusion from the viewpoint of a bright Martian observer. But it is not a humanly acceptable conclusion in advance of the event. Ingenuousness, alas, is all too humanly acceptable. But it is an insult to human intelligence and a powerful contribution to rendering real life in due course desperate in practice. There is no categorically more reassuring and splendid form of collective life, lurking just over the brow of the hill (or in the sybilline pages of Karl Marx or Kropotkin or John Rawls or Hayek or Schumacher) to which we can hope suddenly to break through: just less unpromising ways of continuing the forms of social life which have made us what we are and which we reproduce and refashion as we live our lives.

There are no *solutions*: just better and worse things to do and say and feel. Professional social theorists cannot cure the degeneracy of modern political life[39] by devising and applying their own patent nostrums. But what they can do is to resist its ravages within their own imaginations and strategies of emotional self-gratification, and try to do the same, as unprivileged fellow citizens, in the wider arenas in which all our fates as social creatures will in the end be determined. In their professional capacity itself they have better opportunities than anyone else enjoys to try to narrow the widening gap between the causal and moral complexity of the predicaments with which all modern political communities are confronted and the causal and moral adequacy of the understanding which they can collectively bring to bear upon these predicaments.

It would not be hard to use these opportunities better.

What modern politics most needs to recapture is a sense of the openness and the ineliminably problematic character of collective social life, of the complicated and imperfect nature of political and economic choices and of the universality of our responsibility for coping with the problems and choosing between the options that politics and economics present and will always continue to present. In recapturing this sense both Liberalism and Socialism have very evident disabilities as well as very evident strengths. The centre of gravity of each ideology is occupied by an image of unproblematic value, framed in each case by the bland presumption of a well-nigh automatic progress in human social life: the powerfully rationalizing and energizing impact of a pervasive market and the evident moral authority of the systematic rational planning of the collective production and distribution of material goods. Each of these two images of unproblematic value retains a keen critical force: the efficacy of the market in the face of the dispiriting shambles of socialist production and the dubieties of the distributive arrangements which issue from this in all actual socialist states, and the socialist image of a clear and considered public good in the face of durable mass unemployment and the rickety and disquieting structures of the world market. But neither has more than a perfunctory claim to resolve the political difficulties of the world in which we now live. As doctrines of political agency, accordingly, each offers the mirage (rather than the substance) of an effective solution to these difficulties; and by proffering the mirage it is apt to deplete still further the limited resources of imagination and energy of which human beings at any time dispose for confronting the challenges of history.

Even democracy, the least contentious, if also the vaguest,[40] of modern political values, can on its own offer little aid in meeting these challenges. True, no other simple principle of political justice has much chance of eclipsing the claims of equality of adult entitlement to political power. But this principle has already been formally conceded over much the greater part of the earth. And, as we all know, its formal concession bears pretty lightly upon practical realities. Even as an abstract standard of political value it has very palpable limitations: echoing fluently, if insincerely, a certain oecumenical modern smugness which is the very antithesis of political wisdom. As a boast of universal political prowess or an affirmation of privilege universally and justly accorded, democracy offers all too responsive a mirror to modern narcissism. It is an apt political equivalent to the sophisticated versions of liberalism advanced by American thinkers like Rawls or Dworkin which centre on the conception of an equal dignity for the values of life plans of all human beings. Only in a more anxious and fraternal form can democracy still expect to be a benign political presence in the tangled world of today. It is democracy as an acknowledgement of shared fallibility and shared vulnerability – not democracy as a boast of political capacity or a claim to political privilege – of which modern politics stands so urgently in need.

It is in this setting, I think, that the value of prudence can once more serve to steady and deepen modern political understanding. What modern politics most pressingly requires is a democratization of prudence, a spreading out of the burden of judging and choosing soberly about political questions across the entire adult populations of particular societies. A modern political community – the only genuine form of political community now possible on the scale of a nation state – would be a community which faced and accepted the need to judge and choose together, a community whose members were reared and educated on the premise that this was the responsibility which lay ahead of them at the core of adult life: this and not the opportunity to consume whatever pleasures prove to be accorded by their current market efficacy or made available to the dutiful citizen by the kind and provident ministrations of the state power.[41]

To see prudence as the central political value, central for citizens just as much as for rulers, yields a permanent reminder that all human beings may judge badly and choose, and perceive the world, greedily and intemperately. It is to see collective, like individual, life as a challenge in the face of which few are likely to have much occasion for well-founded self-satisfaction. The democratization of prudence would not be a recipe for the good life on the scale of the modern world (a prescription which may safely be left to moral philosophers or partisans of intermediate technology). It could in any case hardly suffice by itself as a recipe for the good life because it is founded on too thin a specification of human value. But what it would do is to thrust aside the presumption, as compulsively attractive to modern political moralists like Lenin or Mao or Hayek or the paladins of social democracy[42] as it was to Plato or Cardinal Richelieu, that the solution to the problems of politics is to concentrate power in just the right hands or at the service of just the right values. (This is, of course, an altogether natural perspective for those engaged in practical politics. What is the point of winning if not to press one's own choices home?)

To propose the democratization of prudence is to insist that we now understand political, social and economic life well enough to be confident of just one conclusion: that it is irretrievably problematic, and that its problems are ours to cope with for the rest of human time. Over the generations that are to come (if there are indeed generations to come), the democratization of prudence will be a precondition for anything at all resembling a good life to be in question for the vast majority of human beings: perhaps, indeed, for any life at all to be in question for them. Politics, at least, must learn to cope effectively with the preconditions for a good life before it busies itself too self-importantly with the content of such a life.

Notes

1: 11 118 1
2: 8 11 1
3: 4 136 1

1 Introduction

2

2

1 Quentin Skinner, *The Foundations of Modern Political Thought* (Cambridge University Press, Cambridge, 1978), vol. 2, pp. 349–58; and 'The state', in Terence Ball, James Farr and Russell L. Hanson (eds), *Political Innovation and Conceptual Change* (Cambridge University Press, Cambridge, 1979), pp. 90–131.

1

2 Cf. John Locke, *An Essay concerning Human Understanding*, ed. Peter H. Nidditch (Clarendon Press, Oxford, 1975); John Dunn, *Locke* (Oxford University Press, Oxford, 1984), especially pp. 65–76, 80, 83; David Hume, *A Treatise of Human Nature* (2 vols, J. M. Dent, London, 1911).

3

1

3 Cf. Bernard Manin, 'On legitimacy and political deliberation', *Political Theory*, 15(3), August 1987, pp. 338–68; John Dunn, *Rethinking Modern Political Theory* (Cambridge University Press, Cambridge, 1985), chs 9 and 10.

2

4 Cynthia Farrar, *The Origins of Democratic Thinking: The Invention of Politics in Classical Athens* (Cambridge University Press, Cambridge, 1988).

2

5 Quentin Skinner, 'The idea of negative liberty: philosophical and historical perspectives', in Richard Rorty, J. B. Schneewind and Quentin Skinner (eds), *Philosophy in History* (Cambridge University Press, Cambridge, 1984), pp. 193–221.

3

6 Cf. Carole Pateman, *Participation and Democratic Theory* (Cambridge University Press, Cambridge, 1970).

1

7 For some of the reasons why such an approach might prove helpful see Dunn, *Rethinking*, introduction, pp. 1–12; and the essays collected in John Dunn, *Political Obligation in its Historical Context* (Cambridge University Press, Cambridge, 1980).

1

8 Cf. Dunn, *Rethinking*, ch. 4, especially p. 78.

1

9 Dunn, *Political Obligation*, ch. 10.

10 John Dunn, *The Political Thought of John Locke* (Cambridge University Press, Cambridge, 1969), p. x: 'I simply cannot conceive of constructing an analysis of any issue in contemporary political theory around the affirmation or negation of anything which Locke says about political matters.'

11 Compare the judgements of Richard Tuck, *Hobbes* (Oxford University Press, Oxford, 1989), pp. 76, 91, 113, and *Natural Rights Theories* (Cambridge University Press, Cambridge, 1979); and cf. James Tully's analysis of Locke's theory of property in his *A Discourse on Property* (Cambridge University Press, Cambridge, 1980) and a series of subsequent articles culminating in his reply to 'Tully's Locke', in *Political Theory* 1989.

12 This does not entail the judgement that human agents do not have reasons of their own for their actions. See, very helpfully, Adam Przeworski, *Capitalism and Social Democracy* (Cambridge University Press, Cambridge, 1985) and, at a more firmly epistemological level, Bernard Williams, 'Internal and external reasons' in his *Moral Luck* (Cambridge University Press, Cambridge, 1981), pp. 101–13.

13 Cf. John Dunn (ed.), *The Economic Limits to Modern Politics* (Cambridge University Press, Cambridge, 1990) and Dunn, *The Politics of Socialism* (Cambridge University Press, Cambridge, 1984), Istvan Hont and Michael Ignatieff (eds), *Wealth and Virtue* (Cambridge University Press, Cambridge, 1983), especially ch. 1.

14 Compare also the introduction to the 2nd edition of John Dunn, *Modern Revolutions* (Cambridge University Press, Cambridge, 1989), pp. xv–xxix.

15 Cf. also Dunn, *Rethinking*, introduction.

16 Dunn, *Economic Limits* and *Politics of Socialism*.

17 For the distressing precariousness of the value of economic prosperity compare Donal Cruise O'Brien, John Dunn and Richard Rathbone (eds), *Contemporary West African States* (Cambridge University Press, Cambridge, 1989), conclusion.

18 Jean-François Bayart, *L'État en Afrique: la politique du ventre* (Fayard, Paris, 1989).

19 Dunn, *Rethinking*, ch. 7, pp. 119–38.

2 What is Living and What is Dead in the Political Theory of John Locke?

1 John Dunn, *The Political Thought of John Locke* (Cambridge University Press, Cambridge, 1969). Compare now John Dunn, *Locke* (Oxford University Press, Oxford, 1984); John Dunn, *Rethinking Modern Political Theory* (Cambridge University Press, Cambridge, 1985), chs 2 and 3.

2 Dunn, *Political Thought*, p. x.

3 W. V. O. Quine, *From a Logical Point of View* (Harper Torchbooks, New York, 1963), pp. 20–46, and *Word and Object* (MIT Press, Cambridge, Mass., 1960). Hilary Putnam, *Reason, Truth and History* (Cambridge University Press,

Cambridge, 1981); and more extremely Richard Rorty, *Philosophy and the Mirror of Nature* (Basil Blackwell, Oxford, 1980) and *Consequences of Pragmatism* (University of Minnesota Press, Minneapolis, 1982).

4 John Locke, 'Observations upon the growth and culture of vines and olives: the production of silk: the preservation of fruit written at the request of the Earl of Shaftesbury', in *Collected Works*, 7th edn (London, 1768), vol. 4, 645–70.

5 Compare Dunn, *Rethinking*, ch. 1.

6 Compare, for example, Michael Ayers, 'Mechanism, superaddition and the proof of God's existence in Locke's *Essay*', *Philosophical Review*, 90, 2, 1981, pp. 210–51; Dunn, *Locke*, ch. 3.

7 John Passmore, 'The idea of a history of philosophy', *History and Theory*, Beiheft V, 1965, p. 13.

8 Cf. Robert Nozick, *Anarchy, State and Utopia* (Basil Blackwell, Oxford, 1974), especially p. ix; Ronald Dworkin, *Taking Rights Seriously* (Duckworth, London, 1977).

9 Compare chapter 4 below.

10 For a sophisticated expression of this view see J. L. Mackie, 'Can there be a right-based moral theory?', in Jeremy Waldron (ed.), *Theories of Rights* (Oxford University Press, Oxford, 1984), ch. 8. But contrast the (at least equally sceptical) view of Bernard Williams, *Ethics and the Limits of Philosophy* (Fontana, London, 1985) and the less sceptical positions of John McDowell, 'Non-cognitivism and rule-following', in Steven E. Holtzman and Christopher M. Leich (eds), *Wittgenstein: To Follow a Rule* (Routledge and Kegan Paul, London, 1981), pp. 141–63, and Peter Railton, 'Moral realism', *Philosophical Review*, 95(2), April 1986, pp. 163–207.

11 See particularly James Tully, *A Discourse on Property* (Cambridge University Press, Cambridge, 1980); John Colman, *John Locke's Moral Philosophy* (Edinburgh University Press, Edinburgh, 1983); Francesco Fagiani, *Nel Crepuscolo della probabilita* (Bibliopolis, Naples, 1983).

12 John Locke, *Epistola de Tolerantia* (*A Letter on Toleration*), ed. R. Klibansky and J. W. Gough (Clarendon Press, Oxford, 1968), p. 134.

13 Contrast Dunn, 'Rights' with Waldron (ed.), *Theories of Rights*, especially the editor's very helpful introduction.

14 John Rawls, *A Theory of Justice* (Oxford University Press, Oxford, 1972); Nozick, *Anarchy, State and Utopia*.

15 Compare now the very helpful analysis in Jeremy Waldron, *The Right to Private Property* (Clarendon Press, Oxford, 1989).

16 This is the great strength of Nozick's approach. G. A. Cohen is at present developing a searching assessment of its strengths and limitations.

17 Contrast Tully, *A Discourse* with Jeremy Waldron, 'Locke, Tully and the regulation of property', *Political Studies* 32(1), March 1984, pp. 98–106, and the contributions by Waldron, Tom Baldwin and Tully to *The Locke Newsletter*, 13, 1982; and compare Locke's repeated insistence that the central purpose of legitimate political power is the protection of property and his rejection of the possibility of legitimate prerogative taxation with the wide

latitude which he allows to prerogative authority in other aspects (Dunn, *Political Thought*, ch. 11).

18 John Locke, *Two Treatises of Government*, ed. Peter Laslett, 2nd edn (Cambridge University Press, Cambridge, 1967), II, 12, lines 14–17: 'the Phansies and intricate Contrivances of Men, following contrary and hidden interests put into Words . . . truly are a great part of the *Municipal Laws* of Countries.'

19 G. A. Cohen, 'Marx and Locke on land and labour', *Proceedings of the British Academy*, 71, 1985, pp. 357–88, especially pp. 380–1.

20 Locke, *Two Treatises*, II, 37, lines 19–20.

21 Ibid., II, 35, lines 12–13.

22 Ibid., II, 34, lines 1–7. God gave the world 'to the use of the Industrious and Rational . . . not to the Fancy or Covetousness of the Quarrelsom and Contentious'.

23 The best philosophical rendering of this is John Passmore, 'Locke and the ethics of belief', *Proceedings of the British Academy*, 64, 1978, pp. 185–208. For a biographical approach see Dunn, *Locke*, ch. 3.

24 Locke, *Letter on Toleration*.

25 Pierre Bayle, *Pensées diverses sur la comète*, ed A. Prat, E. Cornély (2 vols, Paris, 1911–12), vol. 1, pp. 301–20, 336–50; vol. 2, pp. 5–21, 102–51. For the novelty and importance of Bayle's argument see especially David Wootton, 'The fear of God in early modern political theory', *Historical Papers* (Canadian Historical Association, Vancouver, 1983), pp. 56–80.

26 Contrast Locke, *Two Treatises* with the present position of John Rawls: 'Justice as fairness: political not metaphysical', *Philosophy and Public Affairs*, 14(3), summer 1985, pp. 223–51.

27 See Dunn, *Political Thought*, chs. 2–6, 8, 10, 13.

28 Compare Dunn, 'Consent in the political theory of John Locke', in John Dunn, *Political Obligation in its Historical Context* (Cambridge University Press, Cambridge, 1980), ch. 3.

29 See especially Nozick, *Anarchy, State and Utopia*; Carole Pateman, *The Problem of Political Obligation* (John Wiley, Chichester, 1979); A. John Simmons, *Moral Principles and Political Obligations* (Princeton University Press, Princeton, 1979).

30 Dunn, *Political Obligation*, chs 6 and 7.

31 Compare John Dunn, *Western Political Theory in the Face of the Future* (Cambridge University Press, Cambridge, 1979), ch. 1.

32 Compare Dunn, 'Consent'; Hanna Pitkin, 'Obligation and consent', in Peter Laslett, W. G. Runciman and Quentin Skinner (eds), *Philosophy, Politics and Society, Fourth Series* (Basil Blackwell, Oxford, 1972), pp. 45–85; Simmons, *Moral Principles*: Patrick Riley, *Will and Political Legitimacy* (Harvard University Press, Cambridge, Mass. 1982).

33 Compare Dunn, *Political Obligation*, ch. 10, and *The Politics of Socialism* (Cambridge University Press, Cambridge, 1984).

34 'I cannot distrust that providence that hath conducted me this far.' (*The Correspondence of John Locke*, ed. E. S. de Beer (Clarendon Press, Oxford,

1976), vol. I, 163. For the importance of this orientation in the formation of Locke's personality see Dunn, *Rethinking*, ch. 1.

35 John Locke, *An Essay concerning Human Understanding*, ed. Peter H. Nidditch (Clarendon Press, Oxford, 1975), II, xxvii, 26, lines 26-8, lines 32-5; and see ibid. xxvii, 18 and 19.

36 John Locke, *The Reasonableness of Christianity* (*Collected Works*, III). Cf. Norman T. Burns, *Christian Mortalism from Tyndale to Milton* (Harvard University Press, Cambridge, Mass., 1972); D. P. Walker, *The Decline of Hell* (Routledge and Kegan Paul, London, 1964).

37 On Filmer see Dunn, *Political Thought*, ch. 6; James Daly, *Sir Robert Filmer and English Political Thought* (University of Toronto Press, Toronto, 1979); Gordon J. Schochet, *Patriarchalism in Political Thought* (Basil Blackwell, Oxford, 1975).

38 Compare Dunn, *Rethinking*, ch. 2, *Politics of Socialism*, and chapter 3 below.

39 Compare, for example, Pateman,*Problem of Political Obligation*; Benjamin Barber, *Strong Democracy* (University of California Press, Berkeley, 1980); Philip Green, *Retrieving Democracy: In Search of Civic Equality* (Rowan and Allanheld, Totowa, NJ, 1985); Robert Dahl, *A Preface to Economic Democracy* (University of California Press, Berkeley, 1985). But contrast Joseph Schumpeter, *Capitalism, Socialism and Democracy* (Allen and Unwin, London, 1959), pp. 256-302 (especially pp. 259, 261, 295, 299), and the earlier but more comprehensive political theory of the Abbé Sieyès.

3 Trust and Political Agency

1 Niklas Luhmann, *Trust and Power*, ed. T. Burns and G.Poggi (John Wiley, New York, 1979), p. 30, and 'Familiarity, confidence and trust', in Diego Gambetta (ed.), *Trust: Making and Breaking Cooperative Relations* (Basil Blackwell, Oxford, 1988), pp. 94-107.

2 David Hume, *A Treatise of Human Nature* (1739) (2 vols, J. M. Dent, London, 1911), vol. 2, p. 127.

3 Thomas C. Schelling, *Choice and Consequence* (Harvard University Press, Cambridge, Mass., 1984), ch. 9.

4 Susan James, *The Content of Social Explanation* (Cambridge University Press, Cambridge, 1984).

5 Honesty and loyalty may have been the watchwords of the European *ancien régime*, but they were the canonical values of an intensively imposed system of social discipline, not the spontaneous overflow of grateful hearts (J. C. D. Clark, *English Society 1688-1832* (Cambridge University Press, Cambridge, 1986, p. 86). Contrast William Paley's *Reasons for Contentment addressed to the Labouring Part of the British Public* (1793): 'The labour of the world is carried on by *service*, that is, by one man's working under another man's direction. I take it for granted, that this is the best way of conducting business, because all nations and all ages have adopted it. Consequently service is the relation

which, of all others, affects the greatest number of individuals . . . a continuance of this connection is frequently the foundation of so much mutual kindness and attachment that very few friendships are more cordial or more sincere; that it leaves oftentimes nothing in servitude, except the name; nor any distinction but what one party is as much pleased with, and sometimes also, as proud of, as the other' (cited by Clark).

6 Thomas Hobbes, 'Human nature' (1640), in *The Moral and Political Works of Thomas Hobbes of Malmesbury* (London, 1750), p. 19.

7 Michael Taylor, *Community, Anarchy, and Liberty* (Cambridge University Press, Cambridge, 1982).

8 John Locke, *Two Treatises of Government*, ed. Peter Laslett (Cambridge University Press, Cambridge, 1967), II, paragraphs 7–9.

9 Ibid., II, paragraphs 159–68, 199–243.

10 E. E. Evans-Pritchard, 'The Nuer of the Southern Sudan', in M. Fortes and E. E. Evans-Pritchard (eds), *African Political Systems* (Oxford University Press, London, 1940), p. 294.

11 Locke, *Two Treatises*, II, ch. 5.

12 I take this way of expressing the distinction from an essay of Frank Hahn's (in John Dunn (ed.) *The Economic Limits to Modern Politics* (Cambridge University Press, Cambridge, 1990). For the crucial political importance of accessibility see John Dunn, *The Politics of Socialism* (Cambridge University Press, Cambridge, 1984).

13 Compare John Rawls, *A Theory of Justice* (Oxford University Press, London, 1972).

14 Dunn, *Politics of Socialism*.

15 Alec Nove, *The Economics of Feasible Socialism* (Allen and Unwin, London, 1983); but compare Jon Elster (ed.), *Alternatives to Capitalism* (Cambridge University Press, Cambridge, 1988).

16 Joseph de Maistre, *The Works of Joseph de Maistre*, ed. and tr. Jack Lively (Macmillan, New York, 1964).

17 John Dunn, *Political Obligation in its Historical Context* (Cambridge University Press, Cambridge, 1980), ch. 10.

18 See chapter 9 below.

19 Luhmann, *Trust and Power*, and 'Familiarity'.

20 John Dunn, *Rethinking Modern Political Theory* (Cambridge University Press, Cambridge, 1985), ch. 2.

21 Quentin Skinner, *The Foundations of Modern Political Thought* (2 vols, Cambridge University Press, Cambridge, 1978), vol. 2.

22 Locke, *Two Treatises*, II, paragraph 14.

23 John Locke, *An Essay concerning Human Understanding*, ed. Peter H. Nidditch (Clarendon Press, Oxford, 1975), p. 74; and see also p. 69; and for the judgement compare Bernard Williams, 'Formal structures and social reality', in Gambetta (ed.), *Trust*, pp. 3–13.

24 Neal Wood, *The Politics of Locke's Philosophy* (University of California Press, Berkeley, 1983), chs 5–7; Locke, *Essay*, pp. 353–7.

25 Dunn, *Rethinking*, ch. 3.

26 John Locke, *The Correspondence of John Locke*, ed. E. S. de Beer (Clarendon Press, Oxford, 1976–9), vol. 1, p. 122.

27 Compare Ernest Gellner, 'Trust, cohesion and the social order', in Gambetta (ed.), *Trust*, pp. 142–57.

28 John Dunn, 'Rights and political conflict', chapter 4 below.

29 Dunn, *Political Obligation*, ch. 3.

30 Contrast R. M. Hare, 'The lawful government', in Peter Laslett and W. G. Runciman (eds), *Philosophy, Politics and Society. Third Series* (Basil Blackwell, Oxford, 1972), and 'Political obligation', in Ted Honderich (ed.), *Social Ends and Political Means* (Routledge and Kegan Paul, London, 1976).

31 Patrick Riley, *Will and Political Legitimacy* (Harvard University Press, Cambridge, Mass., 1982).

32 Locke, *Two Treatises*, II, ch. 5.

33 John Dunn, *The Political Thought of John Locke* (Cambridge University Press, Cambridge, 1969), especially ch. 11.

34 Allan Silver, '"Trust" in social and political theory', in G. D. Suttles, and M. N. Zald (eds), *The Challenge of Social Control* (Ablex, Norwood, NJ, 1985), and 'Friendship and trust as moral ideals', unpublished paper, American Sociological Association meeting August 1985.

35 Quentin Skinner, *Foundations*, vol. 2, and 'The state', in Terence Ball, James Farr and Norbert Hanson (eds), *Political Innovation and Conceptual Change* (Cambridge University Press, Cambridge, 1989).

36 James Tully, 'Political individualism', unpublished paper, Canadian Political Science Association meeting, Winnipeg, June 1986.

37 Silver, 'Friendship'.

38 Émile Benveniste, *Le Vocabulaire des institutions indo-européennes* (Editions de Minuit, Paris, 1969), vol. 1, pp. 103–21, especially pp. 118–19.

39 Dunn, *Political Thought*, especially p. 236n; William F. Church, *Richelieu and Reason of State* (Princeton University Press, Princeton, 1972).

40 Dunn, *Political Thought*, chs 15–19; compare C. B. Macpherson, *The Political Theory of Possessive Individualism* (Clarendon Press, Oxford, 1962).

41 Locke, *Correspondence*, vol. 4, p. 148; Dunn, *Political Obligation*, p. 243.

42 Locke, *Two Treatises*, II, paragraph 6, line 9.

43 Dunn, *Political Thought*, p. 148 n. 1.

44 St Augustine, *The City of God*, tr. Marcus Dods (2 vols, T. and T. Clark, Edinburgh, 1884), book 4, ch. 4, in vol. 1, p. 139.

45 John Locke, *Essays on the Law of Nature*, ed. W. von Leyden (Clarendon Press, Oxford, 1954), pp. 204–14.

46 Williams, 'Formal structures'.

47 Luhmann, 'Familiarity'; Silver, 'Friendship'; Elster (ed.), *Alternatives*, p. 6.

48 Compare Raymond Geuss, *The Idea of a Critical Theory* (Cambridge University Press, Cambridge, 1981).

49 Jack Lively and John Rees, *Utilitarian Logic and Politics* (Clarendon Press, Oxford, 1978), ch. 2; William Thomas, *The Philosophic Radicals* (Clarendon Press, Oxford, 1979), ch. 3.

50 L. J. Hume, *Bentham and Bureaucracy* (Cambridge University Press, Cam-

bridge, 1981); Frederick Rosen, *Jeremy Bentham and Representative Democracy* (Clarendon Press, Oxford, 1983).

51 Anthony Downs, *An Economic Theory of Democracy* (Harper and Row, New York, 1957).

52 Robert Dahl, *A Preface to Democratic Theory* (University of Chicago Press, Chicago, 1956).

53 Lively and Rees, *Utilitarian Logic*, ch. 3.

54 Mancur Olson, *The Logic of Collective Action* (Harvard University Press, Cambridge, Mass., 1965).

55 Robert Dahl, *A Preface to Economic Democracy* (University of California Press, Berkeley, 1985).

56 Mancur Olson, *The Rise and Decline of Nations* (Yale University Press, New Haven, 1982).

57 Joseph Schumpeter, *Capitalism, Socialism and Democracy* (Allen and Unwin, London, 1959), p. 229.

58 Gaines Post, *Studies in Medieval Legal Thought: Public Law and the State, 1100–1322* (Princeton University Press, Princeton, 1964), pp. 241–309, 316–18.

59 Church, *Richelieu*, pp. 34–5, 303–15.

60 Niccolò Machiavelli, *The Prince*, tr. George Bull (Penguin, Harmondsworth, 1961), ch. 18.

61 Church, *Richelieu*, pp. 190–6, 205, 244–7, 278–81, 424–6, 433, 501–2.

62 I am indebted to Quentin Skinner for underlining the importance of this point to me.

63 Alan Gewirth, 'Are there any absolute rights?', in Jeremy Waldron (ed.), *Theories of Rights* (Oxford University Press, Oxford, 1984).

64 Compare, later, John McManners, *Death and the Enlightenment* (Oxford University Press, Oxford, 1985), pp. 375–9, 550, 553.

65 Post, *Studies*, p. 305n.

66 Ibid., pp. 266–7.

67 Ibid., p. 376.

68 Skinner, 'The state'.

69 Dunn, *Political Thought*, chs 11, 12.

70 M. I. Finley, *Politics in the Ancient World* (Cambridge University Press, Cambridge, 1983).

71 See, for example, Adam Przeworski, *Capitalism and Social Democracy* (Cambridge University Press, Cambridge, 1985).

72 Alessandro Pizzorno, 'Interests and parties in pluralism', in Suzanne D. Berger (ed.), *Organizing Interests in Western Europe* (Cambridge University Press, Cambridge, 1981), and 'Sulla razionalità della scelta democratica', *Stato e Mercato*, 7, pp. 1–46; but compare Przeworski, *Capitalism*.

73 Paul Bracken, *The Command and Control of Nuclear Forces* (Yale University Press, New Haven, 1983).

74 Gellner, 'Trust'.

4 Rights and Political Conflict

1   H. L. A. Hart, *Punishment and Responsibility* (Clarendon Press, Oxford, 1968), and *Essays on Jurisprudence and Philosophy* (Clarendon Press, Oxford, 1983); Ronald Dworkin, *Taking Rights Seriously* (Duckworth, London, 1977), and *A Matter of Principle* (Harvard University Press, Cambridge, Mass., 1985).
2   W. N. Hohfeld, *Fundamental Legal Conceptions as Applied in Judicial Reasoning* (Yale University Press, New Haven, 1919); Jeremy Waldron (ed.), *Theories of Rights* (Oxford University Press, Oxford, 1984), pp. 5-8.
3   John Dunn, *Western Political Theory in the Face of the Future* (Cambridge University Press, Cambridge, 1979).
4   Compare J. Mackie, *Ethics: Inventing Right and Wrong* (Penguin, Harmondsworth, 1977), and 'Can there be a right-based moral theory?', in Waldron (ed.), *Theories of Rights*, and S. Blackburn, 'Reply: Rule-following and moral realism', in Steven Holtzman and Christopher Leich (eds), *Wittgenstein: To Follow a Rule* (Routledge and Kegan Paul, London, 1981), with J. McDowell, 'Non-cognitivism and rule-following', in Holtzman and Leich (eds), *Wittgenstein*, and J. Raz, 'Right-based moralities', in Waldron (ed.), *Theories of Rights*.
5   D. Malone, *The Story of the Declaration of Independence* (Oxford University Press, Oxford, 1975); G. Wills, *Inventing America: Jefferson's Declaration of Independence* (Doubleday, New York, 1978).
6   Alan Gewirth, 'Are there any absolute rights?', in Waldron (ed.), *Theories of Rights*; A. J. Simmons, 'Inalienable rights and Locke's Treatises', *Philosophy and Public Affairs*, 12(3), 1983, pp. 175-204.
7   Compare R. Nozick, *Anarchy, State and Utopia* (Basil Blackwell, Oxford, 1974) with G. A. Cohen, 'Capitalism, freedom and the proletariat', in Alan Ryan (ed.), *The Idea of Freedom* (Oxford University Press, Oxford, 1979), R. Dworkin, 'What is equality? Part 1: Equality of welfare. Part 2: Equality of resources', *Philosophy and Public Affairs*, 10(3 and 4), pp. 185-246, 283-345, and Gregory Vlastos, 'Justice and equality', in Waldron (ed.), *Theories of Rights*.
8   ? J. Finnis, *Natural Law and Natural Rights* (Clarendon Press, Oxford, 1980).
9   Mackie, 'Can there be a right-based moral theory?', p. 170.
10   Raz, 'Right-based moralities', p. 182; H. Putnam, *Reason, Truth and History* (Cambridge University Press, Cambridge, 1981), pp. 127-216.
11   Compare A. MacIntyre, *After Virtue: A Study in Moral Theory* (Duckworth, London, 1981), Putnam, *Reason, Truth and History*, Raz, 'Right-based moralities', and T. Scanlon, 'Rights, goal and fairness', in Waldron (ed.), *Theories of Rights*, with B. Williams, *Moral Luck* (Cambridge University Press, Cambridge, 1981), pp. 101-13, and *Ethics and the Limits of Philosophy* (Fontana/Collins, London, 1985).
12   Blackburn, 'Reply'; Putnam, *Reason, Truth and History*; Waldron (ed.), *Theories of Rights*; Williams, *Ethics*.
13   John Dunn, *Locke* (Oxford University Press, Oxford, 1984).

14 John Dunn, *Rethinking Modern Political Theory* (Cambridge University Press, Cambridge, 1985), pp. 13–67.

15 'If therefore Men in this Life only have hope; if in this Life they can only enjoy, 'tis not strange, nor unreasonable, that they should seek their Happiness by avoiding all things, that disease them here, and by pursuing all that delight them . . . For if there be no Prospect beyond the Grave, the inference is certainly right, *Let us eat and drink*, let us enjoy what we delight in, *for tomorrow we shall die* . . . Men may chuse different things, and yet all chuse right, supposing them only like a Company of poor insects, whereof some are Bees, delighted with Flowers, and their sweetness; others, Beetles, delighted with other kind of Viands; which having enjoyed for a season, they should cease to be, and exist no more for ever.' (John Locke, *An Essay concerning Human Understanding*, ed. Peter H. Nidditch (Clarendon Press, Oxford, 1975), pp. 269–70.) For the impact on Locke's understanding of rights see A. J. Simmons 'Inalienable rights', especially p. 204.

16 For the cultural and political importance of their subsequent divergence see John Dunn, *Political Obligation in its Historical Context* (Cambridge University Press, Cambridge, 1980), pp. 243–99; Putnam, *Reason, Truth and History*.

17 Compare Williams, *Moral Luck*, pp. 101–13.

18 Mackie, 'Can there be a right-based moral theory?', pp. 170–1.

19 Compare virtually all the contributions to Waldron (ed.), *Theories of Rights*. On a common contemporary philosophical understanding, the design of moral theories is in effect their profession. But compare Williams, *Ethics*; R. Rorty, *Philosophy and the Mirror of Nature* (Princeton University Press, Princeton, 1979).

20 Scanlon, 'Rights, goals and fairness'.

21 S. Scheffler, *The Rejection of Consequentialism* (Clarendon Press, Oxford, 1982); Dworkin, *Taking Rights Seriously* and 'What is equality?'.

22 Nozick, *Anarchy, State and Utopia*.

23 Mackie, 'Can there be a right-based moral theory?'.

24 Raz, 'Right-based moralities'; Dunn, *Rethinking*, pp. 139–89.

25 Raz, ibid.

26 It is conceptually more than a little obscure how such a process is to be understood on a modern liberal theory. But compare R. Geuss, *The Idea of a Critical Theory* (Cambridge University Press, Cambridge, 1981).

27 R. Dworkin, 'Rights as trumps', in Waldron (ed.), *Theories of Rights*, p. 158.

28 Dunn, *Rethinking*, pp. 34–54; A. Kenny, *The Logic of Deterrence* (Firethorn Press, London, 1985).

29 A. MacIntyre, 'The indispensability of political theory', in David Miller and Larry Siedentop (eds), *The Nature of Political Theory* (Clarendon Press, Oxford, 1983); C. Taylor, 'Political theory and practice', in Christopher Lloyd (ed.), *Social Theory and Political Practice* (Clarendon Press, Oxford, 1983); Dunn, *Rethinking*, pp. 119–38.

30 T. Hobbes, *De Cive: The English Version*, ed. Howard Warrender (Clarendon Press, Oxford, 1983), pp. 46, 75, 84, 95, 137–8, 196, 229.

31 Raz, 'Right-based moralities', p. 187.

226 to pages 52-59

32   Dworkin, *Taking Rights Seriously* and 'Rights as trumps'.

33   Raz, 'Right-based moralities'.

34   Dunn, *Political Obligation*, pp. 249–99. For the analogous pressure in social explanation see S. James, *The Content of Social Explanation* (Cambridge University Press, Cambridge, 1984); Dunn, *Rethinking*, pp. 119–38.

35   S. Lukes, *Marxism and Morality* (Clarendon Press, Oxford, 1985). I do not wish to defend the view that this failure is compatible with the fundamental principles of socialism (compare J. Elster *Making Sense of Marx* (Cambridge University Press, Cambridge, 1985); John Dunn, *The Politics of Socialism*, Cambridge University Press, Cambridge, 1984)). I merely note the historical and conceptual pressures involved.

36   O. Gierke, *Natural Law and the Theory of Society 1500 to 1800*, tr. Ernest Barker (2 vols, Cambridge University Press, Cambridge, 1934).

37   J. H. Goldthorpe (ed.), *Order and Conflict in Contemporary Capitalism* (Clarendon Press, Oxford, 1984).

38   R. Tuck, *Natural Rights Theories; Their Origin and Development* (Cambridge University Press, Cambridge, 1979).

39   Dunn, *Rethinking*; Raz, 'Right-based moralities'.

40   This is not in my view an intellectually defensible conception of what an ideology really is – Dunn, *Political Obligation*, pp. 81-111, and *Rethinking*; Elster, *Making Sense of Marx* (Cambridge University Press, Cambridge, 1985). But it is a conception that social scientists are apt to find particularly compelling.

41   Dunn, *Politics of Socialism*, Adam Przeworski, *Capitalism and Social Democracy* (Cambridge University Press, Cambridge, 1985); more equivocally, Elster, *Making Sense of Marx*.

42   Geuss, *The Idea of a Critical Theory*.

43   M. Olson, *The Logic of Collective Action* (Harvard University Press, Cambridge, Mass., 1965) and *The Rise and Decline of Nations* (Yale University Press, New Haven, 1982); Elster, *Making Sense of Marx*.

44   Waldron (ed.), *Theories of Rights*.

45   Q. Skinner, 'The idea of negative liberty: philosophical and historical perspectives', in Richard Rorty, J. B. Schneewind and Quentin Skinner (eds), *Philosophy in History* (Cambridge University Press, Cambridge, 1984), and 'The paradoxes of political liberty', in *The Tanner Lectures on Human Values*, vol. VII, ed. Sterling M. McMurrin (University of Utah Press, Salt Lake City, 1986).

46   Elster, *Making Sense of Marx*.

47   Przeworski, *Capitalism*.

48   Olson, *Logic of Collective Action* and *Rise and Decline*.

49   Dunn, *Political Obligation*, pp. 249–99, and *Politics of Socialism*.

50   And no doubt, more surreptitiously, in every modern socialist society. And perhaps, functionalist social anthropology notwithstanding, in every geographically extended human society there has ever been.

51   J. Lear, 'Leaving the world alone', *Journal of Philosophy*, 79(7), 1982, pp. 382–403; Putnam, *Reason, Truth and History*; Rorty, *Philosophy*.

52 John Locke, *Two Treatises of Government*, ed. Peter Laslett (Cambridge University Press, Cambridge, 1960).
53 Vlastos, 'Justice and equality'; Dworkin, 'What is equality?' and 'Rights as trumps'.
54 Gewirth, 'Are there any absolute rights?'.
55 Simmons, 'Inalienable rights'.

5 Liberty as a Substantive Political Value

1 Quoted in Robin Milner-Gulland, 'Heroes of their time', in Alan Ryan (ed.), *The Idea of Freedom* (Oxford University Press, Oxford, 1979), p. 118.
2 Isaiah Berlin, *Four Essays on Liberty* (Oxford University Press, London, 1969).
3 Ibid., p. 163.
4 Benjamin Constant, *De la Liberté des anciens comparée à celle des modernes*, see Constant, *Cours de politique constitutionelle* (Bechet, Paris and Rouen, 1820), vol. 4, part 8, pp. 238–74. On Constant's thoughts see the introduction to Biancamaria Fontana's edition of Benjamin Constant, *Political Writings* (Cambridge University Press, Cambridge, 1988), which gives an English translation of some of Constant's major political works, and Stephen Holmes, *Benjamin Constant and the Making of Modern Liberalism* (Yale University Press, New Haven, 1984).
5 See, for example, Quentin Skinner, 'The idea of negative liberty: philosophical and historical perspectives', in Richard Rorty, J. B. Schneewind and Quentin Skinner (eds), *Philosophy in History* (Cambridge University Press, Cambridge, 1984), pp. 193–221.
6 Thomas Hobbes, *Leviathan*, ed. Michael Oakeshott (Basil Blackwell, Oxford, 1946), 'A review and a conclusion', p. 465; 'And as to the whole doctrine, I see not yet, but the principles of it are true and proper; and the ratiocination solid.'
7 See John Rawls, *A Theory of Justice* (Oxford University Press, Oxford, 1972), and 'Kantian constructivism in moral theory', *Journal of Philosophy*, 77(9), September 1980, pp. 515–72; and cf. Michael J. Sandel, *Liberalism and the Limits of Justice* (Cambridge University Press, Cambridge, 1982).
8 Skinner, 'Idea of negative liberty'.
9 Niccolò Machiavelli, *Discourses on the First Ten Books of Titus Livy*, see *The Chief Works and Others*, tr. A. Gilbert (3 vols, Duke University Press, Durham, N. Carolina, 1965).
10 Skinner, 'Idea of negative liberty'.
11 John Dunn, *The Politics of Socialism: An Essay in Political Theory* (Cambridge University Press, Cambridge, 1984).
12 Constant, *De la Liberté*, p. 238.
13 Ibid., pp. 238–9.
14 Ibid., p. 239, and cf. Thomas Paine's insistence on the novelty of representative government: *The Rights of Man*, part II (1792) (J. M. Dent, London, 1915), pp. 176–7.

15 Constant, *De la Liberté*, p. 240. For a very helpful assessment of the historical setting of these judgements see Istvan Hont and Michael Ignatieff (eds), *Wealth and Virtue* (Cambridge University Press, Cambridge, 1983), especially the editors' introduction and the chapters by Robertson and Hont.

16 Constant, *De la Liberté*, p. 240.

17 Ibid., p. 241.

18 Ibid., p. 242.

19 Ibid.

20 Ibid., p. 243.

21 Ibid.

22 Ibid., p. 253.

23 Ibid., p. 260.

24 Ibid., p. 265.

25 Ibid., p. 244.

26 Ibid., pp. 244, 250–1.

27 Ibid., p. 244.

28 Ibid., p. 245.

29 Ibid.

30 Ibid., p. 246.

31 Ibid.

32 Ibid., p. 248.

33 Cf. Lord Palmerston's view that 'Half-civilised governments require a dressing down every eight to ten years' (cited in Anthony G. Hopkins, 'Property rights and empire building: Britain's annexation of Lagos, 1861', *Journal of Economic History*, 40(4), December 1980, p. 795).

34 Constant, *De la Liberté*, p. 248.

35 Ibid.

36 Ibid., p. 249. It is this line of thought which has culminated in the modern economic theory of democracy. For an attractive demolition of the latter see Alessandro Pizzorno, 'Sulla razionalità della scelta democratica', *Stato e Mercato*, 7, April 1983, pp. 1–46.

37 See particularly Adam Smith, *An Inquiry into the Nature and Causes of the Wealth of Nations*, ed. R. Campbell, A. Skinner and W. Todd (Clarendon Press, Oxford, 1976), vol. I, pp. 412–22; vol. II, pp. 712 ff.

38 Constant, *De la Liberté*, p. 249.

39 Ibid., p. 251.

40 Ibid., p. 252.

41 Ibid., p. 253.

42 Ibid., p. 257.

43 Ibid., p. 258.

44 Ibid.

45 Ibid., p. 265.

46 Ibid., p. 266.

47 Ibid., pp. 267–8.

48 Ibid., pp. 268–9.

49 Compare John Locke's view – letter to Edward Clarke, 17 October 1690:
   'the zeale and forwardness of you your selves makes it needlesse for us without dores soe much as to thinke of the publique which is the happyest state
   a country can be in, when those whose businesse it is, take such care of
   affairs that all others quietly and with resignation acquisce and thinke it
   superfluous and impertinent to medle or beat their heads about them.' See
   The Correspondence of John Locke, ed. E. S. de Beer (Clarendon Press, Oxford,
   1979), vol. 4, p. 148.

50 Constant, *De la Liberté*, p. 269.

51 Ibid., p. 270.

52 Ibid., pp. 271–2.

53 See Derek Parfit, *Reasons and Persons* (Clarendon Press, Oxford, 1984),
   especially chs 1 and 6 and appendix I.

54 Constant, *De la Liberté*, p. 273.

55 Machiavelli, *Discourses*, p. 137. (I take this presentation of Machiavelli's view
   directly from Skinner, 'The idea of negative liberty'.)

56 Machiavelli, *Discourses*, p. 174.

57 Ibid., p. 176.

58 Ibid., p. 284.

59 Compare John Locke on how human beings would have good reason to live
   if there were no life beyond the grave: 'Men may chuse different things, and
   yet all chuse right, supposing them only like a Company of poor insects,
   whereof some are Bees, delighted with Flowers, and their sweetness; others,
   Beetles, delighted with other kinds of Viands; which having enjoyed for a
   season, they should cease to be, and exist no more for ever' (*Essay concerning
   Human Understanding*, ed. Peter H. Nidditch (Clarendon Press, Oxford,
   1975), p 270).

60 G. W. F. Hegel, *The Philosophy of Right*, tr. T. M. Knox (Oxford, 1942),
   addition to paragraph 324, pp. 295–6.

61 Julian H. Franklin, *Jean Bodin and the Rise of Absolutist Theory* (Cambridge
   University Press, Cambridge, 1973).

62 John Dunn, *Western Political Theory in the Face of the Future* (Cambridge University Press, Cambridge, 1979).

63 Constant, *De la Liberté*, p. 269.

64 Edmund Burke, *Reflections on the Revolution in France* (J. M. Dent, London,
   1910), pp. 38–47. And cf. François Furet, *Interpreting the French Revolution*, tr.
   E. Forster (Cambridge University Press, Cambridge, 1981), especially
   pp. 65, 181–3.

65 Emmanuel Joseph Sieyès, *Qu'est-ce que le Tiers Etat*, translated as *What is the
   Third Estate?* by M. Blondel (Pall Mall Press, London, 1963), and the magisterial analysis of Pasquale Pasquino, 'E. J. Sieyès: la "politique constitutionelle" de la "commercial society"', Kings College Research Centre paper,
   July 1984.

66 Sieyès, *Third Estate*, pp. 53–7, 104, 177, 178, 186.

67 M. I. Finley, *Politics in the Ancient World* (Cambridge University Press,
   Cambridge, 1983).

68   Skinner, 'Idea of negative liberty'; and see Quentin Skinner, 'Machiavelli on the maintenance of liberty', *Politics*, 18(2), November 1983, pp. 3–15.

69   Gerald C. MacCallum Jr, 'Negative and positive freedom', *Philosophical Review*, 76, 1967, pp. 312–34; and, more boldly, Charles Taylor, 'What's wrong with negative freedom?', in Ryan (ed.), *Idea of Freedom*, pp. 175–94.

70   The United States, as Judith Shklar points out, has been having national elections for some two centuries ('The idea of rights in the early republic', Kings College Research Centre paper, July 1984).

71   Compare Ronald Dworkin, *Taking Rights Seriously* (Duckworth, London, 1977), especially ch. 12.

72   No doubt this sensitivity is *in part* a sensitivity to the intensity of political opposition which they are likely to encounter when they do seek to employ such expedients.

73   On Skinner's compelling analysis, just the same, of course, is true of Machiavelli's recension of ancient liberty.

74   G. A. Cohen, 'Capitalism, freedom and the proletariat', in Ryan (ed.), *Idea of Freedom*, especially p. 13; and contrast Taylor, 'Negative Liberty', in the same volume, p. 182.

75   David Hume, *A Treatise of Human Nature* (J. M. Dent, London, 1911), book III, ch. ii, section ii, in vol. 2, pp. 198–200.

76   See chapter 7 below.

77   John Dunn, 'Social theory, social understanding and political action', in Christopher Lloyd (ed.), *Social Theory and Political Practice*, Wolfson College Lectures, 1981, pp. 109–35.

78   Cf. Chalmers Johnson, *MITI and the Japanese Miracle: The Growth of Industrial Policy 1925–1975* (Stanford University Press, Stanford, 1982).

79   Cf. John Dunn, *Western Political Theory*; *Politics of Socialism*; *Political Obligation in its Historical Context* (Cambridge University Press, Cambridge, 1980); *Rethinking Modern Political Theory* (Cambridge University Press, Cambridge, 1985). And for a stimulating contrasting perspective see Larry Siedentop, 'Two liberal traditions', in Ryan (ed.), *Idea of Freedom*, pp. 153–74.

80   Karl Marx, *Contribution to the Critique of Hegel's Philosophy of Law: Introduction*, see Karl Marx and Frederick Engels, *Collected Works*, vol. 3 (Lawrence and Wishart, London, 1975), especially pp. 184–86).

81   Sieyès, *Third Estate*; the significance of the presumed commonality of interest is well emphasized by Pasquale Pasquino, 'E. J. Sieyès e la Rappresentanza politica: Progetto per una ricerca', *Quaderni Piacentini*, 12, 1984, especially pp. 75–81.

82   Dunn, *Politics of Socialism*.

83   Cf. Parfit, *Reasons and Persons*, especially ch. 1.

84   Cf. John Dunn, 'Hoc signo victor eris: representation, allegiance and obligation in the politics of Ghana and Sri Lanka', in Dunn, *Political Obligation*, ch. 7.

85   Dunn, *Western Political Theory*, ch. 1.

86   Dunn, 'The future of political philosophy in the West', in *Rethinking*.

87   H. L. A. Hart, 'Between utility and rights', in Ryan (ed.), *Idea of Freedom*, p. 84.

88   Cohen, 'Capitalism, freedom and the proletariat', and Michael Taylor, *Community, Anarchy and Liberty* (Cambridge University Press, Cambridge, 1982).

89   Dunn, 'Future of political philosophy', and *Political Obligation*, ch. 10.

90   Contrast the works of Joseph de Maistre, Thomas Carlyle and George Fitzhugh. For an excellent presentation of the merits of this release see Pizzorno, 'Sulla razionalità'.

91   Cf. Paul Bracken, *The Command and Control of Nuclear Forces* (Yale University Press, New Haven, 1983).

6 Revolution

1   For the importance of this contrast see Bernard Williams, *Problems of the Self* (Cambridge University Press, Cambridge, 1973), pp. 187–206; and in relation to political understanding see chapter 8 below.

2   Marquis de Condorcet, 'Sur le sens du mot "révolutionnaire"', *Journal d'instruction sociale*, 1 June 1793: 'De révolution, nous avons fait révolutionnaire; et ce mot, dans son sens general, exprime tout ce qui appartient à une révolution.

     'Mais on l'a créé pour la nôtre, pour celle qui, d'un des Etats soumis depuis plus longtemps au despotisme, a fait, en peu d'années, la seule république ou la liberté ait jamais eu pour base une entière égalité des droits. Ainsi, le mot révolutionnaire ne s'applique qu'aux révolutions qui ont la liberté pour objet.

     'On dit qu'un homme est révolutionnaire, c'est-à-dire, qu'il est attaché aux principes de la révolution, qu'il agit pour elle, qu'il est disposé à se sacrifier pour la soutenir.

     'Un esprit révolutionnaire est un esprit propre à produire, à diriger une révolution faite en faveur de la liberté.' M-J-A-N Condorcet, *Oeuvres* (12 vols, Firmin Didot, Paris, 1847), vol. 12, pp. 616–24, at pp. 616–17.

3   Arthur Hatto, '"Revolution": an enquiry into the usefulness of an historical term', *Mind*, NS, 58(232), 1949, pp. 495–517.

4   Compare the discussions in Plato's *Republic*, Aristotle's *Politics* and Thucydides' *History of the Peloponnesian War* with M. I. Finley, *Politics in the Ancient World* (Cambridge University Press, Cambridge, 1983) and G. E. M. de Ste Croix, *The Class Struggle in the Ancient Greek World from the Archaic Age to the Arab Conquests* (Duckworth, London, 1981).

5   Polybius, *The Histories*, 6.2–9, *politeion anakuklosis*, see the translation by W. R. Paton (Loeb Classical Library/Heinemann, London, 1954), vol. 3, pp. 270–89, 288. And see Kurt von Fritz, *The Mixed Constitution in Antiquity* (Columbia University Press, New York, 1954); F. W. Walbank, *Polybius* (University of California Press, Berkeley, 1972), chs 1 and 5; Arnaldo Momigliano, *Alien Wisdom: The Limits of Hellenization* (Cambridge University Press, Cambridge, 1975), ch. 2.

6   For the most expansive presentation of this movement of thought see
    J. G. A. Pocock, *Politics, Language and Time* (Methuen, London, 1972), ch. 4,
    and *The Machiavellian Moment; Florentine Political Thought and the Atlantic
    Republican Tradition* (Princeton University Press, Princeton, 1975). The key
    text is Machiavelli's *Discourses on the First Ten Books of Titus Livius*.

7   Most strikingly perhaps, in the Great Rebellion in mid-seventeenth-century
    England.

8   Jacob Viner, *The Role of Providence in the Social Order: An Essay in Intellectual
    History* (American Philosophical Society, Philadelphia, 1972). Cf. St Augus-
    tine, *City of God*; Adam Smith, *An Inquiry into the Nature and Causes of the
    Wealth of Nations*; Karl Marx and Frederick Engels, *Manifesto of the Communist
    Party* 1848), in Marx and Engels, *Collected Works*, vol. 6 (Lawrence and
    Wishart, London, 1976), pp. 477–519.

9   Hatto, '"Revolution"'; Karl Griewank, *Der Neuzeitliche Revolutionsbegriff:
    Enstehung und Entwicklung*, 2nd edn (Europäische Verlagsanstalt, Frankfurt
    am Main, 1969).

10 John Locke: '*sufficient to establish the Throne of our Great Restorer, Our present
    King William.*' John Locke, *Two Treatises of Government*, ed. Peter Laslett, 2nd
    edn (Cambridge University Press, Cambridge, 1967), preface, p. 155. For the
    context in Locke's own thinking see John Dunn, *Locke* (Oxford University
    Press, Oxford, 1984), chs 1 and 2. For the seventeenth century application of
    the term see Vernon F. Snow, 'The concept of revolution in seventeenth-
    century England', *Historical Journal*, 5(2), 1962, pp. 167–74. There is an
    extensive, if somewhat undisciplined, discussion of seventeenth-century
    usage in Melvin J. Lasky, *Utopia and Revolution* (Macmillan, London, 1976).

11 James Harrington, *The Prerogative of Popular Government*: 'Property coms to
    have a being before empire and government two ways, either by a natural or
    violent revolution. Natural revolution happens from within, or by com-
    merce, as when a government erected upon one balance, that for example of
    a nobility or a clergy, thro the decay of their estates come to alter to another
    balance; which alteration in the root of property, leaves all to confusion, or
    produces a new branch or government, according to the kind or nature of
    the root. Violent revolution happens from without, or by arms, as when
    upon conquest there follows confiscation.' In *The Oceana and other Works of
    James Harrington*, ed. John Toland (Becket and Cadell, London, 1771),
    p. 228.

12 François Guizot, *Collection des mémoires relatifs à la révolution d'Angleterre* (25
    vols, Paris, 1823–5) and *Histoire de la révolution d'Angleterre* (Paris, 1826),
    vol. 1. For Guizot's own political orientation see now Pierre Rosanvallon, *Le
    Moment Guizot* (Gallimard, Paris, 1985), especially pp. 16–25, 'Terminer la
    Révolution'. For the contrasting seventeenth-century application of the
    term see Hatto, '"Revolution"', especially pp. 504–5; Snow, 'Concept of
    revolution' (e.g. Anthony Ascham, *Of the Confusions and Revolutions of Govern-
    ment*).

13 Compare John Kenyon, *Revolution Principles: The Politics of Party 1689–1720*
    (Cambridge University Press, Cambridge, 1977) with the striking account of

Locke's own more concrete hopes and purposes in Richard Ashcraft, *Revolutionary Politics and Locke's Two Treatises of Government* (Princeton University Press, Princeton, 1986).

14 Bernard Bailyn, *The Ideological Origins of the American Revolution* (Harvard University Press, Cambridge, Mass., 1967).

15 Cf. Gordon Wood, *The Creation of the American Republic 1776–87* (University of North Carolina Press, Chapel Hill, 1969) with the quality of reflection chronicled in Durand Echeverria, *Mirage in the West: A History of the French Image of American Society to 1815*, 2nd edn (Princeton University Press, Princeton, 1968).

16 George V. Taylor, 'Non-capitalist wealth and the origins of the French revolution', *American Historical Review*, 62(2), 1967, pp. 429–96; Colin Lucas, 'Nobles, bourgeois and the origins of the French revolution', *Past and Present*, 60, 1973, pp. 84–126; William Doyle, *Origins of the French Revolution* (Oxford University Press, Oxford, 1980); François Furet, *Interpreting the French Revolution*, tr. E. Forster (Cambridge University Press, Cambridge, 1982).

17 Laurence L. Bongie, *David Hume: Prophet of the Counter-Revolution* (Clarendon Press, Oxford, 1965), especially pp. xv, xvi, 59n, 66, 77, 81, 123–4, 126, 159.

18 Keith Michael Baker, 'Enlightenment and revolution in France: old problems, renewed approaches', *Journal of Modern History*, 53(2), 1981, pp. 281–303; 'French political thought at the accession of Louis XVI', *Journal of Modern History*, 50(2), 1978, pp. 279–303; and 'On the problem of the ideological origins of the French revolution', in Dominick LaCapra and Steven L. Kaplan (eds), *Modern European Intellectual History: Reappraisals and New Perspectives* (Cornell University Press, Ithaca, 1982).

19 See particularly Keith Michael Baker, 'A script for the French revolution: the political consciousness of the Abbé Mably', *Eighteenth Century Studies*, 14(3), 1981, pp. 235–63, and the remarkable vision of Diderot in the year 1774, cited in Reinhard Koselleck, *Futures Past: On the Semantics of Historical Time*, tr. Keith Tribe (MIT Press, Cambridge, Mass., 1985), pp. 19–20. Chapters 1 and 3 of Koselleck's impressive book are especially instructive on the character of the modern concept of revolution.

20 See particularly Istvan Hont and Michael Ignatieff (eds), *Wealth and Virtue: The Shaping of Political Economy in the Scottish Enlightenment* (Cambridge University Press, Cambridge, 1983), ch. 1; also Ronald L. Meek, *Social Science and the Ignoble Savage* (Cambridge University Press, Cambridge, 1976) and Donald Winch, *Adam Smith's Politics: An Essay in Historiographic Revision* (Cambridge University Press, Cambridge, 1978).

21 Joseph Barnave, *Introduction à la révolution française*, ed. Fernand Rude (Armand Colin, Paris, 1960), chs 1 and 2; English translation in Emanuel Chill (ed.), *Power, Property and History* (Harper and Row, New York, 1971). There remained, however, a distinct degree of political discomfort: see the illuminating discussion in Biancamaria Fontana, *Rethinking the Politics of Commercial Society: The Edinburgh Review 1802–1832* (Cambridge University

Press, Cambridge, 1985), ch. 1. For the interpretations of English historians in the nineteenth century see Hedva Ben-Israel, *English Historians on the French Revolution* (Cambridge University Press, Cambridge, 1968).

22 Emmanuel Joseph Sieyès, *What is the Third Estate?*, tr. M. Blondel (Pall Mall, London, 1963). (For Sieyès' political thinking see Paul Bastid, *Sieyès et sa pensée* (Hachette, Paris, 1970) and Pasquale Pasquino, 'E. J. Sieyès e la Rappresentanza politica: Progetto per una ricerca', *Quaderni Piacentini*, 12, 1984 and 'E. J. Sieyès: la "Politique Constitutionelle" de la "Commercial Society"', Kings College, Cambridge, Research Centre Paper, July 1984; Thomas Paine, *The Rights of Man* (J. M. Dent, London, 1915).

23 George E. Rudé, *The Crowd in the French Revolution* (Clarendon Press, Oxford, 1959); Albert Soboul, *The Parisian Sans-Culottes and the French Revolution 1793-4*, tr. G. Lewis (Clarendon Press, Oxford, 1964) and 'Some problems of the revolutionary state 1789-1796', *Past and Present*, 65, 1974, pp. 52-74.

24 Sylvain Maréchal, *Manifeste des Égaux*, in Filippo Michele Buonarroti, *Conspiration pour l'égalité dite de Babeuf* (Editions Sociales, Paris, 1957): 'La révolution française n'est que l'avant-courière d'une autre révolution bien plus grande, bien plus solonnelle, et qui sera la dernière' (vol. 2, pp. 94-8, at 95), and the judgement of Buonarroti himself several decades later: 'Il ne tint, peut-être, qu'á un acte de sévérité de plus, que la cause du genre humain ne remportât en France un triomphe complet et éternel' (vol. 1, p. 58n,and see also p. 57n). Compare Karl Marx, *On the Jewish Question* (1844), in Marx and Engels, *Collected Works*, vol. 3 (Lawrence and Wishart, London, 1975), p. 156.

25 Edmund Burke, *Reflections on the French Revolution* (J. M. Dent, London, 1910); Joseph de Maistre: 'L'histoire n'a qu'un cri pour nous apprendre que les révolutions commencées par les hommes les plus sages, sont toujours terminées par les fous; que les auteurs en sont toujours les victimes, et que les efforts des peuples pour créer ou accroître leur liberté, finissent presque toujours par leur donner des fers. On ne voit qu'abîmes de tous côtés.' Maistre, *Du Pape* (Desclée de Brouwer, Lille, 1890), book 2, p. 148. Also Louis-Ambroise de Bonald, *Théorie du pouvoir politique et religieux dans la société civile*, ed. C. Capitan (Union Générale d'Editions, Paris, 1965).

26 Joseph de Maistre, *Considérations sur la France* (1796) (J. B. Pélaguad, Lyon and Paris, 1852), ch. 1, 'Des révolutions', especially p. 5: 'Ce qu'il y a de plus frappant dans la révolution française, c'est cette force entrainante qui courbe tous les obstacles. Son tourbillon emporte comme une paille légère tout ce que la force humaine a su lui opposer: personne n'a contrarié sa marche impunément. . . . On a remarqué, avec grande raison, que la révolution française mène les hommes plus que les hommes ne la mènent. . . . Les scélérats même qui paraissent conduire la révolution, n'y entrent que comme de simples instruments: et dès qu'ils ont la prétention de la dominer, ils tombent ignoblement. Ceux qui ont établi la république,l'ont fait sans le vouloir, et sans savoir ce qu'ils faisaient; ils y ont été conduits par les événements: un projet antérieur n'aurait pas reussi.' Page 7: 'Le torrent révolu-

tionnaire a pris successivement différentes directions; et les hommes plus marquants dans la révolution n'ont acquis l'espèce de puissance et de célébrité qui pouvait les appartenir, qu'en suivant le cours du moment: dès qu'ils ont voulu le contrarier, ou seulement s'en écarter en s'isolant, en travaillant trop pour eux, ils ont disparu de la scène.' page 8: 'On ne saurait troup le répéter, ce ne sont point les hommes qui mènent la révolution, c'est la révolution qui emploie les hommes.' Burke, *Reflections*, especially p. 7: 'liberty, when men act in bodies, is *power*.'

27   R. B. Rose, *Gracchus Babeuf: The First Revolutionary Communist* (Edward Arnold, London, 1978); Elizabeth L. Eisenstein, *The First Professional Revolutionist: Filippo Michele Buonarroti* (Harvard University Press, Cambridge, Mass., 1959); Samuel Bernstein, *Auguste Blanqui and the Art of Insurrection* (Lawrence and Wishart, London, 1971); Alan B. Spitzer, *The Revolutionary Theories of Louis Auguste Blanqui* (Columbia University Press, New York, 1957).

28   Don Locke, *A Fantasy of Reason: The Life and Thought of William Godwin* (Routledge and Kegan Paul, London, 1980); Christopher H. Johnson, *Utopian Communism in France: Cabet and the Icarians 1839–1851* (Cornell University Press, Ithaca, 1974); Barbara Taylor, *Eve and the New Jerusalem* (Virago, London, 1983); Gregory Claeys, 'Owenism, democratic theory and political radicalism: an investigation of the relationship between socialism and politics in Britain 1820–1852', unpublished Ph.D. dissertation, Cambridge University, 1983.

29   Jacques Mallet du Pan (1796): 'There has been formed in Europe a league of fools and fanatics who, if they could, would forbid man the faculty to think or see. The sight of a book makes them shudder; because the Enlightenment has been abused they would exterminate all those they suppose enlightened ... Persuaded that without men of intelligence there would have been no revolution, they hope to reverse it with imbeciles.' Quoted in Norman Hampson, *The Enlightenment* (Penguin, Harmondsworth, 1968), p. 260. Cf. the proposal by Louis de Bonald that the Revolution should be brought to a close by a Declaration of the Rights of God that would nullify the Declaration of the Rights of Man, in Jacques Godechot, *The Counter-Revolution: Doctrine and Action: 1789–1804*, tr. S. Attanasio (Routledge and Kegan Paul, London, 1972), p. 98.

30   For other mechanisms that assisted the continuity of this tradition of sentiment and action see, in its later stages, Patrick H. Hutton, *The Cult of the Revolutionary Tradition: The Blanquists in French Politics 1864–1893* (University of California Press, Berkeley, 1981).

31   David H. Pinkney, *The French Revolution of 1830* (Princeton University Press, Princeton, 1972); William Langer, 'The pattern of urban revolution in 1848', in Evelyn M. Acomb and Marvin L. Brown Jr (eds), *French Society and Culture since the Old Regime* (Holt, Rinehart and Winston, New York, 1966); Charles Tilly, 'The changing face of collective violence', in Melvin Richter (ed.), *Essays in Theory and History* (Harvard University Press, Cambridge, Mass., 1970); and see Tilly (ed.), *The Formation of Nation States in Western Europe*

(Princeton University Press, Princeton, 1975) on the development of the repressive capacities of modern states, along with the March 1895 introduction by Engels to Marx's *The Class Struggles in France*: 'The mode of struggle of 1848 is today obsolete in every respect' (in Marx and Engels, *Selected Works* (2 vols, Foreign Languages Publishing House, Moscow, 1958), vol. 2, pp. 118-38, especially p. 123; and see also pp. 130-4, especially p. 132 on changing weaponry, scale and mobility of modern professional armies.

32 Marx's own interpretation in fact borrowed heavily from the liberal historians of the revolution: Jean Bruhat, 'La Révolution française et la formation de la pensée de Marx', *Annales Historiques de la Révolution Française*, 48(184), 1966, pp. 125-70.

33 Karl Marx, *The Class Struggles in France 1848 to 1850*: 'A new revolution is possible only in consequence of a new crisis. It is, however, just as certain as this crisis.' In Marx and Engels, *Collected Works*, vol. 10 (Lawrence and Wishart, London, 1978), p. 135.

34 For the importance of this perspective see John Dunn, *The Politics of Socialism: An Essay in Political Theory* (Cambridge University Press, Cambridge, 1984).

35 Michael Ellman, *Socialist Planning* (Cambridge University Press, Cambridge, 1979); Frederick L. Pryor, 'Growth and fluctuations of production in OECD and East European countries', *World Politics*, 37(2), 1985, pp. 204-37; Alec Nove, *The Economics of Feasible Socialism* (Allen and Unwin, London, 1983).

36 The most impressive exception is provided by the OECD countries during the post-war boom up to 1973, and by the economy of Japan up to the present day. For the insubstantial cognitive foundations of the former see John H. Goldthorpe (ed.), *Order and Conflict in Contemporary Capitalism* (Clarendon Press, Oxford, 1984) and Mancur Olson, *The Rise and Decline of Nations* (Yale University Press, New Haven, 1982).

37 It has also been applied to an impressive variety of other types of human transformation from the neolithic to the scientific and the industrial. These usages are in every instance posterior to the political impact of the French revolution and despite their evident metaphorical extension of the initial political image it is the scale and decisiveness of the change in question which they principally underline.

38 Cf. Ellen Kay Trimberger, *Revolution from Above: Military Bureaucrats and Development in Japan, Turkey, Egypt and Peru* (Transaction Books, New Brunswick, NJ, 1978); Fred Halliday and Maxine Molyneux, *The Ethiopian Revolution* (New Left Books, London, 1981); and perhaps the nineteenth-century 'revolutions from above' orchestrated by Bismarck and Cavour.

39 The identification of all these dates is, of course, a trifle arbitrary.

40 Karl Marx, *Contribution to the Critique of Hegel's Philosophy of Law: Introduction* (1844), in Marx and Engels, *Collected Works*, vol. 3.

41 A. Walicki, *The Controversy over Capitalism* (Clarendon Press, Oxford, 1969); Franco Venturi, *Roots of Revolution*, tr. Francis Haskell (Grosset and Dunlap, New York, 1966); Teodor Shanin (ed.), *Late Marx and the Russian Road: Marx and the 'Peripheries of Capitalism'* (Routledge and Kegan Paul, London, 1983);

Baruch Knei-Paz, *The Social and Political Thought of Leon Trotsky* (Clarendon Press, Oxford, 1978), pp. 585–98.

42   Michael Löwy, *The Politics of Combined and Uneven Development: The Theory of Permanent Revolution* (New Left Books, London, 1981); Louis Althusser, *Pour Marx* (François Maspero, Paris, 1966), pp. 206–24.

43   For a modern (and admirably disinfected) recasting see Theda Skocpol's (1979) impressive *States and Social Revolutions* (Cambridge University Press, Cambridge) and see John Dunn, *Political Obligation in its Historical Context* (Cambridge University Press, Cambridge, 1980), ch. 9; also Dunn, *Rethinking Modern Political Theory* (Cambridge University Press, Cambridge, 1985), ch. 6.

44   Dunn, *Politics of Socialism* and *Rethinking*, ch. 5.

45   Dunn, *Political Obligation*, ch. 9; Alasdair MacIntyre, 'Ideology, social sciences and revolution', *Comparative Politics*, 5(3), 1973, pp. 321–42.

46   For two spirited attempts to suggest how best to conceive this see G. A. Cohen, *Karl Marx's Theory of History: A Defence* (Clarendon Press, Oxford, 1978), and Jon Elster, *Making Sense of Marx* (Cambridge University Press, Cambridge, 1985).

47   Karl Marx and Frederick Engels, 'Reviews of Chenu and de la Hodde', *Neue Rheinische Zeitung* (1850), in Marx and Engels, *Collected Works*, vol. 10, pp. 314, 318. See Richard N. Hunt, *The Political Ideas of Marx and Engels*, vol. 1 (Macmillan, London, 1975); John M. Maguire, *Marx's Theory of Politics* (Cambridge University Press, Cambridge, 1978); Hal Draper, *Karl Marx's Theory of Revolution: Part I: State and Bureaucracy* (2 vols, Monthly Review Press, New York, 1977); Alan Gilbert, *Marx's Politics: Communists and Citizens* (Martin Robertson, Oxford, 1981). For Marx's hostility to 'clever politicians' and to the political division of labour see Richard Ashcraft, 'Marx and political theory', *Comparative Studies in Society and History*, 24(4), 1984, pp. 637–71, especially p. 664.

48   'A revolution is a purely natural phenomenon which is subject to physical law rather than to the rules that determine the development of society in ordinary times. Or, rather, in revolution these rules assume a more physical character, the material force of necessity makes itself more strongly felt.' Engels to Marx 13 February 1851, in Marx and Engels, *Collected Works*, vol. 38 (Lawrence and Wishart, London, 1982), p. 290. I have taken the translation of the phrase cited in the text from Hunt, *Political Ideas*, vol. 1, p. 280.

49   See note 33 above.

50   Cited in Skocpol, *States and Social Revolutions*, p. 17.

51   Cf. for France in 1789, Georges Lefebvre, *La Grande Peur de 1789* (Société d'Edition d'Enseignement Supérieur, Paris, 1932) and *The Coming of the French Revolution*, tr. by R. R. Palmer (Vintage Books, New York, 1957); for Russia in February 1917 and the succeeding months, Marc Ferro, *The Russian Revolution of February 1917* (Routledge and Kegan Paul, London, 1972); for Iran, see chapter 7 below.

52   John Dunn, 'Understanding revolutions', *Ethics*, 92(2), 1982, pp. 299–315.

53 See Skocpol, *States and Social Revolutions*. It should be clear that the inference drawn here from this emphasis is not one made by Skocpol herself.

54 Cf. Skocpol's emphasis on the international elements in the causation of the French revolution, ibid.

55 This point is forcefully emphasized throughout Skocpol's *oeuvre*.

56 John Dunn, *Modern Revolutions: An Introduction to the Analysis of a Political Phenomenon* (Cambridge University Press, Cambridge, 1972) and 'Understanding revolutions'.

57 Compare James C. Davies, 'Towards a theory of revolution', *American Sociological Review*, 27(1), 1962, pp. 5–13 and Ted R. Gurr, *Why Men Rebel* (Princeton University Press, Princeton, 1970) with Dunn, *Modern Revolutions*, conclusion and James Farr, 'Historical concepts in political science: the case of revolution', *American Journal of Political Science*, 26(4), 1982, pp. 688–708.

58 Contrast Iran (see Theda Skocpol, 'Rentier state and Shi'a Islam in the Iranian revolution', *Theory and Society*, 11(3), 1982, pp. 265–83) and perhaps Mexico (Dunn, *Modern Revolutions*, ch. 2).

59 Cf. particularly Iran.

60 See particularly the incisive discussion in David Wootton, 'Continental rebellions and the English revolution', *Dalhousie Review*, 63, 1983, pp. 349–57, especially pp. 356–7, of Perez Zagorin's (1982) two-volume comparative study *Rebels and Rulers* (Cambridge University Press, Cambridge).

61 For the Great Rebellion see particularly Christopher Hill, *The World Turned Upside Down* (Temple Smith, London, 1972).

7 Country Risk: Social and Cultural Aspects

1 David Kern, 'The evaluation of country risk and economic potential', *Journal of the Institute of Bankers*, 102(3), July 1981, p. 76.

2 T. Fred Bergsten, Thomas Horst and Theodore H. Moran, *American Multinationals and American Interests* (Brookings Institution, Washington DC, 1978), pp. 7–15.

3 Raymond Vernon, *Storm over the Multinationals* (Macmillan, London, 1977), p. 13.

4 Ibid., p. 7.

5 W. Brandt et al., *North-South: A Programme for Survival* (Pan, London, 1980), pp. 70–1.

6 Anthony Angelini, Maximo Eng and Francis A. Lees, *International Lending, Risk and the Euromarkets* (Macmillan, London, 1979)Jonathan Eaton and Mark Gersovitz, *Poor-Country Borrowing in Private Financial Markets and the Repudiation Issue*, Princetown Studies in International Finance, 47, June 1981.

7 Kern, 'Evaluation', p. 77.

8 Ibid.

9   Ibid., p. 79.
10 Ibid., pp. 78-80.
11 Stephen J. Kobrin, 'Foreign enterprise and forced divestment in the LDCs', *International Organization*, 34(1), winter 1980, pp. 84-5.
12 Jon Elster, *Logic and Society* (Wiley, New York, 1978), ch. 3, especially pp. 50-1.
13 See especially Eaton and Gersovitz, *Poor-Country Borrowing*.
14 John Dunn, *Political Obligation in its Historical Context* (Cambridge University Press, Cambridge, 1980), ch. 9.
15 Jacques Rupnik, 'Dissent in Poland, 1966-78: the end of revisionism and the rebirth of civil society', in Rudolf L. Tökes (ed.), *Opposition in Eastern Europe* (Macmillan, London, 1979), pp. 60-112.
16 Harold C. Krogh, 'Guarantees against loss to transnational corporations', *Annals of the American Academy of Political and Social Science*, 443, May 1979, pp. 128.
17 John J. Stremlau, *The International Politics of the Nigerian Civil War 1967-1970* (Princeton University Press, Princeton, NJ, 1977).
18 For helpful, brief critiques of interpretation of work force attitudes in purely cultural terms that bring out the complicated historical interplay between work structure, political experience, and consciousness, see Michael Mann, *Consciousness and Action in the Western Working Class* (Macmillan,London, 1973) and Geoffrey K. Ingham, *Strikes and Industrial Conflict: Britain and Scandinavia* (Macmillan, London, 1974).
19 Lars H. Thunell, *Political Risks in International Business: Investment Behavior of Multinational Corporations* (Praeger, New York, 1977).
20 David A. Jodice, 'Sources of change in third world regimes for foreign direct investment 1968-1976', *International Organization*, 34(2), spring 1980, pp. 177-206.
21 R. J. Rummel and David A. Heenan, 'How multinationals analyze political risk', *Harvard Business Review*, 56(1), January-February 1978, pp. 67-76.
22 Kobrin, 'Foreign enterprise'; Jodice, 'Sources of change', - Dr Jodice subsequently took up a post with the Office of Analytical Methods of the Central Intelligence Agency (p. 178).
23 Vernon, *Storm*, pp. 151, 172; Bergsten et al.,*American Multinationals*, pp. 130-40; Kobrin, 'Foreign enterprise', p. 70.
24 Bergsten et al., cited in Kobrin, ibid.
25 Kobrin, 'Foreign enterprise', p. 73; Jodice, 'Sources of change', pp. 180, 182, 186, but cf. Paul E. Sigmund, *Multinationals in Latin America: The Politics of Nationalism* (University of Wisconsin Press, Madison, 1980).
26 David G. Bradley, 'Managing against expropriation', *Harvard Business Review*, 55(4), July-August 1977, p. 79; Kobrin, 'Foreign enterprise', p. 78; but cf. Jonathan Eaton and Mark Gersovitz, 'Country risk: economic aspects', in Richard J. Herring (ed.), *Managing International Risk* (Cambridge University Press, Cambridge, 1983).
27 Kobrin, 'Foreign enterprise', p. 83.
28 Ibid., pp. 85-6; Jodice, 'Sources of change', pp. 180, 194, 202.

29 Vernon, *Storm*.

30 Thunell, *Political Risks*, ch. 2. Graham T. Allison, *Essence of Decision: Explaining the Cuban Missile Crisis* (Little, Brown, Boston, 1971).

31 Theodore H. Moran, 'Transnational strategies of protection and defense by multinational corporations: spreading the risk and raising the cost of nationalization in natural resources', *International Organization*, 27(2), spring 1973, pp. 273–87.

32 Ibid., pp. 278–9.

33 Ibid., p. 282.

34 Ibid., pp. 284–7. For further discussion of the defensive strategies open to multinational corporations in the face of these risks, see Bradley, 'Managing against Expropriation', William A. Stoever, 'Renegotiations: the cutting edge of relations between MNCs and LDCs', *Columbia Journal of World Business*, 14(1), spring 1979, pp. 5–14, William H. Newman, 'Adapting transnational corporate management to national interests', *Columbia Journal of World Business*, 14(2), summer 1979, pp. 82–8 and Yves Doz and C. K. Prahalad, 'How MNCs cope with host government intervention', *Harvard Business Review*, 58(2), March–April 1980, pp. 149–57.

35 Chalmers Johnson, *Revolution and the Social System* (Hoover Institution Press, Stanford, Calif., 1964) and *Revolutionary Change* (Athlone, London, 1966), but cf. his *Autopsy on People's War* (University of California Press, Berkeley, 1973).

36 Ted Gurr, *Why Men Rebel* (Princeton University Press, Princeton, 1970).

37 Ted Gurr, ibid. and 'The revolution-social-change nexus: some old theories and new hypotheses', *Comparative Politics*, 5(3), April 1973, pp. 359–92; Michael C. Hudson, 'Political protest and power transfers in crisis periods', *Comparative Political Studies*, 4(3), October 1971, pp. 259–94; Gregory B. Markus and Betty A. Nesvold, 'Governmental coerciveness and political instability: an exploratory study of cross-national patterns', *Comparative Political Studies*, 5(2), July 1972, pp. 231–44.

38 Rummel and Heenan, 'How multinationals analyze political risk'.

39 P. Nagy, 'Quantifying country risk: a system developed by economists at the Bank of Montreal', *Columbia Journal of World Business*, 13(3), fall 1978, p. 141.

40 For an attempt to draw inferences from an even less promising tradition in American political science, see Robert T. Green, 'Political structures as a predictor of radical political change', *Columbia Journal of World Business*, 9(1), spring 1974, pp. 28–36.

41 Alasdair MacIntyre, *Against the Self-Images of the Age* (Duckworth, London, 1971), ch. 22; Dunn, *Political Obligation*, ch. 5.

42 Alasdair MacIntyre, 'Ideology, social science and revolution', *Comparative Politics*, 5(3), April 1973, pp. 321–42, and *After Virtue: A Study in Moral Theory* (Duckworth, London, 1981).

43 Theda Skocpol, *States and Social Revolutions* (Cambridge University Press, Cambridge, 1979).

44 John Dunn, *Modern Revolutions* (Cambridge University Press, Cambridge,

1972), *Political Obligation*, ch. 9, and 'Understanding revolutions', *Ethics*, 92(2), January 1982, pp. 299-315.

45 Dunn, *Political Obligation*, ch. 9, and 'Understanding revolutions'.

46 Dunn, *Political Obligation*, ch. 9.

47 Theda Skocpol and Ellen K. Trimberger, 'Revolutions and the world-historical development of capitalism', *Berkeley Journal of Sociology*, 22, 1977-78, pp. 101-13 and Skocpol, *States and Social Revolutions*.

48 Hamza Alavi, 'The state in post-colonial societies: Pakistan and Bangladesh', *New Left Review*, 74, July-August 1972, pp. 58-81; James O'Connor, *The Fiscal Crisis of the State* (St Martins Press, New York, 1973); Nicos Poulantzas, *Political Power and Social Classes*, tr. T. O'Hagan (New Left Books, London, 1973), *Fascism and Dictatorship*, tr. Judith White (New Left Books, London, 1974), and 'The capitalist state: a reply to Miliband and Laclau', *New Left Review*, 95, January-February 1976, pp. 62-83; Jürgen Habermas, *Legitimation Crisis*, tr. T. McCarthy (Heinemann Educational Books, London, 1976); Ralph Miliband, *Marxism and Politics* (Oxford University Press, Oxford, 1977); John Dunn (ed.), *West African States: Failure and Promise* (Cambridge University Press, Cambridge, 1978; John Holloway and Sol Picciotto (eds), *State and Capital: A Marxist Debate* (Edward Arnold, London, 1978); Göran Therborn, *What Does the Ruling Class Do When It Rules?* (New Left Books, London, 1978); Erik Olin Wright, *Class, Crisis and the State* (New Left Books, London, 1978); Theda Skocpol, 'Political response to capitalist crisis: neo-Marxist theories of the state and the case of the New Deal', *Politics and Society*, 10(2), 1980, pp. 155-202; John Urry, *The Anatomy of Capitalist Societies* (Macmillan, London, 1981).

49 Louis Hartz, *The Liberal Tradition in America* (Harcourt Brace and World, New York, 1955).

50 F. A. Hayek, *New Studies in Philosophy, Politics, Economics and the History of Ideas* (Routledge and Kegan Paul, London, 1978).

51 John Dunn, *Western Political Theory in the Face of the Future* (Cambridge University Press, Cambridge, 1979).

52 R. H. Tawney, *The Agrarian Problem in the Sixteenth Century* (Longman, London, 1912) and *Religion and the Rise of Capitalism* (Penguin, London, 1938); Eric Hobsbawm, *Primitive Rebels* (Manchester University Press, Manchester, 1959), *The Age of Revolution 1789-1848* (Weidenfeld and Nicolson, London, 1962) and *Labouring Men: Studies in the History of Labour* (Anchor Books, Garden City, NY, 1967); E. P. Thompson, 'The moral economy of the English crowd in the eighteenth century', *Past and Present*, 50, February 1971, pp. 76-136, and *Whigs and Hunters: The Origin of the Black Act* (Allen Lane, London, 1975); Christopher Hill, *Society and Puritanism in Pre-revolutionary England* (Secker and Warburg, London, 1964) and *The World Turned Upside Down* (Temple Smith, London, 1972); Douglas Hay, Peter Linebaugh and E. P. Thompson (eds), *Albion's Fatal Tree* (Allen Lane, London, 1975); Gareth Stedman Jones, *Outcast London: A Study of the Relationship Between Classes in Victorian Society* (Penguin, London, 1976); and

John Foster, *Class Struggle and the Industrial Revolution* (Methuen, London, 1977).

53 David A. Hume, *A Treatise of Human Nature* (2 vols, J. M. Dent, London, 1911); Adam Smith, *An Inquiry into the Nature and Causes of the Wealth of Nations*, ed. R. H. Campbell and A. S. Skinner (2 vols, Clarendon Pressm, 1976); see also Duncan Forbes, *Hume's Philosophical Politics* (Cambridge University Press, Cambridge, 1975) and Donald Winch, *Adam Smith's Politics* (Cambridge University Press, Cambridge, 1978).

54 John Dunn, 'From applied theology to social analysis: the break between John Locke and the Scottish enlightenment', in Istvan Hont and Michael Ignatieff (eds), *Wealth and Virtue: Political Economy and the Scottish Enlightenment* (Cambridge University Press, Cambridge, 1983).

55 But cf. Barrington Moore, *Injustice* (Macmillan, London, 1978) and, more abstractly, *Social Origins of Dictatorship and Democracy* (Beacon, Boston, 1966).

56 Anthony Giddens, *The Class Structure of the Advanced Societies* (Hutchinson, London, 1973); Mann, *Consciousness and Action*.

57 Sigmund, *Multinationals*, pp. 34, 327–8.

58 Anthony G. Hopkins, 'Property rights and empire building: Britain's annexation of Lagos, 1861', *Journal of Economic History*, 40(4), December 1980, pp. 777–98.

59 Ibid., p. 788.

60 Ibid.

61 Vernon, *Storm*, p. 151; Bergsten et al., *American Multinationals*, pp. 381–95.

62 Eric N. Baklanoff, *Expropriation of U.S. Investments in Cuba, Mexico and Chile* (Praeger, New York, 1975), pp. vi, 15, 21, 113; Sigmund, *Multinationals*.

63 Hopkins, 'Property rights', p. 795.

64 Dunn, *Political Obligation*, ch. 9.

65 Tom Kemp, *Theories of Imperialism* (Dennis Dobson, London, 1967); Roger Owen and Bob Sutcliffe (eds), *Studies in the Theory of Imperialism* (Longman, London, 1972); Michael Barratt Brown, *The Economics of Imperialism* (Penguin, London, 1974); Immanuel Wallerstein, *The Modern World-System* (Academic Press, New York, 1974); Anthony Brewer, *Marxist Theories of Imperialism: A Critical Survey* (Routledge and Kegan Paul, London, 1980); but cf. Benjamin J. Cohen, *The Question of Imperialism: The Political Economy of Dominance and Dependence* (Macmillan, London, 1974); Bill Warren, *Imperialism: Pioneer of Capitalism*, ed. John Sender (New Left Books, London, 1980); Aristide R. Zolberg, 'Origins of the modern world system: a missing link', *World Politics*, 33(2), January 1981, pp. 253–81.

66 Jodice, 'Sources of change', p. 180.

67 Hopkins, 'Property rights'; John Dunn and A. F. Robertson, *Dependence and Opportunity: Political Change in Ahafo* (Cambridge University Press, Cambridge, 1973), ch. 3.

68 James C. Scott, *The Moral Economy of the Peasant: Rebellion and Subsistence in Southeast Asia* (Yale University Press, New Haven, Conn., 1976)

69 John Rawls, *A Theory of Justice* (Oxford University Press, Oxford, 1973);

Robert Nozick, *Anarchy, State, Utopia* (Blackwell, Oxford, 1974); MacIntyre, *After Virtue*, ch. 17.

70 Cf. Harry G. Johnson, 'A theoretical model of economic nationalism in new and developing states', in H. G. Johnson (ed.), *Economic Nationalism and Old and New States* (Allen and Unwin, London, 1968), pp. 1–16.

71 Stefan H. Robock, 'Political risk: identification and assessment', *Columbia Journal of World Business*, 6(4), July–August 1971, p. 13; Harald Knudsen, *Expropriation of Foreign Private Investment in Latin America* (Universitets-forlaget, Bergen, 1974); Baklanoff, *Expropriation*; Jodice, 'Sources of change'; Kobrin, 'Foreign enterprise', p. 87; Sigmund, *Multinationals*, pp. 36–9.

72 Skocpol and Trimberger, 'Revolutions'; Dunn, *Political Obligation*.

73 Baklanoff, *Expropriation*; Sigmund, *Multinationals*.

74 Joe C. Ashby, *Organized Labor and the Mexican Revolution under Lázaro Cárdenas* (University of North Carolina Press, Chapel Hill, 1967); Clark W. Reynolds, *The Mexican Economy: Twentieth Century Structure and Growth* (Yale University Press, New Haven, Conn., 1970), ch. 6.

75 Robert F. Smith, *The United States and Cuba: Business and Diplomacy, 1917–1960* (Bookman, New York, 1960); James O'Connor, *The Origins of Socialism in Cuba* (Cornell University Press, Ithaca, NY, 1970); Dunn, *Modern Revolutions*, ch. 8; Baklanoff, *Expropriation*, pp. 15, 21; Jorge I. Dominguez, *Cuba: Order and Revolution* (Harvard University Press/Belknap Press, Cambridge, Mass., 1978).

76 Dunn, *Political Obligation*, ch. 7, especially pp. 195–205.

77 Bergsten et al., *American Multinationals*; Newman, 'Adapting transnational corporate management'; Stoever, 'Renegotiations'.

78 Sigmund, *Multinationals*; Eaton and Gersovitz, 'Country risk: economic aspects'.

79 Moran, 'Transnational strategies'; Baklanoff, *Expropriation*; Vernon, *Storm*; Bergsten et al., *American Multinationals*.

80 See, for instance, the assessment of a bitter left-wing critic of the Shah's regime given in the first edition of Fred Halliday, *Iran: Dictatorship and Development*, 2nd edn (Penguin, London, 1979).

81 William H. Sullivan, 'Dateline Iran: the road not taken', *Foreign Policy*, 40, fall 1980, pp. 175–86; Said Amir Arjomand, 'Shi'ite Islam and the revolution in Iran', *Government and Opposition*, 16(3), summer 1981, pp. 292–316.

82 Karl Marx, 'Contribution to the critique of Hegel's Philosophy of Right: introduction': 'For *one* class to represent the whole of society, another class must concentrate in itself all the evils of society, a particular class must embody and represent a general obstacle and limitation. A particular social sphere must be regarded as the *notorious crime* of the whole society, so that emancipation from this sphere appears as a general emancipation.' In Karl Marx, *Early Writings*, tr. and ed. T. B. Bottomore (McGraw-Hill, New York, 1964), pp. 41–59, at p. 56. The class terminology does not fit the Iranian case very happily, but the dynamics of the judgements in question are difficult to miss.

83   *The Times* (London), 30 June 1981.
84   George Lenczowski, 'The arc of crisis: its central sector', *Foreign Affairs*, 57(4), spring 1979, pp. 796–820.
85   Robert Graham, *Iran: The Illusion of Power*, 2nd edn (Croom Helm, London, 1979), p. 230.
86   Michael A. Ledeen and William H. Lewis, 'Carter and the fall of the Shah: the inside story', *Washington Quarterly*, spring 1980, pp. 3–40.
87   Halliday, *Iran*.
88   Lenczowski, 'Arc of crisis'; Ledeen and Lewis,'Carter and the fall of the Shah'; Sullivan, 'Dateline Iran'.
89   Lenczowski, 'Arc of crisis', p. 807.
90   London and Lewis, 'Carter and the fall of the Shah'; Sullivan, 'Dateline Iran'.
91   Hossein Mahdavy, 'Patterns and problems of economic development in rentier states: the case of Iran', in M. A. Cook (ed.), *Studies in the Economic History of the Middle East* (Oxford University Press, Oxford, 1970), pp. 428–67; Halliday, *Iran*, chs 2–4.
92   Graham, *Iran: The Illusion of Power*, pp. 235–7; Halliday, *Iran*, pp. 317–18; Arjomand, 'Shi'ite Islam', p. 306.
93   Arjomand, 'Shi'ite Islam'.
94   Graham, *Iran: The Illusion of Power*; Thomas H. Walton, 'Economic development and revolutionary upheavals in Iran', *Cambridge Journal of Economics*, 4(3), September 1980, pp. 271–92; Arjomand, 'Shi'ite Islam'.
95   Richard W. Cottam, *Nationalism in Iran*, 2nd edn (University of Pittsburgh Press, Pittsburgh, 1979), pp. 155–6.
96   Ibid., p. 156.
97   Nikki R. Keddie, 'The roots of the ulama's power in modern Iran', in Keddie (ed.), *Scholars, Saints and Sufis* (University of California Press, Berkeley, 1972), at, p. 229.
98   Hamid Algar, *Religion and State in Iran: The Role of the Ulama in the Qajar Period* (University of California Press, Berkeley, 1969).
99   Hamid Algar, 'The oppositional role of the ulama in twentieth-century Iran', in Keddie (ed.), *Scholars, Saints and Sufis*, at p. 255.
100   Algar, *Religion and State in Iran*; Keddie, 'Roots'; S. Akhari, *Religion and Politics in Contemporary Iran* (State University of New York Press, Albany, 1980); Said Amir Arjomand, 'The Shi'ite hierocracy and the state in pre-modern Iran: 1785–1890', *Archives Européennes des Sociologie*, 22(1), 1981, pp. 40–78 and 'Shi'ite Islam'.
101   Arjomand, 'Shi'ite Islam', p. 300.
102   Donal Cruise O'Brien, *The Mourides of Senegal: The Political and Economic Organization of an Islamic Brotherhood* (Oxford University Press, Oxford, 1971) and 'A versatile charisma: the Mouride brotherhood 1967–1975', *Archives Européennes de Sociologie*, 18(1), 1977, pp. 84–106.
103   Arjomand, 'Shi'ite Islam', pp. 310–13.
104   Algar, 'Oppositional role'; Gustav Thaiss, 'Religious symbolism and social

change: the drama of Husain', in Keddie (ed.), *Scholars, Saints and Sufis*, pp. 349–66.

105 Compare the assessment by Frederick Engels in 1895 of the implications of change in military technology for the prospects of urban risings: Frederick Engels, 'Introduction' (1895) to Karl Marx, *The Class Struggles in France from 1848 to 1850*, in Karl Marx and Frederick Engels, *Selected Works*, vol. 1 (Foreign Languages Publishing House, Moscow, 1958), pp. 130–4. For a useful study of Engels's thinking on this topic, see Martin Berger, *Engels, Armies and Revolution: The Revolutionary Tactics of Classical Marxism* (Archon Books, Hamden, Conn., 1977).

106 Thaiss, 'Religious symbolism', p. 365.

107 Graham, *Iran: The Illusion of Power*; Walton, 'Economic development'.

108 Richard Pfau, 'The legal status of American forces in Iran', *Middle East Journal*, 28(2), spring 1974, pp. 141–53.

109 Algar, 'Oppositional role'.

110 Graham, *Iran: The Illusion of Power*, p. 48.

111 Ibid., p. 161.

112 Ledeen and Lewis, 'Carter and the fall of the Shah'; Sullivan, 'Dateline Iran'.

113 With the essential proviso that attribution of responsibility is characteristically collective between enterprises of common national derivation, deserved odium is a necessary condition for high social and cultural risk. It is not, of course, a sufficient condition for such risk to be actualized.

114 Rummel and Heenan, 'How multinationals analyze political risk'.

115 It has been estimated that $100 million per month of private capital was leaving Iran in the period 1975–8; Graham, *Iran: The Illusion of Power*, p. 199.

116 Halliday, *Iran*, p. 156.

8 Responsibility without Power: States and the Incoherence of the Modern Conception of the Political Good

1 Is pragmatism the sole truly modern metaphysics; or is it simply a more or less effective contemporary specific against metaphysical anxieties? Compare Richard Rorty, *Philosophy and the Mirror of Nature* (Basil Blackwell, Oxford, 1980) and *Consequences of Pragmatism* (University of Minnesota Press, Minneapolis, 1982) with Bernard Williams, *Descartes: The Project of Pure Enquiry* (Penguin, Harmondsworth, 1978), *Moral Luck* (Cambridge University Press, Cambridge, 1981), chs 11 and 12, and *Ethics and the Limits of Philosophy* (Fontana, London, 1985).

2 Cf. Bertrand Badie and Pierre Birnbaum, *The Sociology of the State*, tr. Arthur Goldhammer (University of Chicago Press, Chicago, 1983).

3 Cf. Perry Anderson, *Passages from Antiquity to Feudalism* and *Lineages of the Absolutist State* (New Left Books, London, 1974). There is a helpful discussion of Anderson's approach by Mary Fulbrook and Theda Skocpol in

Theda Skocpol (ed.), *Vision and Method in Historical Sociology* (Cambridge University Press, Cambridge, 1984), pp. 170–210.

4   Badie and Birnbaum, *Sociology of the State*, chs 7 and 8, especially p. 130.

5   For a particularly sympathetic presentation of Fitzjames Stephen which nevertheless maintains a discreet moral and intellectual distance see Eric Stokes, *The English Utilitarians and India* (Oxford University Press, Delhi, 1982), especially pp. 299–300. I do not of course wish to imply any personal political sympathy with any of these markedly diverse political projects.

6   For a very helpful emphasis on the importance of this contrast see Bernard Williams, *Problems of the Self* (Cambridge University Press, Cambridge, 1973), especially, pp. 187–206.

7   For a particularly level-headed presentation of this point of view see H. L. A. Hart, *Punishment and Responsibility* (Clarendon Press, Oxford, 1968), especially ch. 1.

8   This is a question which may in fact sometimes have a cogent answer.

9   See note 1 above.

10 For the sceptical dissolution of individual identity see Derek Parfit, *Reasons and Persons* (Clarendon Press, Oxford, 1984), following David Hume. The attempt to reconstruct practical reason through the elaboration of a moral theory which Parfit essays in the same volume decidedly lacks the force of this sceptical dissolution and reaches by the close of the book a status which is little more than whimsical.

11 See Williams, 'Internal and external reasons' in *Moral Luck*, pp. 101–13.

12 See Charles Taylor, 'Political theory and practice', in Christopher Lloyd (ed.), *Social Theory and Political Practice* (Clarendon Press, Oxford, 1983), pp. 61–86, and *Philosophy and the Human Sciences* (Cambridge University Press, Cambridge, 1985), especially chs 2 and 3; Alasdair MacIntyre, 'The indispensability of political theory', in David Miller and Larry Siedentop (eds), *The Nature of Political Theory* (Clarendon Press, Oxford, 1983), pp. 17–34, *Against the Self-Images of the Age* (Duckworth, London, 1971) and *After Virtue* (Duckworth, London, 1981).

13 I have tried to sketch the indeterminacies that result from this range of considerations in Dunn, *Political Obligation in its Historical Context* (Cambridge University Press, Cambridge, 1980), ch. 10.

14 Compare Quentin Skinner, 'The idea of negative liberty: philosophical and historical perspectives', in Richard Rorty, J. B. Schneewind and Quentin Skinner (eds), *Philosophy in History* (Cambridge University Press, Cambridge, 1984), pp. 193–221.

15 Compare Dunn, *Political Obligation*, ch. 10; Williams, *Ethics*.

16 Cf. Robert Keohane, *After Hegemony* (Princeton University Press, Princeton, 1984) and 'The world political economy and the crisis of embedded liberalism', in John H. Goldthorpe (ed.), *Order and Conflict in Contemporary Capitalism* (Clarendon Press, Oxford, 1984), ch. 1.

17 Cf. Richard J. Herring (ed.), *Managing International Risk* (Cambridge University Press, Cambridge, 1983), chs 2–4.

18 For an illuminating summary see Naomi Chazan, *An Anatomy of Ghanaian*

Politics: Managing Political Recession 1969–1982 (Westview Press, Boulder, 1983). For a broader perspective see chapter 9 below.

19 Cf. Graham T. Allison, *Essence of Decision: Explaining the Cuban Missile Crisis* (Little, Brown and Co., Boston, 1971).

20 See, again, Dunn, 'Political obligation and political possibilities', chapter 10 of *Political Obligation*.

21 Cf. Amartya Sen and Bernard Williams (eds), *Utilitarianism and Beyond* (Cambridge University Press, Cambridge, 1982), introduction.

22 Lawrence Freedman, *The Evolution of Nuclear Strategy* (Macmillan, London, 1981); Michael Mandelbaum, *The Nuclear Question: The United States and Nuclear Weapons 1946–1976* (Cambridge University Press, Cambridge, 1979).

23 Cf. Charles Lipson, 'International cooperation in economic and security affairs', *World Politics*, 37(1), October 1984, pp. 1–23.

24 Paul Bracken, *The Command and Control of Nuclear Forces* (Yale University Press, New Haven, 1983).

25 Ibid. Compare Clausewitz's insistence that real war is distinguished from the blind unleashing of violence because the former 'unfolds slowly enough to remain in submission to the will of a directing intelligence' ('Willen einer leitenden Intelligenz'); Raymond Aron, *Clausewitz, Philosopher of War*, tr. Norman Stone and Christine Booker (Routledge and Kegan Paul, London, 1983), p. 66.

26 Compare Thomas Paine, *The Rights of Man* (J. M. Dent, London, 1915), p. 104: 'Ignorance is of a peculiar nature: and once dispelled, it is impossible to re-establish it. It is not originally a thing of itself, but is only the absence of knowledge; and though man may be kept ignorant, he cannot be made ignorant. The mind, in discovering truth, acts in the same manner as it acts through the eye in discovering objects; when once any object has been seen, it is impossible to put the mind back to the same condition it was in before it saw it … The means must be an obliteration of knowledge; and it has never yet been discovered how to make man *unknow* his knowledge, or unthink his thoughts.' Also Clausewitz: 'When barriers which in fact consisted only in ignorance of what was possible are broken down it is not easy to build them up again' (quoted in Mandelbaum, *Nuclear Question*, p. 99). The Clausewitz formulation, being more cautious, is more obviously cogent. Paine, in the passage in question was attempting to persuade his readers (and those of Burke) that a counter-revolution in France was a natural impossibility.

9 The Politics of Representation and Good Government in Post-colonial Africa

1 On practical reason see in particular Bernard Williams, *Problems of the Self* (Cambridge University Press, Cambridge, 1973), pp. 187–206, especially pp. 203 ('the line between discourse which … has to fit the world, and discourse which the world has to fit') and 156. For the contrasting conception

of theoretical reason see Bernard Williams, *Descartes: The Project of Pure Enquiry* (Penguin, Harmondsworth, 1978) and *Moral Luck* (Cambridge University Press, Cambridge, 1981), ch. 11; John Dunn, *Locke* (Oxford University Press, Oxford, 1984), ch. 3; and Joseph Raz (ed.), *Practical Reasoning* (Oxford University Press, Oxford, 1978), especially introduction and chapter by Wiggins. For the implications of the distinction between theoretical and practical reason in the articulation of social understanding, see Geoffrey Hawthorn, *Plausible Worlds* (Cambridge University Press, Cambridge, 1990). For a relevant instance from African political history see John Dunn (ed.), *West African States: Failure and Promise* (Cambridge University Press, Cambridge, 1978), conclusion. David Blackbourn and Geoff Eley, *The Peculiarities of German History* (Oxford University Press, Oxford, 1984) provide a helpful discussion of the difficulty of focusing an analytically relevant range of counterfactuals in relation to historical examples. See also Jon Elster, *Logic and Society: Contradictions and Possible Worlds* (John Wiley, Chichester, 1978).

2   For the proposal that practical reason should in effect replace theoretical reason in its entirety, see especially Richard Rorty, *Philosophy and the Mirror of Nature* (Basil Blackwell, Oxford, 1980) and *Consequences of Pragmatism* (University of Minnesota Press, Minneapolis, 1982).

3   Compare John Lonsdale, 'Political accountability in African history', in Patrick Chabal (ed.), *Political Domination in Africa* (Cambridge University Press, Cambridge, 1986), and Keith Hart, *The Political Economy of West African Agriculture* (Cambridge University Press, Cambridge, 1982).

4   Compare on a more local scale Jean-François Bayart, 'Civil society in Africa', in Chabal (ed.), *Political Domination*; John Dunn, 'From democracy to representation: an interpretation of a Ghanaian election', in Dunn, *Political Obligation in its Historical Context* (Cambridge University Press, Cambridge, 1980), pp. 112–56; J. D. Y. Peel, *Ijeshas and Nigerians: The Incorporation of a Yoruba Kingdom, 1890s to 1970s* (Cambridge University Press, Cambridge, 1983); Naomi Chazan, *An Anatomy of Ghanaian Politics: Managing Political Recession 1969–1982* (Westview Press, Boulder, 1983). Governmental accountability to a majority grouping in a plural state is not necessarily an unambiguous asset to its polity: compare the responses of the government in Sri Lanka to Sinhalese communal pressures, particularly in the last ten years. (For the earlier background see John Dunn, '*Hoc signo victor eris*: representation, allegiance and obligation in the politics of Ghana and Sri Lanka', in Dunn, *Political Obligation*, pp. 157–205.)

5   'To ask and have, comand and be obey'd.' Christopher Marlowe, *Tamburlaine*, Act II, Scene 5, line 62 (Roma Gill (ed.), *The Plays of Christopher Marlowe* (Oxford University Press, Oxford, 1971), p. 77).

6   See Richard Sklar, 'Democracy in Africa', in Chabal (ed), *Political Domination*.

7   See John Dunn, *The Politics of Socialism* (Cambridge University Press, Cambridge, 1984) and 'Political obligations and political possibilities', in Dunn, *Political Obligation*, pp. 243–99.

8   Dunn, 'Political obligations and political possibilities'.

9 John Dunn, *Western Political Theory in the Face of the Future* (Cambridge University Press, Cambridge, 1979), ch. 1, and compare M. I. Finley, *Politics in the Ancient World* (Cambridge University Press, Cambridge, 1983).

10 See John Dunn, 'From applied theology to social analysis: the break between John Locke and the Scottish enlightenment', in Istvan Hont and Michael Ignatieff (eds), *Wealth and Virtue* (Cambridge University Press, Cambridge, 1983), pp. 119-35; Derek Parfit, *Reasons and Persons* (Clarendon Press, Oxford, 1984), especially part 1.

11 Compare Crawford Young, *Ideology and Development in Africa* (Yale University Press, New Haven, 1982); Robert H. Bates, *Markets and States in Tropical Africa: The Political Basis of Agricultural Policies* (University of California Press, Berkeley, 1981) and *Essays on the Political Economy of Rural Africa* (Cambridge University Press, Cambridge, 1983); Dunn, *West African States*; Douglas Rimmer, *The Economies of West Africa* (Weidenfeld and Nicolson, London, 1984).

12 There are no very explicit modern theories of good government (as opposed to good organization) – in contrast with the dense seventeenth- or eighteenth-century Germanic tradition of *polizeiwissenschaft*. A misleadingly abstract version of the criterion is furnished by modern utilitarianism: compare Amartya Sen and Bernard Williams (eds), *Utilitarianism and Beyond* (Cambridge University Press, Cambridge, 1982) and Stuart Hampshire (ed.), *Public and Private Morality* (Cambridge University Press, Cambridge, 1978), chs 1 and 2. The most impressive elaborations of the standpoint are perhaps given by Hume and Hegel. See Duncan Forbes, *Hume's Philosophical Politics* (Cambridge University Press, Cambridge, 1975); Shlomo Avineri, *Hegel's Theory of the Modern State* (Cambridge University Press, Cambridge, 1972).

13 Dunn, *Politics of Socialism*.

14 Rimmer, *Economies of West Africa*; Tony Killick, *Development Economics in Action: A Study of Economic Policies in Ghana* (Heinemann Educational Books, London, 1978); Andrzej Krassowski, *Development and the Debt Trap: Economic Planning and External Borrowing in Ghana* (Croom Helm, London, 1974); Elliot J. Berg, 'Structural transformation versus gradualism: recent economic development in Ghana and the Ivory Coast', in Philip Foster and Aristide Zolberg (eds), *Ghana and the Ivory Coast: Perspectives on Modernization* (University of Chicago Press, Chicago, 1971), pp. 187-230.

15 Emmanuel Joseph Sieyès, *What is the Third Estate?*, tr. M. Blondel (Pall Mall Press, London, 1963); James Mill, *An Essay on Government* (Liberal Arts Press, New York, 1955). On Sieyès see particularly Pasquale Pasquino, 'E. J. Sieyès e la Rappresentanza politica: Progetto per una ricerca', *Quaderni Piacentini*, 12, 1984, especially pp. 75-81.

16 See Ralph Miliband, *Capitalist Democracy in Britain* (Oxford University Press, Oxford, 1982).

17 John Dunn, 'Social theory, social understanding and political action', in Christopher Lloyd (ed.), *Social Theory and Political Practice* (Oxford University Press, Oxford, 1983), pp. 109-35.

18   Hart, *Political Economy*: Bates, *Markets and States in Tropical Africa*.
19   Rimmer, *Economies of West Africa*, pp. 176, 178.
20   See Cranford Pratt, *The Critical Phase in Tanzania* (Cambridge University Press, Cambridge, 1976); Patrick Chabal, *Amilcar Cabral: Revolutionary Leadership and People's War* (Cambridge University Press, Cambridge, 1983).
21   The best overall assessment of the role of the state in modern African history is John Lonsdale, 'States and social processes in Africa: a historiographical survey', *African Studies Review*, 24 (2–3) (June–September 1981), pp. 139–225. For its role in a single country see John Iliffe's magisterial *A Modern History of Tanganyika* (Cambridge University Press, Cambridge, 1979).
22   Ruth B. Collier, *Regimes in Tropical Africa: Changing Forms of Supremacy 1945–1975* (University of California Press, Berkeley, 1982). But see also the review by Dunn, *International Journal of African Historical Studies*, 16(1), 1983, pp. 93–5.
23   For a local instance see Dunn, 'From democracy to representation'.
24   The best modern study of the concept of representation is Hanna F. Pitkin, *The Concept of Representation* (University of California Press, Berkeley, 1972). On modern representative politics in general see especially, Alessandro Pizzorno, 'Sulla razionalità della scelta democratica', *Stato e Mercato*, 7, April 1983, pp. 1–46, and 'Interests and parties in pluralism', in Suzanne Berger (ed.), *Organizing Interests in Western Europe* (Cambridge University Press, Cambridge, 1981), pp. 247–84.
25   James Mill, *Essays on Government*, pp. 69–72, especially p. 69: 'lessening of duration is the instrument by which, if by anything, the object is to be attained.' On careful examination very similar problems arise within Bentham's analysis of the problem of representation: see L. J. Hume, *Bentham and Bureaucracy* (Cambridge University Press, Cambridge, 1981); Frederick Rosen, *Bentham and Representative Democracy* (Clarendon Press, Oxford, 1983).
26   See William Thomas, 'James Mill's politics: the *Essay on Government* and the Movement for reform', *Historical Journal*, 12(2), June 1969, pp. 249–84 and 14(4), December 1971, pp. 735–50, and *The Philosophic Radicals* (Clarendon Press, Oxford, 1979).
27   See for instance T. B. Macaulay, 'Mill's Essay on Government: utilitarian logic and politics', reprinted in Jack Lively and John Rees (eds), *Utilitarian Logic and Politics* (Clarendon Press, Oxford, 1978), pp. 97–129.
28   The best accounts we possess of the incidence and character of corrupt practices come from the inquisitions conducted by avenging regimes. See, for instance for Ghana Victor T. Levine, *Political Corruption: The Ghana Case* (Hoover Institute Press, Stanford, 1975). For the Ghanaian public service background see Robert M. Price, *Society and Bureaucracy in Contemporary Ghana* (University of California Press, Berkeley, 1975).
29   Abner Cohen, *The Politics of Elite Culture* (University of California Press, Berkeley, 1981); and see *International Journal of African Historical Studies*, 15(14), 1982, pp. 715–18.

30 But see Gavin Williams and Terisa Turner, 'Nigeria', in Dunn (ed.), *West African States*, pp. 132-72.

31 For the Gold Coast see Margaret Priestley, *West African Trade and Coast Society: A Family Study* (Oxford University Press, London, 1969); Edward Reynolds, *Trade and Economic Change on the Gold Coast 1807-1874* (Longman, London, 1974); David Kimble, *A Political History of Ghana 1850-1928* (Clarendon Press, Oxford, 1963).

32 For a particularly strong statement of this theme see Rimmer, *Economies of West Africa*; but see also Hart, *Political Economy*.

33 Karl Marx, *The Eighteenth Brumaire of Louis Bonaparte*, in K. Marx and F. Engels, *Collected Works*, vol. 11 (Lawrence and Wishart, London 1979), pp. 187-93.

34 Barrington Moore, *Social Origins of Dictatorship and Democracy* (Beacon Press, Boston, 1966); James C. Scott, *The Moral Economy of the Peasant* (Yale University Press, New Haven, 1976) and 'Peasant revolution: a dismal science', *Comparative Politics*, 9(2), 1977, pp. 231-48; Samuel L. Popkin, *The Rational Peasant* (University of California Press, Berkeley, 1979); Theda Skocpol, 'What makes peasants revolutionary?', *Comparative Politics*, 14(2), April 1982, pp. 351-75; Joel S. Migdal, *Peasants, Politics and Revolution* (Princeton University Press, Princeton, 1974); J. Wilson Lewis (ed.), *Peasant Rebellion and Communist Revolution in Asia* (Stanford University Press, Stanford, 1974); Henry A. Landsberger, 'The sources of rural radicalism', in S. Bialer and S. Sluzar (eds), *Sources of Contemporary Radicalism* (Westview Press, Boulder, 1977), pp. 247-91; Jeffrey M. Paige, *Agrarian Revolution: Social Movements and Export Agriculture in the Underdeveloped World* (Free Press, New York, 1975); Eric Wolf, *Peasant Wars of the Twentieth Century* (Harper and Row, New York, 1969); and on the early stages in China see Roy Hofheinz Jr, *The Broken Wave: The Chinese Communist Peasant Movement 1922-1928* (Harvard University Press, Cambridge, Mass., 1977).

35 See, for example, Michael Burawoy, 'Karl Marx and the satanic mills: factory politics under early capitalism in England, the United States and Russia', *American Journal of Sociology*, 90(2), September 1984, pp. 247-82. And compare Dunn, *Politics of Socialism*.

36 See, for example, Ralph Miliband, *Marxism and Politics* (Oxford University Press, Oxford, 1977) and *Class Power and State Power: Political Essays* (New Left Books, London, 1983).

37 On the African proletariat see Robin Cohen and Richard Sandbrook (eds), *The Development of an African Working Class* (Longman, London, 1975); Robin Cohen, *Labour and Politics in Nigeria* (Heinemann Educational;, London, 1974); Richard Jeffries, *Class, Power and Ideology in Ghana: The Railwaymen of Sekondi* (Cambridge University Press, Cambridge, 1978); Ralph Grillo, *African Railwaymen: Solidarity and Opposition in an East African Labour Force* (Cambridge University Press, Cambridge, 1973); Bill Freund, *Capital and Labour in the Nigerian Tin Mines* (Longman, London, 1981).

38 See Bates, *Markets and States in Tropical Africa*.

39 Cf. Jeffries, *Class, Power and Ideology*: Freund, *Capital and Labour*; and Jeff

Crisp, *The Story of an African Working Class: Ghanaian Miners' Struggles 1870-1970* (Zed Press, London, 1984). For the concept of occupational community see Graeme Salaman, *Community and Occupation* (Cambridge University Press, Cambridge, 1974).

40 Jeffries, *Class, Power and Ideology*; P. C. Lloyd, *Power and Independence: Urban Africans' Perceptions of Social Inequality* (Routledge and Kegan Paul, London, 1974).

41 On Möser, see Geraint Parry, 'Enlightened government and its critics in eighteenth century Germany', *Historical Journal*, 6(2), 1963, pp. 178-92, especially p. 189. But for evidence of the political indeterminacy of *Lokalvernunft*, see J. W. Burrow, '"The village community" and the uses of history in late nineteenth century England', in Neil McKendrick (ed.), *Historical Perspectives: Studies in English Thought and Society* (Europa, London, 1974), pp. 255-84; and J. W. Burrow, *A Liberal Descent* (Cambridge University Press, Cambridge, 1981), *passim*.

42 For the centrality of this judgement to socialist political theory and the consequent insecurity of the latter, see John Dunn, 'Unimagined community: the deceptions of socialist internationalism', in Dunn, *Rethinking Modern Political Theory* (Cambridge University Press, Cambridge, 1985), pp. 103-18.

43 See Dunn, *Western Political Theory*, chs 3 and 4, and *Rethinking Modern Political Theory*.

44 John Dunn and A. F. Robertson, *Dependence and Opportunity: Political Change in Ahafo* (Cambridge University Press, Cambridge, 1973), chs 2 and 8; Dunn, 'From democracy to representation' and 'The eligible and the elect: Arminian thoughts on the social predestination of Ahafo leaders', in W. H. Morris-Jones (ed.), *The Making of Politicians* (Athlone, London, 1978), pp. 49-65; Martin Staniland, *The Lions of Dagbon: Political Change in Northern Ghana* (Cambridge University Press, Cambridge, 1975); Paul A. Ladouceur, *Chiefs and Politicians: The Politics of Regionalism in Northern Ghana* (Longman, London, 1979); Peel, *Ijeshas and Nigerians*.

45 Max Gluckman, *Custom and Conflict in Africa* (Basil Blackwell, Oxford, 1965), ch. 2, 'The frailty of authority'.

46 It is conceivable, though far from self-evident, that the localization of governmental distribution produced by the recurrent fission of state units within the Federation of Nigeria does on balance enhance local representation.

47 Chazan, *Anatomy of Ghanaian Politics*: Dunn, 'From democracy to representation' and 'The eligible and the elect'.

48 Rimmer, *Economies of West Africa*; Killick, *Development Economics*; Hart, *Political Economy*; Bates, *Markets and States in Tropical Africa*. Compare the somewhat more sanguine judgement of Young, *Ideology and Development*, focused on varieties of political project.

49 Military links with France have continued in many cases to be of the greatest importance for a quarter of a century since independence. (See for example the *Sunday Times*, 23 December 1984, p. 22).

50 Michael A. Cohen, *Urban Policy and Political Conflict in Africa: A Study of the Ivory Coast* (University of Chicago Press, Chicago, 1974); Bonnie Campbell, 'The Ivory Coast', in Dunn (ed.), *West African States*, pp. 66–116; and particularly Y. A. Fauré and J. F. Médard (eds), *État et bourgeoisie en Côte d'Ivoire* (Editions Karthala, Paris, 1982). On rural political economy in recent decades see Eddy Lee, 'Export-led rural development: the Ivory Coast', *Development and Change*, 11(4), October 1980, pp 607–42, and subsequent discussion by Boelman and Lee, *Development and Change*, 12(4), October 1981, pp. 619–33; and Robert M. Hecht, 'The Ivory Coast economic "miracle": what benefits for peasant farmers?', *Journal of Modern African Studies*, 21(1), March 1983, pp. 25–53; for an earlier phase, see Samir Amin, *Le Développement du capitalisme en Côte d'Ivoire* (Editions de Minuit, Paris, 1967).

51 In an impressive range of studies of Kenya in recent decades Colin Leys, *Underdevelopment in Kenya: The Political Economy of Neocolonialism* (Heinemann Educational, London, 1975) remains outstanding.

52 Compare the roles allotted to a planter bourgeoisie in the Ivory Coast case (Campbell, 'The Ivory Coast'; but also Hecht, 'What benefits for peasant farmers?') with that allotted to clerks in Björn Beckman, *Organizing the Farmers: Cocoa Politics and National Development in Ghana* (Scandinavian Institute of African Studies, Uppsala, 1976), especially ch. 8. The fullest recent discussion of the Ivory Coast case is now Fauré and Médard, *État et bourgeoisie*.

53 Such comparisons are difficult to conduct at all fairly. But for Africa as a whole see Young, *Ideology and Development*, and for West Africa in particular see the more incisive studies by Hart (*Political Economy*) and Rimmer (*Economies of West Africa*).

54 Contrast Hart, *Political Economy*; Bill Warren, *Imperialism: Pioneer of Capitalism* (Verso, London, 1980); Sheila Smith, 'The ideas of Samir Amin: theory or tautology?', *Journal of Development Studies*, 17(1), October, 1980, pp. 5–21; and John Sender and Sheila Smith, 'What's right with the Berg report and what's left of its critics', *Capital and Class*, 24, Winter 1984, pp. 125–46, with Samir Amin, *Accumulation on a World Scale*, tr. B. Pearce (Monthly Review Press, New York, 1974); *Le Développement inégal: Essai sur les formations sociales du capitalisme périphérique* (Editions de Minuit, Paris, 1973).

55 Compare Dunn (ed.), *West African States*, conclusion; 'Understanding revolutions', *Ethics*, 92(2), January 1982, pp. 299–315; Hawthorn, *Plausible Worlds*; Killick, *Development Economics*; and Rimmer, *Economies of West Africa*, with, for example, Martin Carnoy, *The State and Political Theory* (Princeton University Press, Princeton, 1984).

56 John Dunn, 'Liberty as a substantive political value', chapter 5 above; and *Politics of Socialism*.

57 Compare Samir Amin, *Développement du capitalisme*; *Développement inégal*; *L'Afrique de l'ouest bloquée: l'économie politique de la colonisation 1880–1970* (Editions de Minuit, Paris, 1971).

58 For a particularly compelling picture see Killick, *Development Economics*,

though this is certainly *not* a study that emphasizes the ease with which changes from ill-considered to better-considered policies can in practice be implemented.

59 See, for example, the case of Guinea: R. W. Johnson, 'Guinea', in Dunn (ed.), *West African States*, pp. 36-65; Claude Rivière, *Guinea: The Mobilization of a People*, tr. V. Thompson and R. Adloff (Cornell University Press, Ithaca, 1977); and that of Tanzania: Andrew Coulson, *Tanzania: A Political Economy* (Clarendon Press, Oxford, 1981).

60 Dunn, *Politics of Socialism*.

61 Young, *Ideology and Development*.

62 See especially Chalmers Johnson, *MITI and the Japanese Miracle: The Growth of Industrial Policy 1925-1975* (Stanford University Press, Stanford, 1982); Bruce Cumings, 'The origin and development of the northeast Asian political economy: industrial sectors, product cycles, and political consequences', *International Organization*, 38(1), winter 1984, pp. 1-40.

63 Contrast the experience of Tanzania with that of Guinea and of Ethiopia.

64 For an especially striking presentation see Judith N. Shklar, *Ordinary Vices* (Belknap Press of Harvard University Press, Cambridge, Mass., 1984).

65 Cf. Robert E. Dowse, *Modernization in Ghana and the USSR: A Comparative Study* (Routledge and Kegan Paul, London, 1969).

66 Much the most cogent account of both stages in this sequence is given by Killick, *Development Economics*. See particularly his stark summary on pp. 206-7.

67 They can, however, also usually be effectively deterred by government molestation or exaction. The main exception to this capacity for independent agency is in the planning and execution of large-scale irrigation projects.

68 Dunn, 'Liberty', and *Politics of Socialism*.

69 The same, of course, also holds true of the best. See Dunn (ed.), *West African States*, introduction and conclusion.

10 Unger's *Politics* and the Appraisal of Political Possibility

1 Alexis de Tocqueville, *The Recollections*, tr. A. Teixeira de Mattos (Meridian, New York, 1959), p. 116.

2 The trilogy discussed consists of Roberto Mangabeira Unger, *Social Theory: Its Situation and its Task* (a preliminary volume); *False Necessity: Antinecessitarian Social Theory in the Service of Radical Democracy*, part 1 of *Politics: A Work in Constructive Social Theory*; and *Plasticity into Power: Comparative Studies on the Institutional Conditions of Economic and Military Success* (all Cambridge University Press, Cambridge, 1987). See also Unger's *The Critical Legal Studies Movement* (Harvard University Press, Cambridge, Mass., 1986) and *Passion: An Essay on Personality* (Free Press, New York, 1984).

3 See for instance, Karl R. Popper, *Objectve Knowledge: An Evolutionary Approach* (Clarendon Press, Oxford, 1972).

4   John Dunn, *Political Obligation in its Historical Context* (Cambridge University Press, Cambridge, 1980), pp. 243–99.

5   Karl Marx, *Theses on Feuerbach* (1845), in Karl Marx and Frederick Engels, *Collected Works*, vol. 5 (Lawrence and Wishart, London, 1976), pp. 1–8, at pp. 4–7.

6   He does offer an elaborate inventory of recommended practices (*False Necessity; Critical Legal Studies Movement*), which, if they were implemented, would presumptively have the effect of avoiding these dangers. But his own analytical views effectively preclude him from presenting a practical diagnosis of how these arrangements can actually be implemented anywhere in particular.

7   Mancur Olson, *The Rise and Decline of Nations* (Yale University Press, New Haven, 1982); Robert O. Keohane, *After Hegemony: Cooperation and Discord in the World Political Economy* (Princeton University Press, Princeton, 1984); John H. Goldthorpe (ed.), *Order and Conflict in Contemporary Capitalism* (Clarendon Press, Oxford, 1984).

8   Paul Bracken, *The Command and Control of Nuclear Forces* (Yale University Press, New Haven, 1983).

9   *Plasticity into Power*, p. 212.

10 Bracken, *Command and Control*.

11 John Dunn, *Rethinking Modern Political Theory: Essays 1979–83* (Cambridge University Press, Cambridge, 1985), ch. 10.

12 Cf. Jeremy Rayner, 'Philosophy into dogma: the revival of cultural conservatism', *British Journal of Political Science*, 16(4), 1986, pp. 455–73.

13 Dunn, *Political Obligation*, ch. 10, Cf. Bernard Williams, *Moral Luck: Philosophical Papers 1973–1980* (Cambridge University Press, Cambridge, 1981), ch. 8.

14 Quentin Skinner, *The Foundations of Modern Political Thought* (2 vols, Cambridge University Press, Cambridge, 1978), especially vol. 1, pp. 44–5.

15 Cf. Norberto Bobbio, *Quale Socialismo?: discussione di un' alternativa* (Giulio Einaudi, Turin, 1976).

16 Cf. Charles Sabel and Jonathan Zeitlin, 'Historical alternatives to mass production', *Past and Present*, 108, 1985, pp. 133–76.

17 Barrington Moore, *Injustice: The Social Bases of Obedience and Revolt* (M. E. Sharpe, White Plains, NY, 1978).

18 Dunn, *Rethinking*, chs 4 and 5.

19 Nicholas Jardine, ' "Realistic" realism and the progress of science', in Christopher Hookway and Philip Pettit (eds), *Action and Interpretation: Studies in the Philosophy of the Social Sciences* (Cambridge University Press, Cambridge, 1978), pp. 127–44; Hilary Putnam, *Reason, Truth and History* (Cambridge University Press, Cambridge, 1981). For those who are not professional philosophers the most influential exponents of this viewpoint in the last two decades have probably been the historian T. S. Kuhn, the philosophers, Paul Feyerabend and Ian Hacking, and the more turbulent influences of Heidegger, Foucault and Derrida.

256 NOTES TO PAGES 167-172

20 Richard Rorty, *Philosophy and the Mirror of Nature* (Basil Blackwell, Oxford, 1980).

21 Dunn, *Rethinking*, ch. 7.

22 Richard Rorty, *Consequences of Pragmatism: Essays 1972-1980* (University of Minnesota Press, Minneapolis, 1982), ch. 11.

23 Alasdair MacIntyre, *Against the Self-Images of the Age* (Duckworth, London, 1971), p. 263.

24 Cf. Alasdair MacIntyre, 'Ideology, social science and revolution', *Comparative Politics*, 5(3), 1973, pp. 321-42.

25 Harry Frankfurt, 'Identification and externality', in Amelia O. Rorty (ed.), *The Identities of Persons* (University of California Press, Berkeley, 1976), pp. 239-51.

26 Charles Taylor, *Philosophy and the Human Sciences*, vol. 2 of *Philosophical Papers* (Cambridge University Press, Cambridge, 1985).

27 Compare the more systematic presentation of his conception of individual psychology in *Passion*.

28 Compare Unger's own misgivings over 'the fatal cult of Meetings', *False Necessity*, p. 610. Unger's evocative preoccupation (especially in *Plasticity into Power*) with the emancipation of men's powers to destroy and with the central historical role of the quest for military efficacy to make Hobbes's challenge all the sharper.

29 Thomas Hobbes, *De Cive: The English Version*, ed. Howard Warrender (Clarendon Press, Oxford, 1983), p. 136.

30 Unger, *Critical Legal Studies Movement*.

31 Mancur Olson, *The Logic of Collective Action*, (Harvard University Press, Cambridge, Mass., 1965); but cf. Russell Hardin, *Collective Action* (Johns Hopkins University Press, Baltimore, 1982).

32 *False Necessity*, especially pp. 407, 608-9.

33 Benjamin Constant, *De la Liberté des anciens comparée à celle des modernes* (*Cours de politique constitutionelle*) Bechet, Paris and Rouen, 1820), vol. 4, part 8, pp. 238-74; compare Unger's uncharacteristically insensitive account of Constant's views in *Critical Legal Studies Movement*, p. 41. Unger's reading of the implications of the civic republican tradition echoes the contrast between David Hume's and Adam Smith's 'Disdain for all Dependency' (Dunn, *Rethinking*, pp. 13, 32) and the social order commended, for example, by Andrew Fletcher of Saltoun (Istvan Hont and Michael Ignatieff, *Wealth and Virtue: The Shaping of Political Economy in the Scottish Enlightenment* (Cambridge University Press, Cambridge, 1983), especially the introduction). Much the best overall presentation of civic republicanism as a tradition of thought and sentiment remains J. G. A. Pocock, *The Machiavellian Moment* (Princeton University Press, Princeton, 1975).

34 Cf. Dunn, *Political Obligation*, ch. 10.

35 Compare, however, Deborah Baumgold, *Hobbes's Political Theory* (Cambridge University Press, Cambridge, 1988) on Hobbes's difficulties in dispensing with analogous degrees of commitment.

36 *Social Theory; False Necessity*.

37   This is not an especially novel line of thought: let alone sentiment.
38   Francesco Fagiani, *Nel Crepuscolo della probabilità: Ragione ed esperienza nella filosofia sociale di John Locke* (Bibliopolis, Naples, 1983); Ian Hacking, *The Emergence of Probability* (Cambridge University Press, Cambridge, 1975); Barbara J. Shapiro, *Probability and Certainty in Seventeenth-Century England* (Princeton University Press, Princeton, 1983).
39   *False Necessity*, p. 519.
40   Theda Skocpol, *States and Social Revolutions* (Cambridge University Press, Cambridge, 1979); Dunn, *Rethinking*, ch. 4, especially pp. 75, 77-8.
41   John Warr, *The Corruption and Deficiency of the Laws of England* (1649), cited from Christopher Hill, *The World Turned Upside Down: Radical Ideas during the English Revolution* (Temple Smith, London, 1972), p. 219.
42   Cf. John Dunn, *Modern Revolutions: An Introduction to the Analysis of a Political Phenomenon* (Cambridge University Press, Cambridge, 1972), *Political Obligation*, ch. 9, and *Rethinking*, chs 4 and 5.
43   Cf. John Dunn, *The Politics of Socialism: An Essay in Political Theory* (Cambridge University Press, Cambridge, 1984) and especially the powerful account in Adam Przeworski, *Capitalism and Social Democracy* (Cambridge University Press, Cambridge, 1985).
44   Cf. David Lewis, *Counterfactuals* (Basil Blackwell, Oxford, 1973).
45   Contrast Williams, *Moral Luck*, ch. 8.
46   *False Necessity*, p. 612. Cf. Dunn, *Rethinking*, ch. 7.
47   John Dunn, 'Trust and political agency', chapter 3 above.
48   *False Necessity*, p. 617.
49   R. B. Rose, *Gracchus Babeuf: The First Revolutionary Communist* (Edward Arnold, London, 1978).

11   Elusive Community: The Political Theory of Charles Taylor

1   Charles Taylor, *Philosophical Papers* (2 vols, Cambridge University Press, Cambridge, 1985), vol. 1, *Human Agency and Language*, p. 1.
2   Ibid.
3   Ibid.
4   Charles Taylor, *The Explanation of Behaviour* (Routledge and Kegan Paul, London, 1964).
5   See Charles Taylor, *Philosophical Papers*, vol. 2, *Philosophy and the Human Sciences*, pp. 58-90. This essay was first published in Peter Laslett and W. G. Runciman (ed), *Philosophy, Politics and Society. Third Series* (Basil Blackwell, Oxford, 1967), pp. 25-57.
6   See Taylor, *Philosophy and the Human Sciences*, pp. 15-57.
7   Ibid., p. 55.
8   Charles Taylor, *Hegel* (Cambridge University Press, Cambridge, 1975) and *Hegel and Modern Society* (Cambridge University Press, Cambridge, 1980).

9   See also Charles Taylor, *The Pattern of Politics* (McClelland and Stewart, Toronto, 1970).

10 Taylor, *Philosophy and the Human Sciences*, pp. 111–13. For a slightly different statement of the same line of thought in the same year see Charles Taylor, 'Political theory and practice', in Christopher Lloyd (ed.), *Social Theory and Political Practice* (Wolfson College Lectures, 1981), (Clarendon Press, Oxford, 1983), pp. 61–85, especially 85.

11 Taylor, *Human Agency*, p. 3.

12 Thomas Nagel, *Mortal Questions* (Cambridge University Press, Cambridge, 1979), pp. 165–80.

13 Compare, for example, the *oeuvres* of Michel Foucault, Richard Rorty, Clifford Geertz and Alasdair MacIntyre; Martin Hollis and Steven Lukes (eds), *Rationality and Relativism* (Basil Blackwell, Oxford, 1982); Norman Geras, *Marx and Human Nature* (New Left Books, London, 1983).

14 Compare *Human Agency*, p. 3 with Clifford Geertz, *Local Knowledge: Further Essays in Interpretive Anthropology* (Basic Books, New York, 1983), especially 36–54.

15 Alasdair MacIntyre, *After Virtue* (Duckworth, London, 1981).

16 Taylor, *Human Agency*, pp. 2, 54–76; note especially p. 57: 'But subject-referring does not necessarily mean self-referring.'

17 Cf. Bernard Williams, *Descartes: The Project of Pure Enquiry* (Penguin, Harmondsworth, 1978).

18 Cf. John Dunn, *Locke* (Oxford University Press, Oxford, 1984), especially ch. 3.

19 P. F. Strawson, 'Freedom and resentment', in Strawson (ed.), *Studies in the Philosophy of Thought and Action* (Oxford University Press, Oxford, 1968), pp. 71–96.

20 He makes the same point, very illuminatingly, about the imaginative appeals of utilitarian ethics: *Philosophy and the Human Sciences*, pp. 244, 266, 269 etc. And compare Derek Parfit, *Reasons and Persons* (Clarendon Press, Oxford, 1984).

21 Hilary Putnam discusses this feature of Taylor's hopes in a review of Taylor's contribution to Richard Rorty, J. B. S. Schneewind and Quentin Skinner (eds), *Philosophy in History* (Cambridge University Press, Cambridge, 1984) in *London Review of Books*, 8(5), 20 March 1986, pp. 3–4.

22 Taylor, *Human Agency*, p. 1 and *passim*.

23 Compare Judith Shklar, 'Squaring the hermeneutic circle', *Social Research*, 53, 1986, pp. 449–73.

24 Taylor, *Philosophy and the Human Sciences*, ch. 1, especially pp. 53, 57.

25 Cf. Shklar, 'Squaring'.

26 *Philosophy and the Human Sciences*, p. 55.

27 Compare John Dunn, *Political Obligation in its Historical Context* (Cambridge University Press, Cambridge, 1980), pp. 81–111.

28 Cf. the complete absence of any such presumption in a sophisticated modern recension of the possibility of insulating explanation from evalua-

tion like W. G. Runciman, *A Treatise on Social Theory*, vol. I (Cambridge University Press, Cambridge, 1983).

29   *Human Agency*, p. 8.

30   Ibid., pp. 10–11.

31   Ibid., p. 11.

32   See particularly, *Philosophy and the Human Sciences*, pp. 187–210.

33   *Human Agency*, p. 12.

34   Dunn, *Locke*.

35   Compare Bernard Williams, *Moral Luck* (Cambridge University Press, Cambridge, 1981), ch. 8, and *Ethics and the Limits of Philosophy* (Fontana, London, 1985); John Rawls, 'Justice as fairness; political, not metaphysical', *Philosophy and Public Affairs*, 14(1), winter 1985, pp. 1–20.

36   Compare John Dunn, *Rethinking Modern Political Theory* (Cambridge University Press, Cambridge, 1985), ch. 7.

37   Taylor, *Philosophy and the Human Sciences*, pp. -152–84.

38   Ibid., pp. 187–210 and *passim*.

39   For a more directly political instance see chapter 4 above.

40   *Philosophy and the Human Sciences*, p. 205 and - for the Kantian origins of this line of thinking - ch. 12.

41   There are similar weaknesses in many of Taylor's judgements of Locke. See, for instance, ibid., pp. 188, 291–2.

42   Cf. Shklar, 'Squaring'; Amy Gutmann, 'Communitarian critics of liberalism', *Philosophy and Public Affairs*, 14(1), winter 1984.

43   On this tradition see J. G. A. Pocock, *The Machiavellian Moment* (Princeton University Press, Princeton, NJ, 1975); Quentin Skinner, *The Foundations of Modern Political Thought* (2 vols, Cambridge University Press, Cambridge, 1978), and 'The idea of negative liberty', in Rorty et al. (eds), *Philosophy in History*, pp. 193–221.

44   *Philosophy and the Human Sciences*, especially pp. 272, 277, 285. Cf. also, over the last twenty years, the work of C. B. Macpherson, most recently in *The Rise and Fall of Economic Justice* (Oxford University Press, Oxford, 1985).

45   *Philosophy and the Human Sciences*, ch. 11; and compare Michael Walzer, *Spheres of Justice* (Martin Robertson, Oxford, 1983); Michael J. Sandel, *Liberalism and the Limits of Justice* (Cambridge University Press, Cambridge, 1982).

46   *Philosophy and the Human Sciences*, chs 1 and 10.

47   Cf. Taylor, *Pattern of Politics*, ch. 5. But note p. 116.

48   Benjamin Barber, *Strong Democracy* (University of California Press, Berkeley, 1984); Robert Dahl, *A Preface to Economic Democracy* (University of California Press, Berkeley, 1985); Philip Green, *Retrieving Democracy: In Search of Civil Equality* (Rowman and Allanheld, Totowa, NJ, 1985).

49   *Philosophy and the Human Sciences*, p. 317.

50   This fact is in itself of very considerable importance for the politics of advanced capitalist societies: John Dunn, *The Politics of Socialism* (Cambridge University Press, Cambridge, 1984).

51   Cf. Robert J. Smith, *Japanese Society: Tradition, Self and the Social Order* (Cambridge University Press, Cambridge, 1983).
52   Ronald P. Dore, *Shinohata: A Portrait of a Japanese Village* (Pantheon, New York, 1978), especially p. 283.
53   Benjamin Constant, *De la liberté des anciens comparée à celle des modernes* (*Cours de politique constitutionelle*) (Bechet, Paris and Rouen, 1820), vol. 4, part 8, pp. 238–74.
54   Adam Smith, *An Inquiry into the Nature and Causes of the Wealth of Nations*, ed. R. H. Campbell, A. S. Skinner and W. B. Todd (Clarendon Press, Oxford, 1976), vol. 2, pp. 780–90, especially pp. 781–2, 788. (And see Donald Winch, *Adam Smith's Politics* (Cambridge University Press, Cambridge, 1978), especially pp. 113, 116, 119.) Dugald Stewart, *Lectures on Political Economy*, vols 8–9 of his *Collected Works*, ed. William Hamilton (10 vols, Thomas Constable, Edinburgh, 1854–60), vol. 9, especially pp. 327–49. On Stewart's view of the political problems of elite and popular educability see also *Dissertation Exhibiting the Progress of Metaphysical, Ethical and Political Philosophy*, in *Collected Works*, vol. 1, pp. 503–23; and on the impact of his Political Economy lectures see also John Veitch, *Memoir of Dugald Stewart*, in *Collected Works*, vol. 10, pp. xlvi–lv. (And see Stefan Collini, Donald Winch and John Burrow, *That Noble Science of Politics* (Cambridge University Press, Cambridge, 1983), ch. 1, and Biancamaria Fontana, *Rethinking the Politics of Commercial Society* (Cambridge University Press, Cambridge, 1985), especially pp. 106–11.)
55   Constant, *De la liberté*, pp. 271–3.
56   John Locke, *Two Treatises of Government*, ed. Peter Laslett (Cambridge University Press, Cambridge, 1960), II, paragraph 128, p. 370.

12 Reconceiving the Content and Character of Modern Political Community

1   I have tried to spell out this viewpoint more extensively and to indicate the assemblage of judgements which lies behind it in earlier writings: particularly *Western Political Theory in the Face of the Future* (1979), *Political Obligation in its Historical Context* (1980), *The Politics of Socialism* (1984) and *Rethinking Modern Political Theory* (1985) (all Cambridge University Press, Cambridge). I shall make no attempt to summarize the theses of these works here. For a brief exercise in applying the viewpoint to contemporary political judgement see *Politics of Socialism*. Much of the present paper has been prompted by the commentaries of Charles Taylor and John Pocock on *Rethinking Modern Political Theory* at the Canadian Political Science Association meeting at Winnipeg in June 1986. I am extremely grateful for their searching interrogations.
2   See especially Dunn, *Rethinking*, ch. 10.
3   Much the same still remains true of the major ecological menaces – de-

forestation, desertification, atmospheric degradation: Dunn, *Western Political Theory*, ch. 3, especially pp. 78-9.

4 Compare Filippo Michele Buonarroti, *Conspiration pour l'égalité dite de Babeuf* (Editions Sociales, Paris, 1957), vol. 1, p. 25.

5 See chapter 8 above.

6 See especially chapter 8 above.

7 Hobbes' position is stated unequivocally in *Leviathan* and elsewhere. For Locke see John Dunn, *Locke* (Oxford University Press, Oxford, 1984), ch. 3. Especially John Locke, *An Essay concerning Human Understanding*, ed. Peter H. Nidditch (Clarendon Press, Oxford, 1975), II, xxi, 55 (pp. 269 line 29 to p. 270 line 11) and I, iii, 6 (p. 69 lines 10-13).

8 For Locke on everlasting damnation see especially *The Reasonableness of Christianity as Delivered in the Scriptures*, in *Works*, 7th edn (London, 1768), vol. 3.

9 Compare Robert Dahl, *Controlling Nuclear Weapons: Democracy versus Guardianship* (Syracuse University Press, Syracuse, 1985) with Dunn, *Western Political Theory*, pp. 17-18.

10 William F. Church, *Richelieu and Reason of State* (Princeton University Press, Princeton, 1972).

11 For an exemplary analysis, cast in marxist terms, see Adam Przeworski, *Capitalism and Social Democracy* (Cambridge University Press, Cambridge, 1985).

12 Cf. Dunn, *Political Obligation*, ch. 10.

13 For an admirably clear statement, drawing on Habermas, see Raymond Geuss, *The Idea of a Critical Theory* (Cambridge University Press, Cambridge, 1981).

14 Denis Diderot, *Rameau's Nephew*, tr. L. Tancock (Penguin, Harmondsworth, 1966); Plato, *Gorgias*, tr. and ed. Terence Irwin (Clarendon Press, Oxford, 1979).

15 Contrast Alasdair MacIntyre, *After Virtue: A Study in Moral Theory* (Duckworth, London, 1981) with the works of Michel Foucault, especially *Discipline and Punish*, tr. Alan Sheridan (Penguin, Harmondsworth, 1979).

16 See Dunn, *Rethinking*, ch. 7.

17 For fuller discussion see John Dunn (ed.), *The Economic Limits to Modern Politics* (1990), *Modern Revolutions* (1972), *Dependence and Opportunity*, with A. F. Robertson (1973) and Dunn (ed.), *West African States: Failure and Promise* (1978) (all Cambridge University Press, Cambridge); together with chapter 8 above and works cited in note 1 above.

18 But compare the moving fictional reconstruction of Tokugawa efforts to extirpate Christianity in seventeenth-century Japan in the novels of Shusaku Endo: *The Samurai*, tr. Van C. Gessel (Penguin, Harmondsworth, 1983), *Silence*, tr. William Johnston (Quartet, London, 1978), etc.

19 John Rawls, 'Justice as fairness: political not metaphysical', *Philosophy and Public Affairs*, 14(3), summer 1985, pp. 223-51. I am also indebted here to an unpublished paper of Richard Rorty, amplifying Rawls's point (delivered at the International Institute for Advanced Studies, Caracas in December

1985). See also the treatment of Locke's development of the argument for toleration in John Locke, *A Letter concerning Toleration*, ed. James H. Tully (Hackett, Indianapolis, 1983) and in Richard Ashcraft's *Revolutionary Politics and Locke's Two Treatises of Government* (Princeton University Press, Princeton, 1986).

20   Dunn, *Western Political Theory*, chs 1 and 2.

21   See especially Charles Taylor, *Philosophy and the Human Sciences* (Cambridge University Press, Cambridge, 1985).

22   Benjamin Constant, *De la Liberté des anciens comparée à celle des modernes* (*Cours de Politique Constitutionelle*) (Bechet, Paris and Rouen, 1820), vol. 4, part 8, pp. 238-74.

23   See chapter 4 above.

24   Constant, *De la Liberté*, p. 246. It also requires a system of adjudication consciously devoted to ensuring it. See Ronald Dworkin's very interesting *Law's Empire* (Harvard University Press, Cambridge, Mass., 1986).

25   Dunn, *Politics of Socialism*; *Rethinking*, chs 4-6; *West African States*, introduction and conclusion; and chapter 9 above.

26   Compare Joseph Schumpeter, *Capitalism, Socialism and Democracy* (Allen and Unwin, London, 1959), pp. 256-64, especially p. 261: 'What strikes me most of all and seems to me to be the core of the trouble is the fact that the sense of reality is so completely lost. Normally, the great political questions take their place in the psychic economy of the typical citizen with those leisure-hour interests that have not attained the rank of hobbies, and with the subjects of irresponsible conversation. . . . he expends less disciplined effort on mastering a political problem that he expends on a game of bridge.'

27   See especially M. I. Finley, *Politics in the Ancient World* (Cambridge University Press, Cambridge, 1983).

28   John H. Goldthorpe (ed.), *Order and Conflict in Contemporary Capitalism* (Clarendon Press, Oxford, 1984); Peter J. Katzenstein, *Corporatism and Change: Austria, Switzerland and the Politics of Industry* (Cornell University Press, Ithaca, 1984); Gösta Esping-Andersen, *The Social Democratic Road to Power* (Princeton University Press, Princeton, 1984).

29   This is a major theme of Taylor, *Philosophy and the Human Sciences*.

30   Benjamin Constant, *Oeuvres*, ed. Alfred Roulin (Pléiade/Gallimard, Paris, 1957). Of Constant's works only his brilliant novel *Adolphe* has been readily available in English but see now the full translation of his principal political works, *Political Writings*, edited by Biancamaria Fontana (Cambridge University Press, Cambridge, 1988).

31   Taylor, *Philosophy and the Human Sciences*, especially p. 205. This is a major weakness of the sophisticated version of liberalism developed by Ronald Dworkin (see particularly 'Liberalism', in Stuart Hampshire (ed.), *Public and Private Morality* (Cambridge University Press, Cambridge, 1978), pp. 113-43 and 'Is there a right to pornography?', *Oxford Journal of Legal Studies*, I, 1981, pp. 177-212). It is a lacuna which his impressive recent statement, *Law's Empire* (1986), fails to fill.

32   This is plainly a very controversial and somewhat elusive issue. What really

are the fundamental forms of the productive order? Is it indeed even analytically correct to conceive a productive order as having a fundamental (and determining) form? Cf. G. A. Cohen, *Karl Marx's Theory of History: A Defence* (Clarendon Press, Oxford, 1978); Adam Przeworski, *Capitalism*.

33 Jean Bodin, *The Six Bookes of a Commonweale*, ed. K. D. McRae (Harvard University Press, Cambridge, Mass., 1962); Robert Filmer, *Patriarcha and other Political Writings*, ed. Peter Laslett (Basil Blackwell, Oxford, 1949); Julian Franklin, *Jean Bodin and the Rise of Absolutist Theory* (Cambridge University Press, Cambridge, 1973). For the practical background see Perry Anderson, *Lineages of the Absolutist State* (New Left Books, London, 1974); Church, *Richelieu*; John Elliott, *Richelieu and Olivares* (Cambridge University Press, Cambridge, 1984).

34 John Locke, *Two Treatises of Government*, ed. Peter Laslett (Cambridge University Press, Cambridge, 1967), II, 90, especially lines 1-3: '*Absolute Monarchy*, which by some Men is counted the only Government in the World, is indeed *inconsistent with Civil Society*, and so can be no Form of Civil Government at all.'

35 Another, at least equally important and equally baffling, is, as already argued, that between official, professional and amateur theories of effective self-defence and self-protection.

36 See Stefan Collini, Donald Winch and John Burrow, *That Noble Science of Politics* (Cambridge University Press, Cambridge, 1983), chs 1 and 2; Biancamaria Fontana, *Rethinking the Politics of Commercial Society; The Edinburgh Review 1802-1832* (Cambridge University Press, Cambridge, 1985). Compare Constant, *Oeuvres*, pp. 1118 and 1112: 'Ceux que l'indigence retient dans une éternelle dépendance, et qu'elle condamne à des travaux journaliers, ne sont ni plus éclairés que des enfants, sur les affaires publiques, ni plus intéressés que des étrangers à une prospérité nationale, dont ils ne connaissent pas les éléments, et dont ils ne partagent qu'indirectement les avantages.'

37 See especially Boyd Hilton, *Corn, Cash, Commerce: The Economic Policies of the Tory Governments 1815-1830* (Clarendon Press, Oxford, 1977).

38 For a defence of this judgement about the past see Dunn, *Politics of Socialism*; *Rethinking Modern Political Theory*, chs 5 and 6. See now particularly, Alec Nove, *The Economics of Feasible Socialism* (Allen and Unwin, London, 1983).

39 Which is itself, in any case, not necessarily more marked in the round than the degeneracy of any pre-modern form of political life.

40 Dunn, *Western Political Theory*, ch. 1.

41 Compare Schumpeter, *Capitalism, Socialism and Democracy*, especially pp. 259-61.

42 See chapter 8 above, and Dunn, *Western Political Theory*, ch. 4, and *Rethinking Modern Political Theory*, chs 7-10.

Index